STUART JEFFRIES

works as an editor and contributing
and is currently based in its Pari
middle England in 1962, and used to edit the *Walsall Observer*'s children's page

More from the reviews:

'A very funny Proustian parody (the smell of a custard tart sends him back to memories of watching the Flowerpot men) sets the tone for this breezy, intelligent yet irreverent overview of the place of television programmes in Jeffries' life. Sport, cartoons, the news, sitcoms and soaps provide the backdrop to a highly entertaining social history in a sort of *TV-Times*-meets-Edward-Said style of writing . . . A joyous account, illuminating and quite brilliant'
BRIAN BOYD, *Irish Times*

'Often unnervingly clever and witty, *Mrs Slocombe's Pussy* uses the autobiographical form as a means of talking about how television affects our lives – how we see our own experience reflected or refracted on the screen; how our lives sometimes seem to reflect or refract patterns learned from TV . . . Jeffries has excellent taste and is acute and persuasive on individual programmes.'
ROBERT HANKS, *Independent*

'Jeffries is particularly entertaining – almost sidesplittingly so – in his Freudian analysis of fade-out routines at the end of children's programmes.'
VAL HENNESSY, *Daily Mail*

'The format of this extremely entertaining book borders on genius . . . its strength lies in the thousand hooks that line the edges of the writing. You can't help but repeatedly snag on simple recognition. "Yes! I remember that!" you will shout a thousand times during the course of this book as some fleeting televisual joy floats past your memory.'
MICK MIDDLES, *Manchester Evening Post*

'Quite irresistible, perceptive and thought-provoking . . . with a neat twist in the tail.' HUGH MASSINGBRED, *Daily Telegraph*

'Intense and very original' BYRON ROGERS, *Spectator*

'A romp back through all our yesterday teatimes and furtive, late last nights with acute personalised twist, a logical literary successor to those other warm, self-deprecating, thirtysomething male confessional memoirs . . . deftly executed, clever and intuitive' KATHRYN FLETT, *Observer*

'Jeffries' knowledge is wondrous to behold and his writing frequently delightful. He makes a powerful case that at its best TV can be as stimulating as Tolstoy. This is a book of great depth and subtlety.' JAMES RAMPTON, *Scotland on Sunday*

'Entertaining' BRIAN CASE, *Time Out*

'Immensely entertaining, Stuart Jeffries covers everything from *Andy Pandy* and *Friends* to the Gulf War and the dramatisation of the Hillsborough disaster. His tone is genial, his style breezy and his eye acute. This collection provides ample proof that television doesn't rot the brain. It isn't a question of what you watch but how you watch it . . . Above all, *Mrs Slocombe's Pussy* is enormous fun, rattling along on a rollercoaster of high spirits. There are so many areas where Jeffries scores bull's-eyes that it's hard to single out any in particular . . . Most intellectuals have to be sound on sport but Jeffries is particularly good. Until he reminded me, I'd completely forgotten about those extraordinary TV colours in the Mexican World Cup of 1970.' DAVID CHATER, *Ham & High*

'Likeable and unashamedly heartfelt' *Glasgow Herald*

'A perspicacious *Fever Pitch*-style memoir which mixes anecdotal experience with critical insight, an approach well suited to that most effervescent of media and makes for some unusually persuasive, sharply pitched arguments.' *Sight and Sound*

MRS SLOCOMBE'S PUSSY

Growing Up in Front of the Telly

STUART JEFFRIES

Flamingo
An Imprint of HarperCollins*Publishers*

Flamingo
An Imprint of HarperCollins*Publishers*
77–85 Fulham Palace Road,
Hammersmith, London W6 8JB

www.**fire**and**water**.com

Flamingo is a registered trademark of HarperCollins Publishers Limited

Published by Flamingo 2001
1 3 5 7 9 8 6 4 2

First published in Great Britain by Flamingo 2000

The Publishers would like to note that this book
is not associated with or endorsed by Mollie Sugden,
the BBC or the makers of the programme *Are You Being Served?*

ISBN 0 00 655175 0

Set in Plantin Light by
Rowland Phototypesetting Ltd,
Bury St Edmunds, Suffolk

Printed and bound in Great Britain by
Clays Ltd, St Ives plc

For KAY

‘People stared at the fire before television. I think they always felt the need for moving pictures.’

FRANÇOIS TRUFFAUT, ***La Nuit Américaine***

CONTENTS

INTRODUCTION

The Way Dandy Nichols Sat

In 1991, Channel 4 broadcast a sitcom about a man called Martin Tupper. He was a recently divorced thirty-six-year-old New Yorker. What made the show interesting to me was that Martin was a child of television: he had watched TV for more than three decades and it had become the most important thing in his life. The opening credit sequence made that plain. First, we saw him as a doe-eyed child sitting on a mat in front of the TV, by turns giggling, looking puzzled, seeming engaged. In the next shot, he was an adolescent, still on the mat. In the next, a man, still on the mat.

Martin had been abandoned when he was very young to that surrogate breast, television. He was sucking all the nutrition out of it, and television, perhaps by way of revenge, was immobilising him, holding him captivated. As a result, he could not make sense of what happened to him in the real world without reference to a TV programme. His every feeling was expressed by a clip from a classic TV series from the fifties, and his reactions to real-life events were said not by him but by Jack Benny, Ronald Reagan,

Jackie Gleason or Lucille Ball – those great moralists of the television age.

But television didn't help Martin Tupper. In fact, it ruined his life. His ex-wife later married Dr Richard Stone, an internationally known genius. Any fool could see why she had left Martin for Richard. Martin was a watcher, Richard was a doer. Often, when Martin watched TV, he would come across a report on Dr Stone's latest achievement – writing a symphony, climbing a mountain, performing life-saving surgery, going into space. If only Martin hadn't watched so much television he could have been as great as Dr Richard Stone.

Like Martin Tupper, I am thirty-six and have watched a lot of television. Unlike him, it hasn't framed my life. I could never be a contestant on Noel Edmonds' *Telly Addicts*. I am not addicted to television, although if you could just move to the left, there is a very funny car advertisement on right behind you just now. Bit further. That said, I do worry that television has taken up too much of my life. Where are my symphonies? When will I go into orbit?

My life of TV viewing started when I was very young. I can't remember the first programme I saw, but it may well have been *Pinky and Perky*. Two little blank-faced pig puppets with high-pitched voices sang, told jokes and introduced us to their friends – Vera Vixen, Basil Bloodhound, Bertie Bonkers the baby elephant, Horace Hare. Pinky and Perky were identical except that Pinky wore blue and Perky red. But at that time we all had black and white televisions, so that information was worse than useless. In fact, Perky also wore a hat when on camera, which helped.

I can't remember whether Perky lost the hat when colour television arrived in Britain in 1967, but by then I didn't care which was Pinky and which was Perky. I was more interested in Carol Hersey who, from 1967, was, as if by a miracle, always on television when the TV repair man came round. She had a cheeky stare and a thin smile. Her expression said she had done something very naughty or was just about to and didn't feel guilty at all. She was my kind of girl. I loved to sit on the Parker Knoll sofa, while men in overalls put their tool boxes in the middle of the living room carpet and set to work on adjusting her complexion. Carol, in her red dress and matching Alice band, had perfectly-combed, well-conditioned hair as was the fashion then. She sat in a circle in the middle of the test card. There was a blackboard behind her and a rag doll clown, inert and grinning on her right. She had turned round to face us with a long bare arm holding a piece of chalk aloft. Carol had begun a game of noughts and crosses on the blackboard. But who was playing against Carol? This was one of the great puzzles of my early childhood. There was an X and 0 on the board and Carol seemed to be reaching with that lovely arm to draw another mark. Had that slumped invertebrate of a clown briefly acquired a spine and made his mark on the board before collapsing back into a semblance of lifelessness just before the test card came on screen? Or maybe Carol was showing me how the game worked so that we could play together secretly later. Perhaps that was why she smiled so naughtily: she was communicating directly with me, and only me, and thus contravening the very principles of television.

Carol finally left television screens in the early 1980s when the vulgarity of daytime TV eclipsed her poignant charms. In the intervening years I had played lots of games with lots of girls, but Carol, whenever I stumbled across her image in a book or in some TV nostalgia programme, was still that enigmatic foster child of silence and slow time. She helped me recall sitting and staring on the sofa when I should, surely, have been doing something more profitable. The image of Carol helped me to remember a childhood in which there seemed to be time, lots and lots of time, in which to stare at things and, in so doing, store up a bank of memories that might help me later on.

Time was slower then, or at least it seems so in memory, and I had time to consider all the lines on the test card and the patterns they made. Then, too, I had time to appreciate the Pye television which had a large knob for changing channels. I loved that knob. It consisted of a chrome-effect, knobbly plastic circumference, and a central disc that was divided into thirds by three strands of silvery plastic. This disc too was plastic but coloured green, a subterranean sparkling green of emeralds, moss and wine bottles. The knob clicked into five positions, even though there were only three channels then. It was a television that was ready for the future. For a small boy with a little hand span, it was quite difficult to turn the knob and so the choice of channels required some reflection and commitment. No wonder my family mostly watched BBC1 for days at a time.

Now I have three remote controls and two porn channels. The remote controls have little buttons rather than one big knob the size of my hand. In total, I have 150 channels at my disposal, a VCR and a television set whose only distinguishing mark is the manufacturer's logo, which is hardly as appealing as the green marble inlays of television knobs. I have swapped Carol for a world of entertainment, including Greek, German, Italian, French, and Indian stations. I have a choice of nearly 50 films a day. I have far too many channels that purport to show classic television, even though not one of them shows *Pinky and Perky*, *The Herbs*, early *Dr Who*, *The Woodentops* or Carol.

But none of them can give me what I really want. I don't want the characteristic experience of watching television to be flipping endlessly and never really finding anything to delay my attention for more than moments; I don't want to feel this dizzying loss of centre and choices that never satisfy; I don't want to feel anxious – that overwhelming spirit of our age, our age of apparent choices and apparent satisfactions; instead, I want to watch television as I did in the late sixties, to be absorbed by very little. But this cannot be. After all, television was not invented to show a still image of a little girl playing noughts and crosses. Television cannot, nor indeed can anything else, stay still.

INTRODUCTION

Television is rarely invoked as a medium that provokes tender memories. Instead, television is much more readily blamed for all kinds of evils. The anti-television group TV Free America, for example, blames television for insomnia, depression, obesity, illiteracy and profligate spending.

According to them, the average American spends eleven years in front of a television set during a seventy-two-year lifespan. The average Briton probably doesn't watch any less television than the average goggle-eyed stiff from Des Moines. And I am more average than most, so by the time I reach seventy-two, I will have spent eleven years in front of the television. In fact, if England's football team had progressed further in World Cup competitions, if the UK's gold medal tally in the Atlanta Olympics had even approached double figures, if the British sitcom wasn't in its death throes and if *Coronation Street* had had a really juicy incest storyline last year, then, according to my scrupulously researched estimates, I would have spent the equivalent of 12.75 years in front of the idiot box by the time I reached the age of seventy-two. Given the illiteracy, insomnia, depression and horrible sandwiches endemic to our inner cities, not to mention our outer cities and rural bits, something has clearly gone wrong with British society and with people like me. And it's all television's fault. No, it is. Why, I was watching a really good documentary about just that only the other day.

And yet, and yet. Eleven years is a long time. Eleven years? Dandy Nichols looked as though she'd been watching TV for fifty years non-stop. True, she was the ideal foil for her ranting husband. But gormless and open-gobbed, she would sit for long periods of *Till Death Us Do Part* in her armchair saying and doing nothing. For me the Couch Potato of TV Demonology looks like Dandy Nichols in the early seventies. I dread winding up like that.

Eleven years! Eleven years that I could have spent learning Sanskrit, gambolling with lambs in spring fields, longing and loving, loving and longing, improving the design of the trouser press, inventing and building a spacecraft and then visiting Mars in it, curing cancer and really sorting out my trampoline technique.

I could have been Dr Richard Stone, but instead my eleven years have been spent and may well continue to be spent doing the indefensible. Watching television. In a culture so beset by anxiety about how we should live our lives and uncertain about where we are going, eleven years of television viewing sounds like a waste of time. You should spend every moment in some gainful pursuit, shouts the horseman whipping time's winged chariot close to our scurrying heels. It's a brilliant rhetorical device that bears not a moment's scrutiny: vast portions of everyone's lives will be spent doing things that contribute nothing to human well-being or self-fulfilment, but instead measure out the distance between birth and death like coffee spoons. But the deeper argument here is that television viewing is a chain of coffee spoons leading through an unfulfilled, worthless life.

But I refuse to admit my life, or that part of it spent watching TV, is worthless. Instead, for me, watching television has been a much more complicated experience and I want to do justice to it. During my lifetime in front of the television, I've fallen asleep with it, woken up with it, and told it – I don't know how many times – that one of us has to go, and it's not going to be me, if you get the picture. It's been a complicated relationship filled with laughter, tears, furious scenes, sulky looks over the teapot. Everything, in fact, apart from make-up sex, because that would be to press this analogy between watching television and having a meaningful relationship with a loving partner just a little too far. But, the complexity and intensity of my relationship with television does explain why this book is is sometimes light-hearted, sometimes serious and at other times consists of the ranting of a very, very angry man.

In years to come, no doubt, few people will be able to understand the intensity of my engagement with television. But I grew up in a peculiar era during which television was a very special medium. Since the coronation of Elizabeth II in 1953, the most important national events in Britain have been primarily television events (the 1966 World Cup, Charles and Di's 1981 wedding, Diana's funeral, general election after general election), forging a powerful national bond that politicians could only dream about. Whatever ethnic, regional, gender, and class differences existed in Britain, everyone everywhere could talk as equals about how depressing *EastEnders* was last night. Until recently, too, there were some inalienable rights which each and every Briton could insist upon for the price of a licence fee, rights which usually involved access to national sporting events – Cup Finals, Wimbledon, test match cricket.

But the era in which TV was the chief cultural national unifier – that strange time during which I have grown up – is coming to an end. The growth of satellite, cable and digital broadcasting has heralded the death of televisually homogeneous Britain.

In this book, I want to show what it has been like to grow up during that era. For me, British television has hardly ever been a retreat from the real world. Instead, it has brought the world, and in particular that British corner of the world, to me in all its vileness, degradation, selfishness, violence, dysfunction, malnourishment and repressiveness – and presented all that for my entertainment and critical reflection.

The texture of watching television is nearly always smoothed to oversimplification by everybody from historians to TV critics. The story of what it is like to grow up watching television deserves to be told with more sensitivity and understanding than it has been. Once you realise that the history of watching British television is bound up with guilt and shame, denial and occasional bombast, fiercely guarded privacy and social awkwardness – those defining characteristics of the British psyche at the end of the millennium – you'll realise that it's a story worth telling.

CHAPTER 1

1967: Bill and Ben's Hats

MEMORIES OF EATING CUSTARD TARTS

When I was a very young boy, my mother would take my brother Neil and me to Nanny Lewis's in Wednesbury every week for lunch. In my memory, we had the same meal every week. We started with lamb chops, potatoes, peas and gravy, and for pudding we had little custard tarts in tin foil cups, bought that morning from Robinson's the bakers in Sedgley's Bull Ring.

I ate my custard tart like this. I held the tart in the palm of my right hand, brought it up to my face and turned it slowly in a circle so that I could nibble off the serrated pastry edges with my two front baby teeth. When I completed the circle, I plunged my tongue through the thick, nutmeggy skin into the soft custard below. Then I ate all the custard, licking around the bottom of the pastry shell until there was hardly anything left to lick. After that, I turned the tin foil cup upside down, popped out the pastry shell and began eating the walls of the tart while I held the base in the palm of my hand. As for the last, soggy disc of custardy pastry – I placed that on my tongue, custard side down, and let it melt there.

I used to eat Bourbon biscuits and Custard Creams in similar ways, though they were just poor substitutes for custard tarts. I would take a Bourbon in one hand and lever off the lid with my two front teeth. Sometimes I would be lucky enough to lever off the whole lid this way, but mostly not: it usually snapped in the middle, so after eating one half, I would turn the biscuit around and repeat the prising action with my teeth on the second half. Next I ate the chocolatey-cream filling. I did this in one of two ways depending on my mood. The first was to dredge the filling from the base with my two front teeth, leaving teeth tracks across the remaining filling until the last dredge when the smoothness of cream surrendered itself to the crunchiness of the biscuit base below. When I tried this way of eating Bourbon chocolatey-cream filling later, after my milk teeth had fallen out of my head, the gap between my new teeth left a long raised strip of cream across the biscuit. When I looked at this cream furrow it seemed to tell me that I was deformed.

The second way was to lick the cream off, but this demanded a very strenuous tongue indeed, particularly if the biscuits had been stored in a cool place and the cream had consequently hardened. I ate Custard Creams in much the same way as Bourbons, though obviously there was less chance of lid fracture since Custard Creams are squarer than Bourbons.

Many years later, I read a novel by John Updike called *Memories of the Ford Administration* in which he wrote about a vagina. Critics loathed this description, and found it symptomatic of Updike's misogyny. For him, the vagina looked frilly, and when I read that I thought immediately of the serrated edge of a Robinson's custard tart. Nowadays, western Europe is overrun by custard tarts that are not frilly at all, fancy-schmantzy Portuguese ones with flaky pastry and custard, which, although it tastes wonderful, will not stay in place when you nibble the walls. The custard explodes over your face. I've made a mess of myself in enough cafés from Lisbon to London to realise that the firmness, the pertness of the egg custards of my youth are qualities that have not transmuted themselves to the, in many ways superior, Portuguese versions.

Worse than that, though, Portuguese-style custard tarts do not come in tin foil cups. They come wrapped in paper, and not even rice paper which one might eat. This is a terrible development, at least for Neil and myself. Because, for us, tin foil cups house more than custards. They are homes for delicious memories. After I had swallowed the last bits of the disc of pastry that lay at the base of the custard tart, I would take the empty tin foil cup, turn it upside down and put it on my head. Then I would look across the dining table at Neil and say 'Flobadopalop!'. Neil, who had been eating his custard tart in a way that may or may not have been as consummately disgusting as mine (I don't know how he ate his, to be honest, because I was too lost in my own sensual world), then put his tin foil cup on his head and would reply: 'Flobadopalop!'

It was, you see, twenty to two in the afternoon and time for *Watch With Mother*. Whenever we visited my nan's, it seemed, *Bill and Ben the Flowerpot Men* was on television. Neil and I sat at the dining table while my mother and her mother did the dishes in the adjoining kitchen. The adults had retreated from this childhood world, but not very far. Even though the programme strand in which *Bill and Ben* appeared was called *Watch With Mother* we sometimes watched without mother. And this made a lot of sense. After all, Bill and Ben only came to life when the Gardener left his potting shed and went up the garden path for lunch. Similarly, Neil and I only became Bill and Ben when we were alone. This conceit was fundamental for programmes for very young children, at least those that were shown on BBC1 from the mid-fifties onwards created by Freda Lingstrom, who was Head of the BBC's Children's Department: while the authority figures were away, the children played. They came to life and leapt out of their hiding places in little pots. They put on tin foil hats and spoke an incomprehensible vernacular. At least they did in certain dining rooms of the Black Country in the late sixties.

Bill and Ben were very nearly identical. 'Was it Bill or was it Ben?' said the voice of the narrator Peter Hawkins, asking which of them was responsible for some piece of naughtiness. This was not a difficult question to answer, even for a very young boy. Bill had his name painted on his back and so did Ben. What's more, Bill had a voice that was nearly an octave higher than Ben's. True, Bill and Ben's command of English was non-existent and so they could never tell us which was which, but that didn't seem to be an insuperable problem to Neil or me.

Bill and Ben were made mostly from pots. Their torsos were big pots, their legs and arms were made out of pots. They wore thick gardening gloves (or maybe these were supposed to be their actual hands) and they had hobnail boots on their feet. On their heads were painted faces, each with a pair of huge, blank, staring eyes. Each head was topped by a little cap which looked uncannily like a tin foil cup turned upside down, even if, proportionately, they were bigger than the ones Neil and I wore.

Bill and Ben's world was an innocent one, or at least it seemed that way. They had a little autonomous world at the bottom of the garden where, for a time, they could play. But that autonomy was not all it should have been. Unlike my nan's dining room, this place was fraught with menace. What was it that made them shy of revealing themselves to the Gardener? This was the paradox of the Flowerpot Men: the Gardener's absence made Bill and Ben come to life and made their innocent games possible; but the threat of his return fell like a shadow over their play time, and made me worried. The pair would make their appearances each week by rising over the huge flowerpots in which, we were to suppose, they slept, or perhaps cowered while the Gardener worked in the potting shed. First, up popped Bill from his pot. Or maybe it was Ben. Then he popped down again. And then up. And then down. And then up. It wasn't exactly an adaptation of Proust, but Neil and I and the rest of the children in the TV audience were immediately caught up in playing with the Flowerpot Men. But, again, that primal game was tainted since, even though Bill and Ben were playing at hiding from the friendly audience, this was just the simulation of the real hide and seek that they played with the Gardener. And, if they *were* found by the Gardener, I feared that they would surely suffer some terrible fate. After all, they had been obliged to enlist their friend Weed as a look-out while they played. But, to me, Weed was hardly the stoutest of allies: a character whose catchphrase was a high, whiney 'Weeee-eeee-eed!' was hardly going to be much help when the chips were down and the Gardener came marching back down the garden path from lunch, filled with lamb chops and custard tarts.

Why did Bill and Ben need to hide? Why did each episode end with them scrambling so quickly back into their pots? It was all very upsetting since there seemed to be a darkness and strangeness to Bill and Ben's world that was only made worse by the Little House who we often saw at the end of the programme, that house that wore a smile which Peter Hawkins told us suggested that it 'knew something about it, too'. This house with windows for eyes and a smile became the stuff of my nightmares. But the Little House, like Bill and Ben, could not tell us what it knew. It could not tell us that Bill and Ben scampered into their pots so quickly when the Gardener returned from lunch because, if he'd found them, he would have crushed their faces with his hobnail boots, he'd have reduced their blank eyes to even blanker dust, he'd have pulled off their gloves and boots and kept them for himself. And then, finally, he would have snapped off their arms and legs and used their torsos for planting geraniums. That's what I feared. Childhood innocence quickly became a world of theft and subterfuge: theft, because these pots and gardening clothes from which Bill and Ben were made had probably been taken from the Gardener's potting shed – yes, that might explain why they had to hide from him, because their very selves had been somehow stolen from his shed; subterfuge, because games and playing were not things that thunder-browed adults would allow, and so Bill and Ben had to pretend not to exist rather than be caught playing in pots.

Guile, wit and deceit – these were what were needed to keep the threat of the Gardener, that vague, threatening adult presence, at bay. After Neil and I had licked the custard out of the tarts and eaten the pastry, we put tin helmets on our heads not just in play, but at the same time to begin the disturbing, lifelong battle of being human, the fight to hold on to what was good and innocent and true.

ANDY AND TEDDY ARE WAVING GOODBYE

In *Beyond the Pleasure Principle*, Freud wrote about a game called Fort-Da. He had watched his grandson throw a toy from his pram and then pull it back on a piece of string. 'Fort!' he yelled as he hurled it out, and then 'Da!' as he yanked it back. Fort-Da, Fort-Da, gone-here, gone-here. It worked on the same principle as Bill and Ben's game of peek-a-boo. According to Freud, his grandson was symbolically mastering the absence of his mother, showing himself that he could control the world – make something absent and then reassuringly bring it back into his presence again. Later, the French psychoanalyst Jacques Lacan argued that the loss of the mother drives us onward in our lives, in an endless metonymic game-playing quest to find substitutes for her body.

When my mother was in the kitchen doing the washing up

with Nanny Lewis, Neil and I were in the dining room finding substitutes. Sucking on tarts, watching television. Sometimes, I feel sure, my mother would look around the door to see if we were all right – just as my mom or dad would do when we were tucked up at night. And then she was gone. And then back. And then gone.

Or when my Grandad Lewis would sit me on his knee in that same Wednesbury dining room. He had a thing about fake body parts. Sometimes he would take out his false teeth and present them to me and then put them back. In and out, in and out. Sometimes, he would pull at my nose with the second joints of the index and middle finger of his right hand. Then he would try to deceive me: he would show me my nose which he had pulled off with his fingers. There it was between index and middle finger. He had pulled my nose off! This 'nose' was really his thumb which he had inserted in the gap between the two fingers. Then he would gently press my 'nose' back into place. I can still feel his thumb on my real nose as he pressed it gently on to my face. Then he took it off again, showed it to me, and put it back. Again and again until I giggled with delight.

All this helps explain why Bill and Ben's peek-a-boo game with the audience at the start of *The Flowerpot Men* was so appealing to me and why the final farewell was utterly distressing. When Bill and Ben disappeared into their pots at the end of the episode, their absence seemed to be a fort with no da, a goodbye with no soothing.

Goodbyes need to be dealt with very carefully at the end of children's television programmes. Children need to be reassured that there will be a da, that next week or tomorrow Bill and Ben, Zebedee and the rest of the Magic Roundabout, Andy Pandy and Teddy, or the Teletubbies, will come back. Why else do the Teletubbies spend so much time saying goodbye? I initially found the Teletubbies farewell sequences ludicrous. Tinky Winky and Laa-Laa said farewells to each other and to us, and, just when I thought they'd finished, they started the whole goodbye ceremony again. 'Look,' adult me wanted to say, 'this isn't Chekhov, you know. Just say goodbye once, and then hit the bricks, you big-bottomed freaks, you.'

But if you're a very young child, these farewells are profoundly reassuring. There is nothing sweet about the sorrow of parting, be it from your mother at bedtime or from your favourite TV character at teatime, but if the goodbye is abrupt the pain is worse. Zebedee's injunction 'Time for bed' on the *Magic Roundabout* just before the 5.45 p.m. news was to me a desperately upsetting, peremptory dismissal. It would be followed by a strum on the harp and then the hurdy-gurdy theme tune that signalled the unbearable – children's television was over for the day and the adult world of news and weather was taking over.

As a child, I remember the exquisite pain at the end of *Andy Pandy*, when Valerie Cardnell would sing 'Time to Go Home' – a song which was later significantly renamed 'Time to Stop Play', as if the spirit of seriousness must now descend like night. 'Andy and Teddy are waving goodbye, goodbye . . .' sang the adult Valerie, and then added the really heartless last two syllables '. . . goodbye'. Like the last scene of *Uncle Vanya*, all that was left was the bleakly quotidian. And if you were very, very young, as I was then, there were no sleigh bells and vodka to take the edge off the long night of Andy and Teddy's absence.

At the end of the episode called 'Trampoline', for example, during which Andy and Teddy had spent a lot of time jumping up and down on a trampoline (the titles never lied in Andy Pandy land: 'Trampoline' was about jumping on a trampoline, 'Tea Party' was about a tea party and 'Jack in the Box' wasn't an analysis of chaos theory), the storyteller Vera McKechnie said sharply: 'That's enough now, Andy. We have to say goodbye until the next time. Wave to the children!' And then Vera spoke to us watching at home: 'It's time to leave them now, children, but we'll see them again soon. Goodbye Andy Pandy. Goodbye Teddy.'

Then the trio of clarinet, flute and piano would begin what was, to me, the most mournful, heart-rending tune that has ever been played, and Valerie Cardnell would start to sing in a voice of chilly purity:

Time to stop play,
Just for today,
Andy and Teddy must now go away.
Andy is waving goodbye,
Goodbye
Goodbye.

The 'just for today' was intended to be reassuring – Andy and Teddy would be back, children. There was really no need to fret so. Then the instrumentalists would take up the melancholy tune themselves and we would see the title card. The card was made up of the letters ANDY across the top and PANDY across the bottom in an elegant serif font, with a picture of Andy, Teddy and Louby-Lou in the middle. But when it appeared at the end, each letter of ANDY PANDY would be replaced by a daisy head, starting at the first A and ending at the last Y. When the last Y became a daisy, it was over, all over.

And yet, weekly repetition made Andy and Teddy's farewells as ritualised as a Russian ceremony of goodbyes. This repetition made me realise that they would be back. And one week the narrator would sing, 'Andy and Teddy are waving goodbye', and the once childish viewer would tell the screen: 'You think I care? I'm reading Dostoevsky now. And by the way, the strings pulling Andy's hands are as thick as my forearms.'

This is a quite natural process of growing up. Instead of being upset by the farewells of Andy and Teddy or Bagpuss and his toy friends, they should eventually mean nothing. This is how it should work: we should play Fort-Da with children's TV and, as we grow up, come to a point where we fling it finally away and never again pull those puppet toys back by their strings. 'Fort, Clangers! Fort, Noggin the Nog! Fort, Pippin and Tog! Fort, if I can lift you out of the pram, Bagpuss, you great lump!'

But, during my adult years, barely a month has gone by without the promise of the return of some children's TV show from the late sixties or early seventies, as those who were children then intensify their stranglehold on the media. 'Da, Bill and Ben! Da, Wombles! Da, Captain Pugwash, you salty old cove!' In the late nineties, there was loose talk of plans to remake *The Flowerpot Men*, who would feature in a programme hosted by Noel Edmonds. No, for the love of God, no! True, Bill and Ben have more class than Mr Blobby, but not Noel Edmonds, no! On learning that there were plans to remake *The Flowerpot Men*, the *Daily Mail* ran an interview with Bill and Ben, intentionally forgetting, it seemed, that the only replies to the interviewer's pressing questions could and should have been 'Flobadopalop'. But there was such a huge audience for this kind of device, which serves up the poignant characters of childhood television in such an acceptably ironic context that it does not really matter that *The Flowerpot Men*'s memory was traduced. Who cared about the authenticity of Bill and Ben's quotes? In this re-creation frenzy, where programme makers and journalists are under pressure to allude to childhood bliss, authenticity is not everything.

When I read of the plans to re-create *Bill and Ben*, I was upset. It was as though someone had burgled my heart and taken away something that meant a great deal to me. And worse, that by taking that very private thing and making it public, it risked becoming ruined and losing any value for me. But what was it that I feared losing? I feared losing something as fragile and tender as the custard in a tart, my memories of watching *Bill and Ben* on television and all the innocence and warmth that I associated with that early part of my childhood. All that despite the fearful scramble to Bill and Ben's pots at the end of the programme.

I was upset, too, at the plans to remake *Captain Pugwash* and to introduce a new, green Brazilian character into *The Wombles* to make the programme even more fashionably eco-friendly. I felt, once more, that something was being taken from me and given to others who couldn't love it as much as I did. As a result it would be ruined forever. I feared that the Pugwash I loved and who was, all-too-clearly, a piece of card, bobbing in his equally rudimentary ship on waves that looked as though they were carved with a Stanley knife from old boxes, was going to be upgraded and thus lost to me for good. Pugwash was going to become a fully animated captain with a fully animated ship and crew. Cut-throat Jake was probably going to be improved too, which was a very terrible prospect.

What kind of misguided, unfeeling brutes would do this? I felt sure that the programme makers and commissioning editors associated with these re-creation projects were around the same age as me and yet had misguidedly decided to honour their nostalgia for the children's TV of their youth by making it again and making it better. But this was a mistake, I quickly realised, since in the process of upgrading what was going to get lost was the very lack of polish of *The Flowerpot Men*, the obviousness of Andy and Teddy's strings, the early-seventies particularity of *The Wombles*.

Or maybe these TV people sought to give these cherishable old characters a new life in order to entertain a new generation of young children. I particularly hated that possibility. If that was the case then they couldn't have them! They couldn't have my childhood memories. They were mine and these little boys and girls should get their own!

The strength of these feelings surprised me, since I'd always thought I'd flung away children's TV for good. Out of my heart and into oblivion. And yet, here was I, in my mid-thirties and worrying about the fate of bits of old card and puppets apparently made from flowerpots. I had not thrown those childhood puppets away, I now realised, nor had the programme makers and commissioning editors. I wanted something like what those people wanted, I wanted a return to custard tarts at my nan's table. But I didn't want a computer-generated *Pugwash.* I wanted what I couldn't have: I wanted my childhood back.

I realised as if for the first time that I and many other adults didn't want to relinquish our childhoods but instead wanted to keep them near, that some of us were having trouble saying goodbye for the last time. Especially since what we held dearly, locked away in our hearts, was the notion that these childhoods were pristine and perfect in ways that later life could never be.

All this feverish interpretation, re-interpretation and misinterpretation seems to me to be a big game of Fort-Da in which adults keep yanking the puppets back into their prams but pretend they're doing something if not more mature, then acceptably ironic; whereas really, I suspect, they're refusing to accept the loss of their or their audience's childhoods and the pain such a loss would entail.

Journalists write articles about Bill and Ben, Dougal or Andy Pandy; publishers put out books for adults based on old kids' TV shows; programme makers plan new versions of old series, new ways of helping us overcome or even obliterate that loss. But they can never quite succeed, since what we have lost we can never have back. If we cannot have our childhoods back, then we must do what we can to protect ourselves from the awful pain of that irredeemable loss. We must try to anaesthetise ourselves.

But this seems to me a hopeless project, since memories of TV are so fraught with feelings that will not be easily stilled. Surely this is because television itself, not just children's TV but the whole medium, is a substitute for one's mother. When she leaves to do the washing up in the next room, television is there to provide a consolation. When she leaves for longer periods, television can become a substitute – and sometimes an improvement. Unlike her, television is eternal: it is, and always will be, there. It is in what sociologists call a constant flow, since if you turn it off it is still there; if you turn it on, it is there as if it had never gone away – which, in a sense, it did not.

Television is different from the toy that Freud's grandson threw out of the pram. By throwing out the toy the baby was having a fantasy about destroying it; television is invulnerable to that kind of destructive fantasy.

The point is best made in *The Simpsons*. Ten-year-old Bart and eight-year-old Lisa regularly hug their television set, often in preference to their parents. They do so because it offers consolation – it seems and perhaps does give the stable 24-hours-a-day nurturing and pleasure that mom and dad could never manage. 'Bart? Lisa?' yelled their father Homer from upstairs. 'You're not hugging the TV again are you?'. But *of course* they were. For Bart and Lisa television is much more dependable than mere parents who are prone to drink beer in stupefying quantities, completely forget about their children, go on sordid sex weekends and have blue hair.

And for that infantilised adult Homer Simpson, too, television is more reliable than anything else. It is, he once said, 'friend, mother, secret lover'. It is a consolation, a socially acceptable comfort blanket. Homer is as much a child as his children, perhaps even more so. I have often felt that Homer is partly able to be childish because he never said goodbye to television, but kept it in his home and embraced it. No wonder then that on the one occasion when television betrays his trust, his world fell apart.

But how could that happen? How could television betray Homer's trust? In one episode, TV figured as the dominant, destructive force in the family's life. Homer was accused in a TV programme of sexually harassing his childminder. The programme had got hold of a video recording that purported to show him drooling over the woman and pinching her bottom as she got out of his car. Feminist mobs demonstrated outside his house, Marge doubted him in the face of the authoritative condemnation of TV newscaster Kent Brockman, even Bart and Lisa looked on their dad with renewed contempt.

In fact, though, another video clip shot from another angle (life, if it is anything on US TV, is something that is shot from multiple angles) showed that Homer was drooling over the Gummy Bear that had got stuck to his childminder's bottom and which he peeled off to satisfy his lust for jelly. Homer was an id in muck or a mouth on legs, not a harasser on heat. In the end, the television programme cleared him (and hundreds who had been wrongly accused like him, by means of small-print names rushing insanely quickly from the bottom to the top of the screen).

Then, when Marge and the kids had gone to bed, he looked left and right to make sure no one was watching him and then threw his arms around the TV set. 'Let's not argue again,' said Homer, pitifully, hugging the television as though he was, indeed, speaking to his secret lover.

For Homer, it would be a devastating blow to lose his television and its world of comfort. For me, about the same age now as Homer is, it is rather different. What was upsetting to me as a child were the daisies that replaced Andy Pandy's name; what is threatening to me now is that those lovely childhood memories, bound up with pain and loss, should be taken away. All of which is a way of saying that television has never been as important to me as it was in my childhood. Let's go back there again.

*

THE DARK SIDE OF LOUBY-LOU

In the 'Trampoline' episode of *Andy Pandy*, the story was wonderfully wholesome. Or at least it seemed that way. Valerie Cardnell, in a gay voice a world away from her mournful goodbye song, set the scene:

Andy Pandy's coming to play
La-la-la-la-laa-la.
Andy Pandy's here today
La-la-la-la-laaa!

Da, Andy! Da, Teddy! All the daisies had been replaced by letters and it was time for innocent fun. Andy was here again! Andy and Teddy were in their nursery. 'Here they are, and they're jumping!' exclaimed Vera. Yes, they were! And Valerie was singing!

Jumping, jumping,
Jumping up and down
Jumping, jumping
All around the town!

'See if you can jump when Andy and Teddy do,' Vera asked us. And so I did. 'One, two, three – jump!' I was jumping! Jumping around the living room!

But that wasn't all. Later, Andy and Teddy were shaking little bells that were tied to their wrists (and paws) with ribbons. Valerie sang:

Shake your bells and make them ring
Ting-a-ling
Ting-a-ling
Ting-a-ling
Ting!

Then Vera suggested that us children in the audience could have bells of our own. After all, Andy and Teddy's instruments were made up of toy bells sewn to ribbons. 'You could ask somebody to make some bells, couldn't you?' she asked. 'You could shake them next time, but this time let's pretend.' For the rest of the episode I shook my non-existent bells in time with Andy and Teddy.

Children's TV presenters were always inviting their young viewers or their young viewers' parents to make something. This was wholesomeness, this was TV playtime extended into the real world of making and glueing. Worst of all in this respect was *Blue Peter*, which caused a global shortage of egg boxes, sticky-back plastic and washing-up liquid bottles that saw no parallels until Delia Smith's Christmas recipe book caused a remarkable run on world cranberry stocks.

Once, I saw an edition of *Blue Peter* in which one of the presenters – probably John Noakes, conceivably Peter Purves, but surely not Valerie Singleton – suggested that I should make a brush. Inspired, I followed their instructions, such as I remembered them (which probably wasn't much). This brush, I felt sure, would be just the thing for a Christmas present for my mother. I took a wire coathanger, folded it in two and then asked my mother if I could have two balls of wool, one yellow and one blue. I wound the wool around the coathanger as if I was dancing around a maypole, covering it with alternating stripes of blue and yellow. I looked at my handiwork. It was a great disappointment to me. This 'brush', I knew, would never be used to clean anything. Maybe I had missed some vital stage in *Blue Peter*'s exposition, but, nonetheless, I gave this brush to my mother as a present. I think she smiled thinly, said little, and later put the brush in a drawer. Nothing more was said on the subject.

Andy and Teddy had finished playing in the nursery and went through the French windows into the garden to show Vera their trampoline. 'Show us what you can do,' Vera suggested to Andy, who bounced in a rather rudimentary way. 'That's splendid!' Then Teddy, his legs rotating around his torso, made an unconvincing leap on to the trampoline – there was one point at which the puppeteer seemed to hold him in mid-air just before he stood on the trampoline – just as though they were pausing at this crucial moment for a crafty drag on their cigarette.

Then Vera suggested that Andy and Teddy have a rest. There were milk and buns laid out inside for the pair of them. I imagined that, while Valerie was singing, Vera had spread a red-and-white-check tablecloth in a sunny corner of the room. On it she had placed a cool jug of milk and two glasses, along with a plate of fragrant buns, still warm from the oven. How soothing, how nourishing after all that jumping!

While they were inside, Louby-Lou appeared by the trampoline outside. We had seen her before while Andy and Teddy jumped in their room. Then she had been lying in the nursery rocking chair as stuffed with straw as Andy and Teddy were full of beans. But now, while Andy and Teddy were away, she came to life.

Who, who is Louby-Lou?
Little rag doll who plays with you.

So sang Valerie, but Louby-Lou's identity was a much more puzzling affair. This blonde, yellow-plaited Galatea in her dancing slippers topped with pom-poms and dotty skirt of blue and white was a puzzle. Why did she come to life only when Andy and Teddy were gone? Perhaps Andy and Teddy were not as nice as they seemed and, if they knew that she jumped on their trampoline they would punish her severely.

Louby's look-out was Valerie. 'Look out Louby, they're coming back,' she exclaimed, and, quick as a flash, Louby hurried off or fell plop into a seat, only the gleam in her button eyes suggesting that she was anything other than a stuffed doll.

But this deception was very different from Bill and Ben's subterfuge. In *The Flowerpot Men*, adults were the threat, which was easily comprehensible to a childhood viewer, particularly when I could imagine all kinds of horrible things about the unseen Gardener. And Bill and Ben's look-out was Weed, who was probably a child weed. In *Andy Pandy*, though, the look-out was adult Vera, which didn't make much sense in my childish philosophy. Here, it was important that Louby's ability to dance and play was not revealed to Andy and Teddy. They were the threat. But Andy Pandy and Teddy were puppets and thus honorary children. In fact, Andy was a child, just like you and me. Wasn't he?

We would never know. Like Louby-Lou and Teddy, Andy did not speak or at least not to us. Perhaps he confided in Vera – but, no, let's not think about that. That would have been a terrible betrayal.

The television programmes I watched when I was young teemed with Galateas like Louby, puppets that came to life. The sight of life apparently breathing through an inert rag doll was uncanny to me and even frightening. It was as uncanny as the scene in Shakespeare's *The Winter's Tale* in which Leontes sees a statue of his dead wife Hermione and that statue comes to life. Unlike Hermione, who forsakes marble and becomes fleshly-warm to the touch, Louby could never become human: those button eyes were always signs that she was really a doll, though she had a strange life of her own. Stranger yet, after she had danced for the conspiratorial children in the TV audience, Louby-Lou fell back into seeming lifelessness – not death, since she weekly made it seem to Andy and Teddy that she had never been alive. And not real lifelessness either, since as she slumped, concealing from them that she was out of breath after all that dancing, she was still alive.

This toying with life and lifelessness was a common trope of much children's television. In *Bagpuss*, for example, all the toy animals lay lifeless in sepia inside the lost and found shop until Emily came in carrying the premise for that week's episode in her hot little hands. She always brought an object which she hoped to have repaired by Bagpuss and his friends. But first she had to wake him from his slumbers with her magic spell:

Bagpuss
Oh Bagpuss
Oh fat furry cat puss
Wake up and look at this thing
That I bring.
Wake up, be bright
Be golden and light
Oh Bagpuss
Hear what I sing!

And, with that, Bagpuss roused himself, and his sepia coat would become pink, as though he had lost the ancient aura of Victoriana and found the bright new colours of the seventies. But it wasn't only the old furry cat puss who awoke but also the mice at the mouse organ, Professor Yaffle the woodpecker bookend, Madeleine the rag doll (Louby-Lou's distant cousin) and Gabriel the little toad who strummed a banjo. A whole menagerie came to life to see, but more importantly to help, Emily play.

This was meant as a playful, fantastical affair, but the gloomy Gothic quality to Bagpuss's lost and found shop alienated me. I was not alienated from Bagpuss himself, because he was a lovely lump who, I imagined, had a zip sewn across his stomach into which I could stuff my pyjamas. But Professor Yaffle – even though the animators Peter Firmin and Oliver Postgate had created a wonderful image of severe bookishness – always scared me. He was so pointy that I feared he would leave his wooden perch and anoint my head with his beak. His wooden feathers looked to me like chainmail, so that he was wearing a warrior bird's uniform. And his severe expression seemed suited to nothing so much as hurting me, to pecking me again and again and again until the blood flowed.

My very young self was worried by these TV puppets. Not just those that seemed scary by design – like Professor Yaffle or the Soup Dragon from *The Clangers* – but almost all of them, since each week many of them came alive and later fell back into lifelessness. They could never be my friends while they played so, not least because the point of the subterfuge behind these peek-a-boo games with life and lifelessness was always either darkly disturbing (as in *Bill and Ben*) or darkly obscure.

I imagined a great deal about these puppets' inner lives. Behind those empty stares, I was convinced, were souls in torment. Sometimes I thought that Sooty, for instance, looked at me enviously because he was unhappy with his existential lot. His eyes followed me around the room, just like Lord Kitchener's did in the World War One recruitment poster. But Sooty was more troubling than Lord Kitchener's image because he wasn't an image but a puppet who had come to a semblance of life – and a life which, I feared, he didn't like living.

Sooty, I thought in later years, was like the Greek philosopher Cratylus. Cratylus found the world and his role in it so distressing that he was reduced to communicating by waggling a finger. I supposed Sooty was similar. Sooty didn't even have a finger to waggle, just a pair of inarticulate paws. Like Cratylus he long ago took a vow of silence to express his fundamental frustration at the world. I knew and know that he did and does whisper the odd remark into the ear of Harry Corbett, or, latterly, to Matthew: 'Why did you bring Sweep into the world? Don't you love me enough?' he hisses. 'Why do you find strings of sausages funny *every* week?' he sighs. Otherwise, though, like Andy, Teddy and Louby-Lou, he has been effectively mute for many years.

I imagined Sooty's life. When he leapt with newborn vigour on to Harry's hand more than half a century ago, Sooty was full of himself. Since then, though, he has been filled with someone else. Initially, it was the existential absurdity of his predicament that reduced Sooty to silence. When somebody (sometimes Harry, but selfish Matthew made a habit of it) failed to trim the fingernails of the hand that went up Sooty's backside, he became inexpressibly angry. When Sooty emerged from the rinse cycle to find that he was still covered in suds and had to go through the whole undignified process again – well, you can imagine, it would drive even a stuffed bear to desperate measures. And so it was with Sooty.

Perhaps it is no surprise that children's puppets seemed so threateningly alien to me. After all, they're treated in rather the same disgraceful way as domestic cats. We lure cats into our homes with tins of food and thus infantilise them. They can no longer hunt properly and so are utterly dependent on us. And yet, we expect them to be grateful. Sometimes when my cats stare at me, without (really) a thought in their soft little heads, I fear that they are resentful of me, that they are plotting to revenge themselves on me for what I did to them. It's rather the same with Sooty. We ripped out his heart and his other vital organs, stuck him on the end of a hand and expected him to entertain us.

This is perhaps fanciful, yet it explains at least to my satisfaction why I never felt a close affinity with Sooty, Sweep, Soo, Ramsbottom or any other puppet. They were too alien, too facially immobile. They were always rather scary, since behind those blank eyes that would never leave me alone were souls that resented me. When they came to life I feared there was more than a chance that they would hurt me in revenge for what humans did to them. I imagined myself like Tippi Hedren in *The Birds*, but pecked and bitten and scratched by outraged puppets, all rushing into battle against me after Andy Pandy had given the signal by lowering his general's arm awkwardly.

THE INDISPUTABLE LEADER OF THE GANG

As I grew up, it became clear that television was not something that one only experienced alone. It was not just a private world of fears, fantasies and pleasures. It had a public character, and it was demanded of me that I share my experiences of what I had seen with schoolfriends. There was a risk in all this – that by sharing I would mangle what made the experiences pleasurable. But there was also comfort, since sharing experiences or pretending to share experiences helped me to make friends.

When *Top Cat* was shown in Britain, for example, we stood in the playground of my primary school and meditated on why the cartoon was listed in the *Radio Times* as *Boss Cat*. Did the stuffed shirts at the BBC think that we didn't get the jive, daddio, that us Limeys wouldn't understand the phrase Top Cat, that it needed to be translated into English vernacular? No it couldn't be that. In any case, it didn't make sense for the show to be called *Boss Cat* because the sometime eponymous hero was referred to throughout the programme as Top Cat, or TC, or even, by his closest buddies, as Teece. Why were we being misled? Years later, I found out that there was a short-lived brand of cat food called *Top Cat* and to prevent inadvertent promotion of it, the show was re-titled.

But the facts always slightly eluded us, and we imagined all kinds of things to fill in the gaps. When someone pointed out to me recently that one of the words in the closing song was the word 'Vip', an acronym that was pronounced rather than spelled out, my world view changed significantly. For years, decades probably, I had sung:

He's the boss
He's a pip,
He's the championship.
He's the most tip-top
Top Cat!

In my heart of hearts, I knew that no male alley cat would be called a pip, and certainly it ill-behoved a little boy to run around a playground singing lyrics that drew attention to the attractiveness of a mature tom cat, but at least the word sounded like a word that would be used in fifties New York (admittedly in reference to a woman, or at least a particularly hot girl cat, one of those curvy cuties cartoon male cats fell for to the accompaniment of sleazy sax music). It just about fitted. And, while

He's the boss
He's the Vip,
He's the championship.
He's the most tip-top
Top Cat!

makes more sense – TC is a very important person as the moniker Top Cat would suggest – really, has anyone in polite conversation ever said Vip, as they would say Acas or quango? No, they have not. VIP is not an acronym that one pronounces. VIP was spelled out, like TGWU or UNHCR. I came to realise that the proper lyric was silly and written on a very thin day, inspiration-wise.

But fidelity to the actual lyrics of children's TV songs was hardly my strong suit. Nor did it matter much to my school-friends. After all, we would march around the playground singing:

Top Cat, he's ineffectual
Ba-daah! [that was our simulation of the horns]
Top Cat,
His intellectual
Ba-daah! [so was that]
close friends
get to call him TC.
They have bread and dripping for tea.

Yeah, right. Wise-guy Brooklyn alley cats had bread and dripping for tea, just as I did on Sunday evenings. Why, they probably had little sticks of celery, too, and fairy cakes. And what was that stuff about TC being ineffectual? Where did pre-pubescent boys get that kind of language? But at least these were songs that you could sing outside your living room. Andy Pandy's *Jumping, jumping, jumping up and down* was not the same.

Debating issues that arose from children's programmes on television and singing their title songs in public were two of the main ways in which I became a social animal. We used to sing: *Get on board, get on board, get on board, with the Double Deckers!* And we would sing lyrics that had been modified by older, delinquent boys:

I'm Bayleaf the gardener
I rise at early dawn
And go to the shop
To buy a lot of porn.

Sometimes, too, we would run in tight little circles, chasing non-existent tails:

I'm Dill the dog
I'm a dog called Dill

we shouted to anyone who cared to hear.

And we used to try to piece together the lyrics of *Magpie*, too, even though it was shown on ITV and thus was fearfully common, certainly in comparison with its goody-goody BBC1 rival, *Blue Peter*.

One for sorrow
Two for joy
Three for a girl
And four for a boy
Five for silver
Six for gold
Seven for a secret
Never to be told
Eight's a wish
And nine's a kiss
Ten is a bird
You must not miss.

Maa-aaaa-aag-pie!

But, even more important than these nice debates about television and the performances of songs, were the large questions of group identity. If you could choose who you would be in TC's gang, who would it be? This was a very difficult question to answer, not just in the privacy of my bedroom, but worse, much worse, when it had to be decided among friends, among fellow gang members. Only the very reckless or very good at fighting would lay a claim to be Top Cat himself.

I never wanted to get involved in all that. I didn't want to spend my years back-talking Officer Dibble or explaining to teachers and parents where I got a black eye and a fat lip. But then who else could I want to be? Not Benny the Ball, all chubbiness and well-meaning incompetence, even though he was an heir to some Manhattan fortune. And not Fancy-Fancy, since ladies' men were as yet incomprehensible to me and my gang. Nor Brains, because he was too nerdy. Nor Spook, just because the name sounded scary. Instead, I wanted to be Choo Choo, who wore a long turtleneck and spoke with a high monotone. Chooch was the kind of guy who would have a life apart from TC's Bilko-esque scheming. He was semi-detached and yet still part of the gang – which was the arrangement that I wanted. Choo Choo had a life in the Village, I now suspect, sitting hunched in a pair of shades, clicking his fingers in a groovy beatnik juice bar. Maybe, too, he dug the cultural life of the city in a way inconceivable, say, to nice-but-dim Benny, who was voiced by Maurice Gosfield, the same man who played nice-but-dim Private Doberman in *The Phil Silvers Show*. Yeah, that's right – Chooch would hang out wherever Miles Davis blew, or where Allen Ginsberg sucked. His turtleneck, that symbol of fifties difference, told me something of all this when I was very young.

Years later, I was dozing on the sofa with a black and white movie on the screen. It was a courtroom drama. The judge asked the stenographer to read back a piece of testimony, and suddenly I was transported to TC's alley. It was Chooch's voice, every bit as distinctive as Benny's, but more whiney, more Noo Yawk, more autennick. I stretched long and languorously on the sofa like a cat in a turtleneck: I was right to choose Chooch.

It was easier to choose which member of International Rescue you would be. The leader of the Thunderbirds gang was Jeff Tracy and, let's face it, he was a dad and so could be no boy's first choice as a role model. I had one friend who wanted to be Parker, the comedy English chauffeur, perhaps because he got to drive Lady Penelope around in a pink Rolls-Royce, but he wasn't a close friend.

When I was a boy, I immediately plumped for Virgil Tracy. True, he was fatter necked and more sweaty than Scott, and true, he did play appalling sixties cocktail jazz on the piano as they relaxed in the lounge of their island home, waiting like firefighters for the call that would turn them from lounge lizards into professional emergency service puppets. What's more, Scott was second in command, and flew Thunderbird 1 which was a rocket that pumped a reassuringly large amount of exhaust fumes towards the Tracys' swimming pool when it took off.

Those considerations notwithstanding, I wanted to be Virgil. John was in orbit at the helm of Thunderbird 5, whose role in the drama was chiefly to pass on messages retrieved from satellites to his dad back at the island HQ. He was the Greta Garbo of the Tracys, and nobody in my gang would have been pleased if I had chosen him. John, the anti-social Thunderbird. I could have chosen to be Alan who flew the orange rocket that was Thunderbird 3, but that was too similar to Thunderbird 1. And who would want to be Gordon in Thunderbird 4? After all, he only drove a yellow submarine, so he was only going to be at the heart of the action occasionally. No, it had to be Virgil. He flew the green Thunderbird, which would carry the tools for various rescue missions. Virgil was always at the centre of the action and, better than that, each week he went through the same elaborate take-off ritual. As his engines speeded up on the runway, a little flap would open on the ground to catch the exhaust fumes. Where did the fumes go after that? Perhaps to fill canisters with carbon monoxide that would one day – oh, yes, one day – be used to poison the evil Hood in his Thai retreat. After the fumes had disappeared underground, the palm trees that fringed both sides of the runway entrancingly bent away from Thunderbird 2 as it sped towards take off.

The larger, political questions did not engage us as children. But they do now. On what authority was International Rescue acting? And what was the deal with the Hood? When his eyes lit up red as he inflicted some 'hoodoo' on his adversaries, was this some rather sinister critique of orientalism? I think that it was.

The choice of role models that children's television offered helped me work out where I wanted to be in social groups. I didn't want to lead, nor was being subsumed by a group at all appealing. Being completely alienated from the gang was no option either. And yet, like Chooch, like Virgil, I wanted to be sufficiently autonomous to have a life of my own. I could walk away from the gang and be on my own, like Virgil the puppet poppet of a Thunderbird, any time I wanted, my hands dangling heavily at my sides and my legs skipping just a little implausibly.

THE BUSTY SUCCUBUS

In the playground, we also showed off by lying about how late we had stayed up to watch television. It was a sign of one's relative maturity if one had seen programmes designed for adults. When I was about ten, it became socially imperative that I see *Monty Python's Flying Circus*. Not just that this was on late, but because even I could tell that this was a cultural event of great moment and transgressive cachet, and it would impress my mates if I had seen it. I knew this to be the case because my parents moaned about it, were revolted by it and wouldn't let me stay up to watch it.

Only once did I see *Monty Python* when I was very young. The one sketch I recall from that show upset me a lot. It was the one in which Michael Palin plays a milkman who found a busty woman in a negligée leaning on her door jamb provocatively. In a disturbing dumb show of sorry heterosexual seduction, she lured him inside and up the stairs. Bliss, his reptilian face suggested, was what he expected to find with this succubus at the top of the stairs. She ushered him into the bedroom where, instead of bliss, he found the room crowded with milkmen like him. They looked at him miserably – another patsy for the collection. He looked at them, slowly realising what had happened. They sat on the bed in their caps and matching tunics, or leaned against the window ledge. They were her prisoners and their bottles of milk which they clutched bleakly were her booty.

I didn't find this sketch funny at all, even though the laughter track suggested that it was supposed to be amusing. What was going to happen to these men? Would they be kept there forever, long after their milk had gone sour, until they rotted in their uniforms and the smell alerted the neighbours? Why didn't the dairy tell the police to mount a search for all these missing milkmen, who had all disappeared on the same route, leaving their floats parked in the street? Well, why not? Or maybe something else was going on. Maybe she was collecting these milkmen until she had got a complete set and then she would drain them, one by one, like milk bottles, drain them easily and finally. Either way, it didn't look so hot for Michael Palin and his chums.

The following day, I couldn't talk about these questions at school to my friends. Instead, I related a mildly titillating version of the sketch, akin, no doubt, to the surface reading that had made the studio audience laugh, or had prompted the director to add canned laughter. And yet, I had to tell something of what I had seen: after all, there was great social capital in having been allowed to see *Monty Python*, especially when it clearly seemed to have something to do with something as strange as sex.

THE CULTURAL SIGNIFICANCE OF DR MOPP'S CAR

Thomas Tripp, the milkman in *Camberwick Green*, was never lured indoors by a scantily clad female customer. Nothing like that happened in *Camberwick Green*. Nothing untoward happened in Trumptonshire, nothing that would be symptomatic of deep-seated social neuroses.

In Trumpton, society ran like clockwork, like the big town clock that we saw at the start of the episode, or like the clockwork waltz that the fire brigade band played in the bandstand at the end.

At nearby Camberwick Green, life ticked by on the same orderly lines. The first shot was of a musical box which the narrator, Brian Cant, assured us was 'wound up and ready to play', and, as it wound down, the segments on the top would slide apart and one of the puppet characters from the show would be raised up by means, I have always supposed, of a tiny hydraulic lift knocked up in his spare time by Mr Crockett at the garage. But the ticking musical box was a metaphor for how life should be lived: it was measured and rarely, if ever, disturbing. In *Camberwick Green*, everyone had sensibly diversified into specialist trades that made the town work as a well-regulated organic entity. Not only was there Thomas Tripp, but there was PC McGarry (number 452), Mickey Murphy, the baker, Peter Hazel, the postman, Mrs Dingle, the postmistress, Jonathon Bell, the farmer, Mr Carraway, the fishmonger, Roger Varley, the chimney sweep, Windy Miller, who lived at Colley's Mill, Mr Crockett at the garage. Nothing here went very awry: when Windy Miller drank too much cider, for example, he became sleepy rather than fist-fightingly drunk, and dozed off propped up against his mill as the sails turned around him, coolly fanning his sweaty face. Mrs Honeyman, the chemist's wife, was a gossip, it is true, but she was a tolerated social necessity. Gossiping, after all, is an important trade that oils the wheels of other people's industry. It was not clear in which era *Camberwick Green* was set, but Mrs Honeyman did have a long skirt with a hint of the bustle about it, and Dr Mopp wore a top hat and drove a boneshaker of a car. Perhaps the creators of *Camberwick Green* were striving to link their town with the Edwardian past: back to a time when the car had just been invented and yet everything was not yet ruined by technology's acceleration. Indeed, many films of the sixties had a fascination with this period, from *Chitty Chitty Bang Bang* to *Mary Poppins* and *Bedknobs and Broomsticks*. Perhaps this was as near to a time of good order and innocence as British people could imagine in the late twentieth century, as they looked back to those childish days when the century was not even in its teens.

If there was a minor mishap in *Camberwick Green*, though, it would be resolved by Captain Snort and Sergeant Major Grout, who commanded the troops at Pippin Fort. The troops were pleasingly unreal. They sat in two rows facing each other in their army truck that transported them, like the Tracy brothers of International Rescue but on a smaller, more British, less technologically accomplished scale, to deal with an emergency. They wore red tunics and their helmets were of the kind worn by soldiers on the lids of tins of Quality Street. They may have even been made of chocolate themselves: certainly, they looked good enough to eat, but not mean enough to fight. There was no problem that these boys could not sort out; no higher authority that could be appealed to in case of some dire emergency.

It was similar in Trumpton where, when the firemen assembled, we knew that whatever problem the town faced would be sorted out quickly. As the Trumpton clock ticked, Captain Flack in his marvellous helmet and matching, equally marvellous moustache, would summon his men: 'Pugh, Pugh, Barney McGrew, Cuthbert, Dibble, Grubb'.

It still remains one of the most memorably rhythmic pieces of poetry I know. But, heaven forfend, if one of these men was not there or did not answer his call, everything would fall apart – not only Captain Flack's moustache, but Trumptonite order. Each man would snap smartly to attention and then they would climb aboard the fire engine and ride through the town. Fire brigade recruiting officers couldn't buy that kind of publicity: subliminally, this weekly scene made firefighting seem as though it was the best of professions, one where you could be a hero during every shift and everybody in society admired you.

After disaster had been averted, the firemen would go to play at the bandstand. What a fine town in which to live! After a hard day's work, one would take one's hat and cane, link arms with one's good lady wife and stroll through peaceful streets backlit by the declining sun, to hear clockwork waltzes, music that was so potently emblematic of the social structure we all enjoyed. Could life get any better than this?

The Camberwick-Green-Trumpton-Chigley military-industrial-complex hove into view at the end of the sixties, as London swung, as Paris revolted and as I ate custard tarts blithely ignorant that there were sit-ins in art schools all over the Birmingham–Black Country conurbation. The world was going crazy and, or so it seemed, Trumptonshire would have none of it. Camberwick Green, probably unwittingly, supplied me with a conservative counter agenda to the counter-culture. I had jumped aboard a Wellsian time machine, back to the Edwardian era where Dr Mopp drove unimpeded through the country lanes of England under the summer sun to fulfil his duties, and back to the time when the force of law and order, and indeed anybody in a uniform, was prized.

In this context, *Dad's Army*, which was first broadcast in 1968, was an ironic critique of the presumptuousness of Trumptonshire's vision of British society. *Dad's Army* told us that in Britain, thank heaven, nothing worked like clockwork. That only happened in Nazi Germany. There, perhaps, employees would go dancing across the shop floor after the whistle blew; there, perhaps, townspeople would gather as one to hear the fire brigade band play at the bandstand in the park. But not in Britain.

In *Dad's Army*, if anyone thought otherwise – that, in fact, Britain was a perfectly well run society that made Nazi Germany seem like pre-fascist Italy – they were gently mocked. Indeed, anyone who expressed strong political views about British superiority would be mocked. Once, for instance, Private Pike made Captain Mainwaring a cup of tea. Inadvertently, he spilled some sand in the cup rather than sugar. But Mainwaring took the cup without having noticed this. He sat back in his chair and took a long, refreshing drink. Marvellous stuff! Mainwaring said to Sergeant Wilson: 'I bet they're not drinking anything like this over in Germany.' No, agreed Wilson, exchanging a conspiratorial glance with Pike. They were not.

Then Mainwaring went into one of his homilies about Nazism: 'Blind obedience, Wilson. Blind obedience.' True, perhaps, but Wilson held to a different view, even though he was no Nazi. He believed that the Germans wore 'awfully smart' uniforms and, let's face it, he was right, certainly when one compared Nazi uniforms with the ill-tailored bits of sack the Home Guard wore, God bless them. But such subversive thoughts could not have been expressed in a perfect society such as Camberwick Green: there, no criticism of the military or indeed of the social structures of society would have been tolerable.

And yet, in Walmington-on-Sea, there was a small-town orderliness akin to those model societies of Trumptonshire. Everyone had their place in a civilian command structure that was echoed by the ranks of the Home Guard. Mainwaring was the bank manager and thus one of the most powerful men in town; Wilson was his deputy at the bank and thus was also properly his deputy in the Home Guard; Pike was their office boy. Jones, not only because of his military past evoked chiefly by his memories of bayonet charges during the Boer War ('They don't like it up 'em, sir! They don't like it up 'em!'), but also because he was a butcher and thus in wartime, temporarily at least, a figure of huge socio-economic leverage, was a corporal. Frazer, the stereotypically dour, miserly Scotsman was an undertaker – one of the few trades that was not represented in *Camberwick Green*, perhaps because it was thought that children should not be encouraged in their earliest years to think of death. Godfrey was a fancy-free gadabout, or at least he would have been if his bladder had been less troublesome, while it was his sister Dolly who did the work, keeping Walmington supplied with upside-down cakes.

Walmington wasn't quite upside down, then, but it was a place where social tensions were comically rife. It had, for instance, a class system. Warden Hodges was an uppity prole who, while he condemned Mainwaring for being a Napoleon, was every bit as vainglorious and bumptious as his rival (if not quite as physically similar as Arthur Lowe was to the stout Corsican). No, Warden Hodges was only a greengrocer in Civvy Street and, now and again, Wilson, the effete public schoolboy, would have occasion to remark to Mainwaring, the middle-class bastion of wartime Walmington, that Hodges' fingernails were filthy. For once there was unanimity between the upper and the middle class of Wilson and Mainwaring, a conspiracy of white-collared men against the commoner who put potatoes and carrots into ladies' shopping bags, day in day out.

And yet, when I was a little boy, I realised quickly, too, that *Dad's Army* was part of the nostalgia industry that held this country by the throat. This sitcom idealised a past when we were first and foremost British and, even if some of us did have dirty fingernails, that was not an overwhelming problem, still less a reason to overturn society. It was a kinder, gentler, more appealing age than the real one of the late sixties.

Much later, I read a novel by Alison Lurie set in the late sixties that expressed a similar distaste for the present. In *The War Between the Tates*, Erica Tate has lost her husband to a student, lost her children to adolescence and lost her bearings in the world: 'I don't care about nineteen-sixty-nine at all. I don't care about rock festivals or black power or student revolutions or going to the Moon. I feel like an exhausted time traveller. All these new developments they have, maybe they're interesting . . . but they have nothing to do with real life.'

Real life was back when nothing was problematic, when her husband loved her, her children were cute and nobody had burned down the A & P. In Britain this sentiment is much more widely expressed. We are encouraged to want to live in the past where society was more homogeneous and people were more strongly, even sentimentally linked, or rather in a past that is all the better for never having really existed. Hence some of *Dad's Army*'s enduring appeal. Hence, too, much of the soothingly orderly quality to Camberwick Green and Trumpton, those mythical towns which borrowed freely from a better Britain's past.

But this mythical, recycled British past is nothing if not ubiquitous. In the Christmas 1998 edition of the Past Times catalogue, for instance, from which you could have chosen from a selection of 'fine gifts inspired by the past', there were sections on Medieval, Tudor, Stuart, Edwardian, Victorian and 20th-Century gifts. In the 18th-century section there was a picture of Admiral Nelson boxer shorts, pure silk and machine washable, and inscribed with the words said by Horatio, Lord Nelson before the Battle of Trafalgar at which he was killed in 1805: 'England expects that every man will do his duty.' A few pages back, you could have bought three *Dad's Army* videos and a book entitled *Dad's Army: A Celebration* of the BBC sitcom that 'still holds a special place in the nation's hearts'. Next to the *Dad's Army* videos was a picture of a World War One storm lighter, only £12.99. It was a better version of the kind of lighter that the soldiers of World War One made from used bullet cases. Better because it had a smooth sliding case which guarded the flame from any draught and extinguished it when lowered, and better because it was not made of used bullet cases but of brass. Similarly, *Dad's Army* was not made from bullet cases, nor forged in the heat of battle, even though battle raged and blood spilled freely nearby, but remade the past in such a way that we might – we ought to – want to make it our home. Thus, Britain recycles its history, remakes it better without the taint of blood and violence, leaving it mythical and thus safe for us to live there for the first time.

By the end of the sixties, I had learned a lot about Britain from watching television. For me, it was a baby in a pram, hurling its past away and then dragging it back, all the while trying to make it something that it was not, to exercise some mastery over a recalcitrant toy that wouldn't yield easily, that wouldn't become what the baby wanted without a struggle. Only after a long wrangle would this toy become smashed into what the child wanted it to be, and then it would be ready to be adapted into a sitcom or a costume drama or into a children's programme that might encourage a growing boy to love his country rather than try to destroy it.

CHAPTER 2

1970: Gordon Banks's Stomach

BREAKFAST IN MEXICO

Football became important to me in 1970, when I watched the World Cup finals from Mexico on television. I was too young for England's victory in the 1966 World Cup to make much sense. That contest couldn't have supplied a personal memory, but rather became, thanks to endless repeats, part of a public memory that I shared with all England football fans. Instead, 1966 was to me as much as to later English footballers, an overbearing legacy, a singular triumph which Englishmen could only aspire to repeat. And, in those ensuing decades of fruitless aspiration, we lived in a world of pain. When Frank Skinner and David Baddiel sang 'Three Lions' before the Euro '96 tournament, one line in the patriotic lyric cut through the usual, proverbial banality of football song sentiments:

Three lions on the shirt
Jules Rimet still gleaming
Thirty years of hurt
Never stopped me dreaming.

Thirty years of hurt! At long last a football song that dared to declare its emotions. At last a song that spoke to me about football. Of course, it wasn't just hurt that I felt for thirty years: it was exasperation, anger, revulsion, self-disgust (What was I *doing* supporting this inert team? What was this fragment of patriotism doing, winking at me from the dust into which I thought I had crushed such impulses?), and the occasional, very occasional moment of joy. I felt joy, for instance, when I sat with friends watching England versus Scotland in Euro '96. Gazza lobbed the ball over Colin Hendry, caught it on the volley and blasted it past Jim Leighton at Wembley. I felt joy because I couldn't believe that English footballers could create a footballing moment of such athletic grace and beauty. But mostly I have felt pain. When that German whose name I don't want to recall did his peacock strut after scoring the penalty that knocked England out in the semis a few days later, I felt pain.

And more pain. There was pain when, say, I watched England draw with Poland in 1973, on the dark night of the soul when Jan Tomaszewski, the goalkeeper wrongly described as a clown by Brian Clough, defied expectations, when petite Alan Ball foolishly squared up to massive Jerzy Gorgon and the late substitute, Kevin Hector, failed to scramble the ball into the net from inside the six-yard box, and so England could not go to the finals in Munich. There was pain, too, when the late substitutions of Kevin Keegan and Trevor Brooking, those by-then-old war-horses come to save the day, had negligible impact against Spain in the last minutes of England's involvement in the 1982 World Cup finals. There was pain when Chris Waddle shot over the bar in the quarter-final penalty shoot-out against Germany in Italia '90. There was pain when, in Euro '96, Gareth Southgate – oh, God, no, I can't think about that now. And there was mature resignation when, in France in 1998, David Batty turned to face the camera, his penalty a joke trickle, his mouth pulled downwards. I say there was mature resignation, but a lot of cats got kicked that night round my way. I have a wealth of TV memories of England's failure, more than thirty years of hurt, pain, upset and frustration watching long, long minutes in the second half of some game knowing, *knowing* that, despite all their pressure, England will never score. And yet staying in front of the screen until it is all over.

The legacy of 1966 stands there in black and white TV re-runs, as proud as the Wembley divots that lay across the turf in the final minutes of extra time as Geoff Hurst bore down on the left – what pace after nearly two hours of running! – and unleashed a shot into the top corner to the commentary by Kenneth Wolstenholme that is engraved on England's national memory: 'They think it's all over – it is now!'

But that's all ancient history now – as dim and other-worldly as some of the other scenes from the 1966 World Cup that I've seen on re-runs. When the Soviet Union and West Germany – those nations that once made history, but which now *are* history – played each other in the semi-finals at Goodison Park, for instance, there were no advertising hoardings around the touchline for the BBC to broadcast free of charge, only the alphabet painted large along a low wall by the half-way line, as though the groundsmen could think of nothing more than simple lettering as suitable decoration for the ground and for improving the verbal skills of young schoolchildren in the television audience. Or when North Korea took on Portugal in an earlier round, the editor cut to a crowd of Englishmen in ties and raincoats, applauding the underdogs, even though they were communists. Were these crowds football fans, or editors from Faber & Faber on a day out with only literary conventions of the nature of sport to guide them as to how to behave in such circumstances? The latter, clearly.

But the most suggestive moments of the 1966 World Cup came in the England–Portugal semi-final. Bobby Charlton, having scored with a fine shot, trotted back towards the centre circle, and was greeted by a Portuguese player, who shook his hand! It was the sort of gesture that never occurred in the world of football I was used to. I was used to televised football in the seventies – with all the on-terrace hooliganism, on-pitch kissing and thoroughgoing unpleasantness that that implies. He shook Charlton's hand, as if to say: 'Setting aside our national differences, I have to congratulate you on the excellence of the goal. Perhaps, sir, when this contest is over, you might consider accepting my hospitality in Lisbon? My daughter is unattached and I am sure would be be delighted to receive your attentions and perhaps, ultimately, take your hand in marriage.' And, in a later moment, the great Portuguese striker Eusebio put a penalty kick past Gordon Banks. Then he picked up the ball from the back of the net and ran with it back to the centre spot, stopping only to gently, tenderly even, pat Banks's neck. It's hard to convey the strangeness of this gesture since it is now a commonplace one, used by a striker to convey triumph mixed, patronisingly, with disdain, but there was no sense of these qualities in Eusebio's considerate, sporting pat.

Portugal, then, is a lovely land of revolutionary custard tarts and has a proud heritage of nobility in defeat on the football field. But these weren't my main conclusions from watching re-runs of the 1966 World Cup. Rather, my main reflection was that the very fact that the 1966 World Cup was shot in black and white highlighted how the absence of colour has become, in my mind, fundamental to the visual language of monumental history on television. In this sense, there was little difference for me between the 1966 World Cup and *The World At War* – both were historical records of impossibly distant eras. The black and white photography of the World Cup in 1966 cemented together all those other qualities – the gentlemanliness, the lack of commercialism, the sight of rows of men in ties applauding – and made them look ancient and alien. It was also important for me that this black and white history was filmed in England, since this confirmed for me the image of the country before I was aware of a national consciousness: this was a colourless land, even as London swung, even in the heat of the summer, even at the noon apex of England's sporting achievement.

National football for me has always had to be a television event, because I can't bear to share a stadium with my compatriots. The only time I saw England play when I was in the stadium was in 1984, when I went into Wembley supporting England and came out supporting Ireland, their opponents. I was surrounded on the terraces by compatriots I wanted to disown. Racist, stupid, graceless, miserable, thuggish, ugly, worthless – these were the English fans who were taunting the Irish as we walked up Olympic Way from the Tube. When the game began, and Ireland played with spirit and England with their customary indecisiveness in the final third of the field, that old heavy feeling returned to me, that feeling born of hours watching England's post-1966 failures, the feeling that disclosed my team would never play with panache or gusto. Panache and gusto, anyway, weren't English words. I remember one man standing near me holding a cross of St George flag with the words Peterborough United written on it. He booed every Irish kick and then, late in the second half, loudly told his mates they should stay behind to beat up some Irishmen in the crowd. I wanted to yell deep into his face the lyrics of the best anti-racist song I know, 'Burn It Down' by Dexy's Midnight Runners. It's a song that consists of a chanted chorus of some of the greats of Irish literature: *Oscar Wilde, Brendan Behan, Sean O'Casey, George Bernard Shaw. Samuel Beckett, Edna O'Brien, Laurence Sterne.* I wanted to pit these writers against his thuggishness. But the song doesn't end there. After the chorus, Kevin Rowland, the lead singer, shouts angrily as if into the face of a very thick Englishman, like this man from Peterborough, one who wouldn't recognise any of these names: *Shut it! You don't understand it. Shut it! That's not the way I planned it. Shut your mouth till you know the truth.*

Instead, as the game drew to an end and my friends began singing, without passion, without pride, but with a wet sentimentality, the song the man from Peterborough had begun: 'We love you England! We do/ We love you England! We do' – I knew they wouldn't be friends for much longer. Only connect? Yes, but not here and not with these people.

Since then, I've never seriously contemplated going to see an England match because the team attracts the wrong elements. Instead, I follow my country's football progress as often as not alone. If television has been a national unifier since 1953 – bringing Britons together in a virtual community to share the spectacle of the Queen's coronation, to witness Margaret Thatcher quoting St Francis of Assisi on the steps of 10 Downing Street, to take in a world of catchphrases from television that would later become part of what it is to be British in the second half of the 20th century – then football broadcasting has shown more than anything else the paradox of the unified culture television has produced. We watch football together as a country, but in the privacy of our own living rooms, linked by technology rather than warm hugs on the terraces. And we do this, not only because it is more convenient, cheaper, less easy to miss the key moments of a game, but, partly at least, because we don't like our compatriots enough to want to stand with them for even ninety minutes in a large football stadium. For me, this isn't a small matter, since when I support the English football team this is one of the few times I experience patriotic feelings that otherwise I regard as contemptible. The paradox is reinforced because, when we watch football, we are exposed to a community of footballers who, when one of them scores, hug, and do, for a few moments at least, share their feelings. Perhaps you could get something of this experience watching the game down the pub – but in England only if you prepared yourself for emotional abandonment by getting thoroughly drunk beforehand.

In 1970, I was only seven, so the option of going down the

pub to follow England was not feasible or even comprehensible, still less because the most important reports from the World Cup in Mexico were broadcast during breakfast. This was many years before programmes were broadcast regularly on British television at breakfast, and so was a singular luxury.

The appeal of watching these football highlights over toast and tea was enhanced by the vibrant colour of the images. Was it my imagination or was colour more intense in Mexico than it was in England? There were lots of stories then about the England players sweating seven or eight pints during a game, and this contributed to the fanciful aura that surrounded my first World Cup. I brought in the milk from the step: eight of these had poured from Martin Peters' glands during a football match? Surely not. But along with the dry heat of Guadalajara was the image of the sun, high in the sky, burning into the top of Bobby Moore's head as he thought on his feet, as he wondered whether he should thread the ball up to Hurst or square it to Mullery. There was, in reality, no confusing this sun with the one that had grudgingly released a few rays on the Wembley turf four years ago. Still less was there any confusing the black and white images from Wembley in 1966 with the shocking colour from Mexico in 1970. Here the grass was an incandescent green and the yellow of the Brazilian team's shirts was so vibrant that it did not define their chests, but spilled over them exuberantly into the stadium, as if each player had a pulsing penumbra of yellow around him. This looked odd, even hyperreal to me: the only other manifestation of this uncanny phenomenon of the glowing penumbra I had witnessed was in the TV advertisements for Ready Brek. In these, a boy walked through the driving rain of a bleak English morning to school surrounded by the glow of warmth that had been installed there thanks to his breakfast cereal. But this wasn't the 'central heating for kids' of the advertising slogan; this was the Brazilian football team, the greatest team that ever played football, at the height of its powers, and it seemed appropriate that they glowed joyously as they danced the ball into the net.

But before I could properly fall in love with Brazil, I had to watch England be destroyed. In the school playground, we were obsessed with Bobby Moore, the England captain, a man who expressed, in his lean athlete's frame, all the virtues of English sportsmanship: uprightness, resolve, muted delight in victory, handshakes and silent showers in defeat. He wasn't evil enough to be a role model to us. He wasn't a manipulative tumbler in the 18-yard box like Frannie Lee. Nor was he as devilishly brilliant as George Best. And Bobby Moore was not, not at all, a long-haired bad boy yob like Arsenal's Charlie George who was to lie spread-eagled and exultant, unEnglishly and to the affront of my mother as she watched the game on television, after he scored an FA Cup final goal a year later in 1971. No, Moore inhabited a hero's realm to which the likes of us could not legitimately aspire but only look upon with awe; here was a man, after all, who had wiped his hands deferentially on the ceremonial cloth before accepting the Queen's greetings and the Jules Rimet trophy at the royal box in 1966. No Englishman could do more than that. He had held that gleaming trophy aloft!

And then, suddenly, the image was tarnished. Just before the 1970 World Cup finals, Bobby Moore was arrested for allegedly stealing some jewellery from a shop in the England team's hotel in Bogota. The moral confusion of seven- and eight-year-olds in the playground mutated into that older child's more calculated reaction, disbelief, and then disbelief gave way to anger as Moore was released without charge. Anger that he had been falsely accused; anger that his training had been interrupted by a week; anger that England's chances might suffer as a result.

They didn't. What really messed up England's chances was Gordon Banks's stomach. It was too upset for him to play against West Germany, and instead Peter 'The Cat' Bonetti was picked as goalkeeper. How could this be! we protested at school. In the previous round, against Brazil no less, Banks had pulled off what commentators (at least English commentators) regularly call the greatest save in the history of football. Ever. Picture the scene. Jairzinho pulled the ball back from the byline and Pelé leapt far above the defender (how could such a small man leap so high?), nodding the ball powerfully into the ground before it bounced up, seemingly devastatingly, towards the goal before Banks swept it away for a corner. The freeze-frame image of Banks doing this is forever on my memory, right arm flicked up, body airborne and yet compressed (perhaps there is some foreshortening in this remembered image, since the action replay of him is shot from the right touchline, rather than full on), heedless of the looming goalpost. We couldn't do without Banks.

Like Banks's stomach, I was upset as I watched the quarter final. Even England's quickly established two-goal lead could not soothe me; nothing could soothe me until the final whistle, until the football was over. No wonder for me Gordon Banks's stomach has become an emblem of what it is to watch football: it's always an upsetting business. I can never watch football to relax. I've been this way ever since I was seven and England played for the last time in the 1970 World Cup. Then, I knew I was English, and when the game went into extra time I knew something else: it was desperately important that West Germany lose.

It didn't happen. Francis Lee received a little kick and fell on his knees. I knew then we were dead. He wasn't injured by the tackle, just ruined by running in unremitting heat. I imagined a milk float filled with empty bottles: England had sweated themselves dry – pint after pint of English sweat had fallen on to the Mexican turf to be burned up by the sun before it could nourish the soil. Disastrously for our chances, West Germany brought on a substitute with a spring in his step, while Sir Alf had substituted Bobby Charlton, the Englishman most likely to score, just before extra time. There was a lot of auguring and boding and portending in the hot Mexican air and none of it did my stomach any good at all. And then the end, the image that stays with me even more vividly than the freeze-frame of Gordon Banks saving Pelé's header: the ball is headed back across the box and Gerd Müller pulls away from his marker, rises into the air from within the six-yard box and volleys the ball into the net. In freeze-frame, I recall him shot from the rear, his powerful right thigh extended, the truncated torso obscuring the ball from my view. But the reverse-angle freeze-frame in my memory is even more devastating: through the net I see Bonetti collapsing hopelessly, while the triumphant, vigorous form of Müller sits above him with the ball at his feet, the coup de grâce just about to be administered. 3–2, over and out.

After that, I wanted Brazil to win, not least because I could rationalise the choice in this way: they had defeated England in the first round, and so they were England's natural successors, and what's more, they weren't German. But also, and not rationally at all, because they were beautiful: their white socks disclosed strong calves, which seemed to have such power and, as I fancied, regal grace as they swept balls upfield with an elegance Europeans couldn't match. I wanted to be Jairzinho, because he wasn't the king like Pelé, but because he was like Virgil from *Thunderbirds*, like Chooch from *Top Cat* – more interesting for not being the leader of the gang, and also because, perhaps, he was very good-looking indeed. And yet, it is the moving image of Pelé that I still recall above all others from this World Cup. When he scored his first goal in the final against Italy, he celebrated with a heavy-limbed, mock-languorous spring from the floor and wrapped his legs around Jairzinho's waist. Jairzinho held him there while Pelé exulted, flicking his fist down towards the other gathering players as though he was a priest with a censer. Of course, when I was seven I could only see the gesture, not its hieratical simile. But that was enough for it to be stored in my memory and embroidered in private; enough, too, for me to see a gesture remarkably like it four years later when, in the Rumble in the Jungle, Muhammad Ali leaned on the ropes between rounds, wristily flicked his gloved hand downwards as Pelé had done before him, and exhorted the crowd to chant the chant that would terrify George Foreman who was impassively sitting on his stool: 'Ali! Kill him!' But with Pelé, the gesture was of proper pride and joy, elegantly expressed. Football, not boxing, is the beautiful game.

A BAD CASE OF MALE PMT

Once, in *Whatever Happened to the Likely Lads?*, Bob lured Terry into a poncy hair salon. It was a terrifying place for Terry to be. Women were there for a start. One of them asked him: 'Do you want the beer, egg or herbal tonic?' 'Nothing to drink for me, thanks.' 'They're shampoos, you fool,' said Bob.

Terry didn't like it here at all, so to reassure him Bob told him that the bloke who ran the salon used to blow-dry the hairdos of half the Newcastle United team. 'Bobby Moncur. Malcolm Macdonald. Malcolm Macdonald uses the same conditioner as me,' said Bob, running his hand through perfectly treated locks. Terry, his hair a haystack, looked grim, his eyes a watery blue and fixed with a thousand-mile stare which said that he didn't like the way the world was going. No, not one bit. When men ran their fingers through well-conditioned hair, then for him, the world had lost all sense.

Then Bob added: 'I mean, have you ever seen a homosexual striker?' In 1973, this was a piece of unanswerable rhetoric, though even a couple of decades later it might well have provoked a retort. Imagine, for instance, if, on *Men Behaving Badly*, Gary had asked Tony the same question. Tony would have replied: 'Not knowingly. But what is all that leaping into each others' arms, Pelé with his legs wrapped round Jairzinho's waist? Isn't this suggestive, perhaps, of sublimated homosexual attraction? I think so.' True, Tony might well be unlikely to express himself with such psychoanalytical acuity, but the point remains: hypothetical homosexual strikers can no longer be the subject of such rhetorical flourishes in sitcoms any more.

In this episode, Bob and Terry had to get through the day without finding out the score of the England–Bulgaria international in Sofia, so that they could enjoy the match when it was broadcast on television in the evening. Flint, who Bob and Terry didn't like very much but who was often nearby, seemed to know the result and yelled it across the street as the pair ran out of the hairdressers', hair still damp and uncut. Flint was played by Brian Glover, fresh from playing the games teacher who acted out the Man U–Spurs match on the school playing field in Ken Loach's film *Kes*. He was still obsessed with football was Glover and still exposing his bald pate by whipping off his cap, as the striker in the Barnestoneworth United episode of *Ripping Yarns* did with his toupee just before kick-off.

Flint had shouted something as Bob and Terry had scampered into the pub. It sounded to them like '2–0!'. Sometimes two syllables are enough to ruin your day. They stood at the bar, their sullen, stunned faces a picture of misery – the misery that, I am sure, fills my face for ninety minutes or more whenever there's football on television. What did 2–0 mean? They went into a nice piece of vernacular analysis: 2–0 probably meant Bulgaria had won since the home team's score was usually mentioned first, reckoned Bob; but then nobody said '0–2' in ordinary speech, countered Terry; it could have been a truncated form of '2–0 we won' or '2–0 we lost', he added. It was useless! How could they know! But Flint had ruined their happy prospect of watching the game on television later that evening: whoever scored first, would go on to win. Bob lifted his newspaper, disconsolately. 'King Keegan lifts attack' said the back page.

But Terry was reflecting on deeper matters: 'Where is Bulgaria?' 'If you're going from Greece towards Russia, it's second on your left,' said Bob. 'Out there where they've had all that terrible flooding. Tragic. Thousands homeless.' Immediately, Terry perked up: 'Well, that's to our advantage, isn't it? Heavy pitch!'

This led Terry Collier into one of the most profound analyses of English national character ever beheld in a British sitcom (hardly a hotly contested title, but bear with me). England were bound to win the match, because the Bulgarians are so unstable: 'All these countries like Persia and Bulgaria and the Middle East, they're all unstable. If they're not having floods it's earthquakes, and if it's not earthquakes it's typhoons. That's what makes them so unstable.' Bob, setting aside his Daily Keegan, inquired: 'Are you really putting that forward as a theory of national character?' 'Certainly. Why, you take Britain. We don't have earthquakes or tidal waves, do we? I mean, we do get those bitter north easterlies in February, but we don't have to pack our possessions and flee south. That's why this country is so stable. That's why we're so dogged and relaxed and calm under crises.' 'But according to you,' countered Bob, neglecting the deep, dark waters of his pint of Newcastle Brown for a deeper, darker mystery, 'we don't have any crises.' 'But if we *did*,' said Terry, superciliously, 'we would be calm under them.'

Good point. How could England not win? Heavy pitch, unstable Bulgars, malnourished players worn out from working on collective farms or in tractor factories. It would be a real kick in the Balkans if England lost. But how could England *ever* lose? The world, as sitcoms of this era told us, if ironically, was populated by two classes – the unstable and the stable. Only Englishmen fell into the latter class.

Bob encouraged Terry to go around the world, deciding the national characteristics of each nation. 'Koreans?' 'Not to be trusted. Cruel people. Much the same as all orientals.' Not at all like the plucky North Korean communists, then, whom our Faber and Faber editors had clapped from the terraces only a few years ago. 'Russians?' 'Sinister.' 'Egyptians?' 'Cowardly.' 'I thought you'd save that for the Italians.' 'No, they're greasy.' 'Germans?' 'Arrogant.' 'Danes?' Terry pondered: what *could* one say about the people of Denmark? Oh yes: 'Pornographic.' And so it went on until he reached the United Kingdom: 'I haven't got much time for the Irish or the Welsh, and the Scots are worse than the Koreans.' 'And you could never stand southerners . . .' 'To tell you the truth, I don't much like anybody outside this town. And there aren't many families down our street I can stand.'

It was a lovely scene, in which the writers, Dick Clement and Ian La Frenais, did what Johnny Speight regularly did with Alf Garnett in *Till Death Us Do Part*, and Harry Driver and Vince Powell did with Jack Smethurst in *Love Thy Neighbour*: let the bigot follow his own logic until he gets an inkling of his own absurdity, and let us see for a second that he has a little self-consciousness of his preposterousness before he buries it, quickly and deep, under a mound of greater absurdity. In this reductio ad absurdum, Terry Collier showed me why, rationally, I should stop supporting England.

And, better than that, why the English national character in the late 20th century could only be defined through absurdity and negativity. England, in Terry's absurd fantasy world and in the absurd real world too, was what was left over when you boiled away the rest of the globe, a fearful place and misguidedly proud of something which it didn't have.

Bob, the aspirant, the relatively successful, was always open to new things, like his new semi, his Vauxhall Viva, men's hair conditioners and the latest fashions – such as they were. He could afford a benign global worldview. Terry could not: he lived in fear of a world gone sour, and that world could only be stopped from going sour and made comprehensible to him by imagining an England that never existed. He even lived at 127 Inkerman Terrace, that street purportedly named in honour of one of the battles of one of the most absurd wars Britain ever fought. Inkerman? You remember – from Greece you go straight on,

Bulgaria on your left, just past the lights, up the Crimean peninsula. Can't miss it.

When Bob and Terry left the pub, they went straight to Terry's sister's flat. There, surely, they would be able to avoid Flint and any other person who would tell them the score. They turned off the telly and the radio. 'If you want anything to eat,' said Audrey, 'I haven't got a thing in.' 'Ah Audrey, man, pet, we can't eat,' said Bob. 'There's too much pre-match tension.'

That very male PMT which, nonetheless, a woman (man, pet) can experience. But what, ultimately, was very disappointing about the Likely Lads' analysis of the misery of football, was that they didn't contemplate that one could suffer DMT, during-match tension, that foul upset that ruins every game and yet is part of what makes it utterly compulsive. Why, when the pair settled down to watch the game, Bob suggested that they could enjoy it. Enjoy it? Was he joking? You cannot enjoy football on television. He turned on the game: it had been cancelled due to a waterlogged pitch in Sofia – that was what Flint had been trying tell them all along. His 2–0 remark had only been a joke. Instead, said the announcer, here were the figure skating finals from Vienna.

NICKY SKATER, THE OLYMPIC SLATER

Figure skating is all very well, as are many other such sports involving cold surfaces that can be watched from the fireside. That said, the 1998 Winter Olympics were ruined, to my mind, by the vulgar antics of the snowboarders. All the competitors, it seemed, had backwards baseball caps and were embroiled in drug scandals. And not even interesting drugs. 'It's all about amplitude,' said the commentator on Eurosport, although it was very late and he may have said aptitude or even hamper food.

One American snowboarder left what, it seems, is called a half pipe and spun in the air before making his descent. 'Look at that!' shouted the commentator. 'All the height and upside down! A double grab and back to back 720s!' But this was just showing off, not sport. A Japanese snowboarder flew out of the arena, knocked over two cameramen, did a smart flip and returned to the ground amid a cataclysm of whoops and high fives. When an Olympic event incorporates brawling with the paparazzi into its most compelling moments, something has gone horribly wrong. One Austrian snowboarder, apparently, trashed her hotel room. Fortunately, two of those nice men who do the brushing in the curling had brought their brooms along and had the place spick and span in no time.

I much preferred the speed skating. It was rather like figure skating but less spangly. Two brightly-coloured condoms whooshed around the ice in spectral calm for ages. I would go out of the room to post a letter or make a soufflé and when I returned, there were still two condoms whooshing. True, the condoms had changed colours, but that didn't necessarily mean that the competitors were different. As in competitive swimming, the identities of the participants are concealed by rubber, and nobody in their right mind cares who wins. The commentary on speed skating from the Winter Olympics was generally too ludicrously boring to be informative. 'If he comes eighth it will be a new Austrian best,' said one. 'He wouldn't win a medal, obviously, but he will win an Olympic diploma.'

Nonetheless, it's a courtly sport. As the skaters skated, they sometimes tucked one arm into the small of their backs. To make the image complete, they should have held bouquets aloft in the other hand so they would look like two Nordic seducers bent on wooing some lucky woman waiting at the finishing line.

There was once a British Olympic skater called Nicky Slater, though it was a while ago and now there are so many new and unlikely Olympic events (snooker, curling, lying very still on the sofa and now and again eating a cashew nut), that it has all become too confusing, and he may well have been called Nicky Skater the Olympic slater. 'Yes, the roof is nearly done. But, what's this, disaster for Skater! He's sliding down the slates towards the guttering! British medal hopes in tatters once more!'

There were condoms, too, in the luge. It was an event which I mistakenly thought was called the louche, and so I stayed up late one night specially to watch it. I imagined Dean Martin in a backless dress, cauliflower-nosed, a martini in one hand and a microphone in the other, singing very risqué lyrics to the tune of 'Little Ol' Wine Drinker Me'. But it wasn't like that at all. Instead, it was a well-filled, vulnerable condom reclining on a tiny tray and racing towards certain death across a sheet of ice. Just try getting life insurance if you're in that line of work.

Much better was the new Olympic sport, curling. It was exquisitely dreary: the delicious contrast between the delicate slide and release of the kneeler and the feverish brushing of the nice brushers held my interest for moments only. On BBC2, Dougie Donnelly set the sport in its historical context: 'It's thought to be nearly 500 years old. There's a stone in Scotland which is dated 1511.' I'll bet there is, Dougie. I'll just bet there is. There was plenty of time for more digressions of this sort as, for hour upon hour, nothing that could claim significance happened.

THE HISSING OF SUMMER IRONS

For hour upon hour, nothing that could claim significance happened. This, to me, is the purpose of sport on television if it is not football. And this appealing lack of significance is not just winter's preserve, but summer's too. Think of five-day cricket on television. Could there be anything more pointless, and thus more restful?

There are two ways of watching cricket on television. One is to turn the sound down and tune into the radio commentary. The other is to leave the sound up and do something else while it is on.

My dad always favoured the first way. He would love to hear the ball-by-ball commentary from John Arlott and Brian Johnston while he watched the match on the screen. I only cared for radio commentary when rain stopped play and they had to fill in by reminiscing about an over of googlies bowled in Hyderabad in 1948 or the proverbially excellent chocolate cake sent in by Mrs Jones of Ripon.

I preferred the second way. Cricket on television was always at its best for me on the fifth day of a test match, with no prospect of rain or a result, and the ground devoid of spectators apart from the likes of Sid and Doris Bonkers with their vast collection of headgear and Tupperware. The commentary from Jim Laker or Richie Benaud was never ball by ball, but barely over by over. Instead, the sound of willow on leather would mingle with distant drunken hurrahs from the pavilion bar in the sound recordist's microphone.

Now and again, the commentator would say something intractable which, in the context of the sultry sounds of silence, would be like the observations of a sun-burned madman: 'A Chinaman plucked from nowhere by Underwood.' 'The batsman's Holding, the bowler's Willey.' 'Rice bowls, Paddy fields.'

There I would stand, ironing things which now sound ludicrous – fitted sheets, three-quarter-length socks, towels even. This was, after all, a household in which sport should not be consumed slumped on the sofa with pizzas and beer, but instead glimpsed between bouts of ironing. And yet, the mixture of summer sounds with the smell of freshly-laundered linen and the hiss as the iron passed over a shirt primed with sprayed water were a Protestant sybarite's guilt-free refuge. This was the weird experience of daytime television in the seventies, before Richard and Judy came to our noon-time screens with their lurid, frankly horrifying show; it was 90 per cent aural, only the odd glimpse from the ironing board would make it in any way visual. There was, and still is, something decadent about daytime TV: while you could spend whole evenings slumped in front of the box, morning and afternoon during summer holidays were times for work.

This way of watching television is very different from the one regularly being proposed in fitness advertisements at the back of listings magazines. Usually accompanied by some man with a six-pack stomach pulling a contraption that looks like it owes a debt to the engineers of the Forth Rail Bridge, while watching *Neighbours*, these advertisements astutely manipulate the guilt we feel when watching television. We should be doing something else at the same time, something that is good for our souls or our bodies.

But these advertisements encourage us to consider television as an instrument of the devil which sucks in our attention, leaving us zombified. It is not: it is a medium over which we can and should exercise control. And sometimes that control should manifest itself in allowing oneself to succumb to television's sometimes banal pleasures without guilt. Sometimes, it is true, ironing or workouts function as the foil which allows us to indulge ourselves by watching things we know have little edifying point – Adult *Oprah* (indistinguishable from Infantile Oprah), *Emmerdale, Randall and Hopkirk (Deceased)*.

But there is a big difference between this relaxing trash and the rest of television's output. It is folly to regard television as a medium of undiluted rubbish. What is lamentable about these advertisements is that they encourage us to engage in some displacement activity for whatever is on the television – be it football, a soap opera or a Tarkovsky retrospective. They also come at a time when the images produced specifically for television – particularly in documentaries – demand more visual attention from the viewer than ever before. It is immoral to do the ironing in front of the television when there is a good film on.

I look back on those days of juvenile ironing now, and think – what strange, slightly embarrassing, private bliss, never to be recaptured. They ended when the VCR made watching videos of movies a possibility; but then, the movies were so visually absorbing that those towels no longer got pressed. I lament the passing of the age of ironing, though: there's no time any more to stand and stare, to leave off one's work for a moment and look, uncomprehending, at a restful view of men in white on fields of green.

A HEADBAND AS BIG AS A BATH TOWEL

Much television sport is utterly restful, the sort of thing that Gordon Banks and I could profit from watching in long winter evenings instead of downing Rennie's tablets like they're going out of fashion.

For years women's tennis was soporific bliss, since it consisted, even at its highest level, of Chris Evert and Yvonne Goolagong trading baseline volleys for days on end. In women's tennis, they changed their surnames faster than the score. You could leave the room with Evert and Goolagong on a deuce point, come back years later and they would still be at deuce, only now it would be Chris Lloyd playing Yvonne Cawley. These were women, too, who would not disgrace themselves if my mother invited them round for cucumber sandwiches. Actually, that's not strictly true: my mother didn't care for the way Chris Evert chewed gum or looked sullen like a bratty teenager under her thick eyeliner; though Chris Lloyd, elder stateswoman of the modern women's game, could come round for tea whenever she fancied.

Men's tennis on television was never quite my cup of Robinson's Barley Water since, even though the languorous, faded playboy voice of Dan Maskell lured you into a world of sunburnt quietude, it all got far too engaging when the game itself began. Too much of the Gordon Banks about it, if you catch my drift. My mother enjoyed it immensely, taking the second week of Wimbledon off work most years if she could manage it, drawing the curtains from the July sun and watching the Men in White.

Borg versus McEnroe was the sort of contest my mother would find unmissable and so too would I, though it upset me more than I could say to watch, as we sat, curtains closed, mouths open. This often-repeated contest wasn't so much a tennis match, after all, as a showdown between two worldviews – Abba v The Dead Kennedys, Sense v Sensibility, Volvo v Harley-Davidson, white headband v red headband, boring good v rampaging evil. There was a twenty-five minute tie-break in the fourth set of the pair's encounter at the men's singles final at Wimbledon in 1980 and during it the world was volleyed back and forth across the still sultry shade of our living room, and we hung on through the stupefying heat and tension wondering which of these gods would hold global sway come twilight.

Some people say that Borg was sexy. They can't be serious. They CANNOT be serious. He made Charles Bronson look facially expressive. He had the charm of a bunion. Hips that belonged to a smaller, narrower person. And yet I would marvel as he accepted police escorts to whisk him past screaming teeny-boppers to court at Wimbledon. Girls reportedly had 'Borgasms' over the Swedish star, whatever that means. If the past is another country, then pubescent sexuality is another planet, where girls fancy blokes with the allure of breezeblocks – the Bay City Rollers, Simon Le Bon, the slightly less ugly one from Bros, Björn Borg.

On court, Borg's game was as blank as his blue Viking's eyes. He was a wall who would return everything for hours, until opponents decided it might be more pleasant to have the afternoon off and do some grouting in the bathroom instead. He never got angry, he had no need for anti-perspirant. He would have been much happier, I suspect, playing in the women's singles, trading baseline shots day in day out with Evert, Lloyd, Goolagong or Cawley – perhaps all four of them at once.

All in all, he was an ideal match for John McEnroe, a man who would invade Mexico if his barley water was slightly warm. But those who called him brilliantly impulsive and artistic had clearly never heard him play guitar. His face always looked as though it was holding back more water than the Hoover Dam; his bath towel-sized headband was surely designed so that in moments of extreme emotional turmoil it would slide down to mop up his tears. If he hadn't existed, the producer of BBC's Wimbledon coverage would have had to invent him, if only to affront the matching blazer and tie of the commentary team, Dan Maskell and John Barrett. 'Oooh, I say!' Maskell would exclaim, and whether the remark was prompted by revulsion for McEnroe's New York coarseness or admiration for a particularly fine volley was a secret that he took to that commentary box in the sky. By contrast, Barrett was more forthright. 'Tennis really does need to uphold authority in some shape or form,' he said as McEnroe welled up once more after complaining about a questionable call. Does it? Does it really?

In retrospect, the second great myth of men's singles (the first is that Borg was sexy) needs to be exploded. This stated that McEnroe was the angry fire to Borg's dispassionate ice. Angry? John McEnroe's problem was that he was always too polite. 'You can't be serious, man. You CANNOT be serious. That ball was on the line.' Excuse me, but that's about as angry as refusing a second cucumber sandwich. Think about it. You're standing at the bottom of a step ladder and some stuck-up, Limey asshole upstairs is telling you: 'The service was good, Mr McEnroe.' And the best you can manage is: 'You're the absolute pits of the world. You know that?' Your reply has all the force of a dink over the net. If a tennis player was really angry he would shake the umpire's ladder until they changed their mind or climb the steps to insert a racquet where the sun doesn't shine. McEnroe's tantrums, like those of other tennis stars, were merely disruptive gamesmanship.

Not that McEnroe wasn't a shock to the Wimbledon system, but then Wimbledon is the sort of place where you could tie your shoelaces too loudly. You could feel neck hairs prickling throughout the Home Counties as he tried to break his racquet over his knees or cut through the niceties of the All-England Tennis Club with the scythe of his New York vernacular, which is why I loved him even as he upset me: he wouldn't defer; he was constitutionally incapable of lying back and thinking of the All-England Lawn Tennis Club.

OPEN THOSE LEGS AS WIDE – WHOO! – AS WIDE AS YOU CAN!

But that's enough lying back and thinking, enough lounging on the couch. Let's pull back the curtains, move the coffee table, roll back the carpet, kick off the slippers, put on something unfeasibly tight and join June Jones in Sydney, Australia!

'Welcome everybody, wherever you are! Europe, Asia, Australasia, America! Let's just start opening everybody's legs now! Just pump down on top of those thighs!'

Ever since the Green Goddess's popularity waned on BBC1's *Breakfast Time*, and Mr Motivator began to endorse those low-fat biscuits in television adverts (didn't he realise that it's a slippery slope from Go Ahead! biscuits to There's a Mobile Cardiac Unit on Standby Triple Chocolate Chip With Extra Molasses! cookies? Didn't he?), ever since then TV aerobics in Britain has been very poor indeed. So poor in fact that we have to go to

June in Australia to get the early morning low-impact choreography that we so richly need.

'Open those legs as wide – whooo! – as wide as you can have them! A little punch. Whoo! Whoo!'

The continued allegiance of Australian TV aerobicists to hi-energy disco music is a wonderful thing. Long after the rest of the world moved on from Hazel Dean and all her works, June Jones and her five maximally-gluted assistants still strut their collective stuff to this relentlessly upbeat, ninety beats-per-minute music.

June was turned out unimpeachably, but her assistant Michelle was wearing a short-sleeved cardigan, which, frankly, made a mockery of the whole proceedings.

No matter. 'We're getting a little sassy, here, having an attitude! Elbows out! Whoo!'

I love June for that thought – the fantasy of sassiness in Lycra. I love her for promoting the virtues of strong squats (whatever they are) while behind her the park on the edge of Sydney Harbour looked extremely clean. In the middle distance, as one looked across the pristine square uncannily devoid of winos and graffiti, were a couple of shoppers resting their tired feet. They looked dully on as June worked up a sweat as clean and wholesome as a neat bowel movement, and shouted increasingly incomprehensible instructions. 'One mambo! Square shave! Grapevine right! Squat down strong! Pump it up!' It was all much simpler in Andy Pandy and Teddy's day. Then there was one instruction which could be easily followed to the letter in the privacy of your living room:

Jumping, jumping,
Jumping up and down
Jumping, Jumping
All around the town!

Life has become a much more complex affair since those days, and so have TV aerobics. Workouts for infantile TV viewers were once Dionysian, all ecstasy and leaping; now they are Apollonian, all order and restraint.

Similarly, the arrival of the least fit person on the planet, Norm Peterson, into his favourite bar, is all order and restraint. The timing, the footfalls, are as precise as a late Samuel Beckett play. First, some broad thighs come shambling down the basement steps. The door opens. The cry goes up: 'Norm!' Then the long, shoulder-shaking sashay of Peterson and his bulk begins across the length of the bar, to the reserved place where, as night follows day, as bum plonks into place, a cold one will be lovingly placed, then lifted and sunk. I'm talking about the choreography of *Cheers*, where, physically, the aerobics are as low impact as is humanly possible.

Did someone say choreography? As Norm wobbles across the bar, some cove always fires off an inquiry. 'Say, Norm. What you up to?' 'About ideal weight if I was 11 feet tall.' He hefts his hunch in his jacket, satisfied at his retort, saliva thickening expectantly in his mouth as he swings into place, all passion spent, all exercise complete.

The only troubling question about Norm Peterson's work-out is this: how does Norm get up those stairs at closing time? Never, in all the long hours I've spent watching Norm Peterson, have I ever seen him drunk, never have I seen him have trouble with those stairs up to the street. These are stairs so steep that they would cause me to have a bivouac half way up after one bitter shandy, still less the vast quantities of aerated hooch Peterson packs away during an evening. The actor who plays Norm, George Wendt, once played my favourite tongue twister, the eponymous hero of Goncharov's novel *Oblomov*. (Goncharov's novel *Oblomov*, Goncharov's novel *Oblomov*, Goncharov's novel *Oblomov*, Goncharov's novel *Oblomov*, Goncharov's novel *Oblomov* – good, isn't it?) He was a guy with motivation issues, a man who couldn't pull himself up into the vertical even though he had slept for twelve hours. And yet, by contrast, Norm, at 2 a.m., awash and wobbly, still scales the north face of the basement bar with nimble aplomb, and sometimes with Cliff Claven. How can this be?

It's very simple. TV aerobics doesn't work. It is contrary to the fundamental principles of television viewing which state that unless you're answering questions in *Mastermind* from your sofa, or you are a child watching and jumping with Andy Pandy, you do not participate. Actually, that's not true: one does participate when one watches wrestling. One shouts, shouts, shouts!

THE RIDDLE OF KENDO NAGASAKI'S MASK

Kendo Nagasaki's mock-Samurai mask almost always stayed on. Despite all those sweaty men who came, rummaged hopefully and yet failed to prise it over his nose. Despite all those long, *tedious* headlocks in the corners of rings from Bethnal Green to Wolverhampton. Despite a million children yelling like me at the screens before the Saturday tea time pools check: 'Pull it off, for crying out loud! Just pull it off!'

Why? Because, as a matter of fact, Kendo was played by the same bloke who played Young Mr Grace in *Are You Being Served?*. Not a tooth in his head. Not an ounce of charisma under that proto-Lycra mask. This was a mask that, nonetheless, evoked so eloquently centuries of Japanese martial culture to an audience of small children in their living rooms and a marauding clutch of handbag-wielding grannies at ringside, off their faces on rum and peps.

The mask had to stay so that the drama would not be spoiled, so that prosaic reality did not intrude too much. So that no one realised that this semblance of a samurai psychopath was in fact a ninety-year-old department store owner.

Legend has it that once Kendo Nagasaki's mask did come off. I find this hard to believe since it flies in the face of all the principles of wrestling. Giant Haystacks tried, but, though this formidable combination of Norseman and hedge prised the mask up just above Nagasaki's mouth, he could not get it all the way off. Big Daddy, that seemingly inflated octogenarian in a tutu, was the man, I am told, who succeeded. I never witnessed the event itself, but people have told me about those few moments in which Nagasaki stood with his face bared. I've stood in noisy pubs and clubs while men have shouted at me about how Big Daddy manoeuvred the mask off and for ten seconds a few people saw his face. They have tried to mime the bitter struggle as Big Daddy prised and Kendo Nagasaki, presumably with his arms and legs pinned, resisted chiefly by clenching his facial muscles and looking as fearsome as he could. 'What did Nagasaki look like?' I shouted across crowded bars with music pumping into my ears. 'Like Young Mr Grace,' they yelled back. 'Perhaps a little older.' Maybe I misheard them. 'A really ugly face. Like a boulder'. Perhaps that's what they said. Or maybe they were making the whole thing up and Nagasaki's mask could never have come off. In the international conspiracy that is televised wrestling, not even Big Daddy would have stooped to pull the mask from the samurai's face and so ruin the mystery. That, at least, is my truth.

American wrestling is rather different. In Britain, wrestling largely consists of two geezers trying to get through a few rounds without losing their toupees, without making their paunches peep through their satin shawls too much. By contrast, the US version concerns men with shoulders the size of aircraft carriers, biceps as big as Warwickshire and nice clean fingernails.

The commentator for WWF Wrestlemania XIV set the scene. 'Can you feel it, ladies and gentlemen, wherever you are?' I feel sure that he wanted to say more but, just then, his ten-gallon hat was sent flying as the mêlée in the ring crossed the ropes and continued in the media enclosure. Feel it? I could virtually taste the baby oil that glistened on the contestants' muscles.

In America, tag wrestling is very popular. Teams are called things like Nation of Domination, Fearfully Butch and Cross As Hell, and Gay Needlepoint Enthusiasts of America. You may not have heard of the last two, since they were eliminated thanks to shockingly homophobic refereeing in the untelevised preliminaries.

Naturally, some of this wrestling is incomprehensible unless you've got a higher degree in the subject. 'Here's Animal,' bawled the commentator. 'Top rope back flip. A drop kick to the jaw. Six foot seven inch, 340 lbs of Karma Mustapha tumbles.' His colleague added: 'Flash Funk, in a second rope black flip, puts Assault in La-La Land.' In the crowd people were still holding up placards that said Austin 3: 16. Why didn't somebody tell me that there was a new edition of the Bible with new books by new prophets? These were references, no doubt, to verses that spelled doom for the likes of Mustapha and his colleague, a man with a fez called Sheikh. The infidels were going to suffer as the verses had foretold.

The referee was felled in a body check by a man who made Giant Haystacks look like Little Titch. Lawlessness ruled, though from the biting, gouging, disregard for table manners and all-round unpleasantness that preceded the referee's neutralisation, it was hard to perceive where anarchy began and supposed order ended. But this, as Roland Barthes noted, is a feature of wrestling: even though a kind of justice is initially enacted, the ring often later collapses into a welcome anarchy.

But nobody had read their Barthes that night. A bloke in cut-off jeans and preposterous musculature leapt into the ring and put the Legion of Doom and the Nation of Domination to flight. He was called Shamrock, thus reinforcing the stereotype that in the States it's Irishmen who are called on to restore order in a world gone mad.

After the tag bouts were over, the main contest began. Shawn Michaels, the Wrestlemania champion was played on by a band as he made the long, lonely walk to the ring, revelling in the pomp which was his due. The band was called Degeneration X and, even in 1998, they were about three years past even being passé. 'Nobody tells us what to wear,' mumbled the singer. 'You think you're better,' he added. It was a pity that he felt obliged to express these sentiments while wearing his dad's tweed cap and a dead uncle's leather jacket.

The fans of the contender, 'Stone Cold' Steve Austin, carried placards that bore interesting legends. Austin 3:16, said one; 100% Degenerate said another; This Way To The Poetry Reading added a third. They all looked ugly enough, but proved much more muted than their angry British contemporaries.

No, in America, the hoopla, such as it is, takes place mostly in the ring. That said, the principles are very similar to those set forth by Mick McManus and Jackie Pallo: make much more seem to happen than actually does; stamp loudly on the echo chamber of the ring when you pull your punches so that the suckers in the circle think grievous bodily harm is being wrought. There's nothing wrong in this, as Barthes noted in his seminal essay on the subject.

What *was* wrong was 'Iron' Mike Tyson. In the middle of this mindless violence, he was like the shy one at some orgy, like an ingénue at a Beckett festival who doesn't remotely grasp the existential concept of the absurd. The meanest, toughest boxer in the history of mean, tough boxing, here he was symbolically castrated, reduced to stasis as Michaels and Austin got medieval on each other's bottoms.

Tyson's role was that of the Enforcer. Like Shamrock he was to step in when the referee was carried out horizontally, his pigeon chest body-slammed by baby-oiled pectorals. But to call on

Tyson, a convicted rapist and flouter of the Marquis of Queensberry's strictures against ear mutilation, to restore law and order was, frankly, a bit rich. He wore a cap-sleeved T-shirt that bore the legend 'S*ck this'. The asterisk, to my mind, was emblematic of the neutering of Iron Mike. What a p*ssy.

But the neutering of sport's hard men on television is a good thing, since it undermines the triumphalist rule of thick Americans with big muscles. In *The Simpsons*, once, Iron Mike was rendered as a killer pugilist with a poncy lisp and a fetish for effete pursuits, such as restaurant-going. As a team of paramedics worked on his opponent's body, Tyson leaned on the ropes and chatted with actor Charlie Sheen in his ringside seat. 'You really should go there, you know,' lisped Tyson. 'They sear the sea bass beautifully.'

For his bout with Homer Simpson, Tyson entered the ring to a rap number about killing someone's mother and eating her viscera. Simpson, the human punchbag, Springfield's answer to Richard Dunn, entered to *Why Can't We Be Friends?*. And yet Homer had a secret weapon: no matter how hard Tyson hit him, Simpson wobbled Weeble-like but wouldn't fall down. Sadly, the same couldn't be said of Shawn Michaels, who was laid out by Stone Cold and counted out by Iron Mike at the evening's piquant dénouement.

THE EVOLUTIONARY CYCLE OF SPORT

Britain may be no good at sports, but it is remarkably successful at inventing them. Americans may have muscles that makes those of Britons look like heat lumps, but by thunder we can come up with games that will occupy the rest of the world for centuries. This is how international sports originate. Someone in a slaughterhouse near Kidderminster finds himself with a spare pig's bladder and an empty afternoon. After a few minutes inflating the bladder, Wayne kicks it around the yard, and then his colleagues, looking for pleasant diversion after working up to their armpits in pig bits all morning, join in. Then the Bewdley Chicken Pluckers, who are passing by after the All-Midland Chicken Pluckers Conference in Bromsgrove, stand transfixed on the edge of the slaughterhouse yard at the sight of grown men kicking an inflated bladder. They too join in, even though, strictly speaking, they weren't invited. Soon it is the Bewdley Pluckers against Kidderminster Butchers, the Pluckers developing a nice one-touch, flowing movement around the yard, over the hedges and down to the river; the Butchers, despite a shocking disciplinary record involving machetes and verbal dissent, profiting from their long-bladder game and ultimately going home with top honours.

But it doesn't end there. Soon the slaughterhouse yard is fringed each afternoon with pluckers and butchers, brewers and bakers, tinkers, tailors, soldiers and talent scouts, all wanting a piece of the action. Now mere possession of the bladder becomes less important and, instead, kicking it between two upright posts becomes the object of the game. Leagues are established, the rules of the contest codified by some solicitors in Wolverhampton. Ultimately, the Kidderminster Butchers are relegated to obscurity, with Wayne, forerunner of Pelé and Jairzinho, and are never heard of again.

Later, the game becomes popular abroad and international tournaments are held. Germans and Italians, Brazilians and Argentinians become so proficient at the game that the regulatory body, the International Association of Pig Bladder Kickers, of Corporation Street, Birmingham, changes the rules. Goalkeepers cannot touch the bladder with their hands when it is passed to them by a member of their own team; an offside clause is added to the rule book; players whose names end in 'o' or 'a' or who like sauerkraut or have a great deal of cultivated facial hair can no longer compete for their national or club pig bladder kicking teams. All this proves so baffling to foreign contestants that

British teams become successful once more and, despite complaints, triumph in international competition. After a few years of British dominance, the foreign teams adjust to the new rules and again win all the top awards. This prompts the IAPBK to adjust the rules once more. This prompts an international revolt: British teams are excluded from international competition by the Federation of International Pig Bladder Kickers based in Zurich. After five years, British teams are allowed to compete on the international stage once more. But it isn't the same: now the rules are codified by international committees and, consequently, British teams hardly ever win anything.

This is the evolutionary cycle of a typical sport: someone invents a game in Britain and once foreigners get to play it they gradually come to dominance. The British response has been to invent games that favour the national temperament. This has been done in two chief ways. First, the rules for a game have been so complex and the seeming point so obscure that other nations' sportsmen and women have for centuries been too baffled to take part. This is clearly true of cricket which, for a very long time indeed, was only played by Britain and her imperial subjects. Indeed, part of the very particular nature of British colonial oppression was that foreigners from Bombay to Barbados were obliged to learn and play a game which they initially could not imagine enjoying, still less becoming successful at. But, in time, even the colonial masters were overthrown in their cricketing dominance by mere colonials. What's more, the rules for cricket were already so obscure that they could not be made any more so to baffle the colonials and so, instead, British sportsmen and women tried the second way of ensuring our national sporting dominance.

The second way essentially involves abandoning sports at which other nations have become dominant and instead devising new sports that favour Britain's natural talents. Britain's national talents chiefly consist of sitting in pubs drinking, moaning and now and again getting up to throw a sharp object at a board and so, as a result, Britain has developed a nice line in that oxymoron, pub sports. Only here can Britons play to their strengths. In these contests, which we call sports and which everybody else calls delusion, we are and will remain supreme. Until, at least, Brazil develops a thriving pub culture.

This national propensity towards sports that must be played with a pint of lager in one hand, a smoke in the other and a vast gut between the contestant and the object of the game, was immortalised in *Indoor League.* The programme, broadcast on ITV on Sunday lunchtimes in the seventies, was hosted by former England fast bowler Fred Trueman. Trueman was from Yorkshire and, consequently, knew what he liked and liked what he bloody well knew.

Trueman's show was an homage to pub sports – bar billiards, darts, skittles and shove ha'penny. *Indoor League* predated the mass popularity of snooker and darts and in many respects paved the way for their acceptance as sports by the TV viewing public. It was set in a pretend pub, complete with lifesized cartoons of seventies people in flares. Trueman, a pipe in one hand and a pint in one hand, greeted TV viewers with a brusque 'Now then' and said farewells to us with his rugged 'I'll see thee'.

But there was more to *Indoor League* than pipes and pints, more to it, too, than questionable cardigans and northern gruffness. The sports that were showcased each week demanded great skill. Consider shove ha'penny. The great darts commentator, Sid Waddell, whose contribution to British culture we are just about to consider at length, once said that 'Shove ha'penny demands more concentration than darts, but the touch must be as light as a butterfly's eyelash.' Trueman himself claimed that shove ha'penny was a game that 'matches the skill and dexterity of the miniature portrait painter'. And they should know. Trueman and Waddell, after all, were great players of the pub game that was invented in the 16th century and referred to by

Shakespeare somewhere as 'shove grout'. Of course, it was only known as 'shove grout' in Shakespeare's heyday because that coincided with the two seasons in which shove ha'penny was merged with competitive bathroom tiling. This was a move made by the British Association of Shove Ha'Penny Enthusiasts in order to thwart Germany's growing excellence at the sport. Germans were then very good at shove ha'penny but temperamentally hopeless at tiling, and so the rule change restored Britain's flagging reputation – until that is the Munich grout disaster of 1597 which led to a rule change and the development of the modern game of shove ha'penny that we know today.

But all that is history. Pub sports are now watched by millions of Britons on television. They no longer need to take place in pubs. After all, it is the work of moments merely to recreate the atmosphere of a pub in a huge hall.

Let us conclude this chapter on TV sport by reflecting on the TV coverage of the 1998 World Darts Championship final which was held at the Winter Gardens in Blackpool. It was, after all, a contest where there was next to no foreign interest and so no danger that a stout Briton would not claim global dominance.

SWEAT AND DONKEYS

The 1998 World Darts Championship final was a remarkable affair, one of the great, and yet in many respects hitherto unsung, moments of British sport. The world number one, stout Rod Harrington was pitted against the even stouter hopeful, Ronnie Baxter. According to the commentator, Sid Waddell, Harrington had the 'physiognomy of a weeping Madonna'. He did, too: not since Bobby Robson stood on the touchline in the 1990 World Cup watching England's hopes dashed, have I seen so many sporting tears dammed in one face. Baxter, too, had his problems: Waddell billed him as the 'TV freezer', chilled into incompetence when performing in front of a mass television audience. But at least his wife Rachel was cheering from the front row: 'She's blowing kisses at a hundred miles an hour at her lad,' shouted Waddell. Together Rod and Ronnie were 'sweating like a pair of donkeys in a savanna swamp,' suggested Sid excitably. 'This is a belter and it could be incredibly tight,' he added. Like the ITV football commentator, Brian Moore, Sid growled increasingly noisily as the action became more compelling. Indeed, you could drift off into a light sleep while watching football on ITV or darts on Sky, safe in the knowledge that you'd be roused by a bellowing commentator if anything interesting happened.

But Harrington and Baxter's sporting contest, gripping though it was, was hardly as engaging as the real battle between Sid Waddell and his commentating assistant John Wynne for the title of the most appealingly flowery commentator in the history of sports broadcasting, a more hotly contested title than any purely sporting honour.

We joined the contest in leg 23 of a 35-leg final from the Blackpool Winter Gardens with, as they say in the commentary box, everything to play for. Sid set the scene. 'Blackpool has become one of the the major destinations in world darts. They love it, the people who come here for their holidays and this is the highlight – as good as the fish and chips and Pepsi Max.' The camera swept around the crowd of men with fags in their gobs and women in posh frocks on their backs. Somebody held up a stuffed monkey toy in a T-shirt which bore the legend 'Hot Rod No 1'. Someone else held up a piece of cloth with 'Da Do One Ron. Ron the Lancastrian' written in felt pen. Another had a sign which read: 'Hello Jamie and all at The Ship (Cardigan)'. So far as one could judge, nobody had graduated from their calligraphy evening class.

Two thousand five hundred people were jammed into the Winter Gardens, three hundred more than had ever foregathered there previously in order to be entertained by a professional darts contest. There was so much smoke and ale fumes there that you could have kippered a shoal of blue whales, or indeed any collective noun of blue whales. You could have cut the tension with a knife, buttered it with the finalists' sweat and served it with chips and Pepsi Max. That's how tense it was.

After Ronnie had won a leg elegantly with two treble 19s and a bullseye, we were allowed to study the Flight Cam, which turned out to be the action replay that they use for televised darts. Sid, studying the footage, hymned the contrasting styles of the two finalists. For a moment his voice was as hushed as that of the snooker commentator Ted Lowe, whose voice was so proverbially muted that you could hear the cue ball parting the green baize as he whispered a frame into narrative being. 'The parabola of the dart,' said Sid, stating his theme. 'Forty-five degree angle in the case of Rod Harrington. The weep controlled against gravity. The slower trajectory of Ronnie's darts rather like Keith Dallas's short – no wiggle or weep, but fighting gravity in the last two feet.'

John, realising that Sid was scoring most of the points, made a wild, looney-tune leap of verbal fancy: 'It's a three-tiered crowd, but in the end there'll be only one man with tears.' Then John modified his prediction. 'Maybe two. Maybe one man with tears of joy and one with tears of sorrow. Already tears of sweat, Sid.'

'The only piece of permanent fixtures not occupied are the chandeliers,' agreed Sid, 'and we have still got a while to go. Even three fat Italians singing *Tosca* couldn't fill them out on three tiers!'

Then Baxter put three darts in a little segment of red on the dart board. 'One hundred and eighty!' yelled the Winter Gardens referee as the partisans brandished their signs for the cameras and cheered.

'That's why!' yelled Sid, alluding to dart's popular superiority over opera. 'Three trebles, never mind three tiers!' retorted John. 'My, my, my!' 'He's still playing like he was six years ago down the boozer having a sly drag and a pint of shandy!' countered Sid. Sid was always fond of reminding his audience of darts' humble origins. Earlier he had said that Baxter was 'playing as though he was down the pub on exhibition night when the trophies are dished out.'

The camera cut to another sign in the audience: 'Rod's no good without Emu', someone had written gnomically. John performed the necessary exegesis: 'Well, he's referring to Rod Hull. But this is a Rod who's certainly not a plonker. He lands them in where he means to put them.'

'Baxter's game will put Rod in the soup', said another sign, an ill-favoured play on the name of the famous Scottish soup manufacturer, perhaps. But that wasn't important any more.

'He's playing as though he was in a pub match for 50p, Baxter,' said Sid, though whether this was intended as a compliment was not clear. 'Baxter can make a hole in this,' countered John, perhaps meaning that he could establish a substantial lead over Rod the Non-Plonker. 'Yes, this lad knows all about Trafalgar,' replied Sid obscurely. Presumably this remark had something to do with British cannons putting holes in the French fleet, but only Sid himself could really adjudicate on the veracity of that analysis. The lager, sweat, smoke and Lancastrian sea air in the Winter Gardens had had a powerful effect on the sign painters in the crowd and the men in the commentary box.

It was 17 legs all and so Rod and Ronnie were thrust into extra time. Quite properly, the commentary went into trans-hyperbolic overdrive. 'It's cruel but it's clinical!' shouted Sid. 'This is called scrapping for your life!' shouted John even louder. This was not about darts now: it was about pride and honour. It was also about the sponsors, Golden Wonder crisps, Skol lager and Bic, purveyors of razors and pens to everyone but the Queen. But more than any of that it was about personal courage, the courage to say things, fanciful, even clichéd things that other commentators would not dare utter. Sid and John were on their own now, right out there on the border between sense and nonsense.

Then, one of Harrington's darts bounced out of the double nine. 'There's no justice in this game,' lamented Sid. 'That's the cruellest twist of fate I have ever seen in twenty-five years of commentating.' 'That was a cruel bounce out,' said John evenly. 'It wasn't even a bounce out. It was a drop out. It was a flop out.'

Sid was rattled by this example of John's commentating poetry, but replied with a flourish: 'One of the biggest crowds for darts watching superabundant brilliance in Blackpool. I wouldn't be surprised if some donkeys chewing carrots came in on their night off to watch this.'

Baxter scored a late 136. Maybe Rod the Non-Plonker's tears of sorrow would be shed after all. '136!' said John. 'Telling and propelling!'

All four were near the edge now. In fact, John had gone into meltdown. Only Sid was still alert: 'Ronnie's tired. Rod's tired. This is testing their very pluck, as Shakespeare would have put it.' John could not answer this, nor could anyone else. After nearly two hours of donkeys and sweat, the tears came down in torrents over the Winter Gardens of Blackpool, rolling down from balcony to stalls. Not Rod's tears, for they remained dammed behind his swollen winner's face, but everybody else cried openly into the wet Lancashire night. And at home, too, millions of viewers, well thousands at least, cried into their remote controls. Tears of joy, tears of sorrow, tiers of tears, but mixed with all those were my tears, tears of laughter mingled with a little national pride. At least Britons are good at one sports-related thing, even if it is only the art of darts commentary. Sid? Sid Waddell? He is the saviour of British sport.

CHAPTER 3

1974: Olivia Newton-John's Waterloo

THE VIRTUES OF MULTI-COLOURED SATIN

I rooted for Olivia Newton-John during the 1974 Eurovision Song Contest because she was singing the British entry. Patriotism can never have been so misplaced. Not only was she Australian, not only was her song 'Long Live Love' unutterably banal (which probably helped its chances of victory), but, worst of all, she was wearing a pale green winceyette-nightie-cum-evening gown. Why, Olivia, why? After all, this was the same black-clad temptress who, only four years later would send a frisson of something or other around my youthful frame, thanks to her bump and grind performance opposite John Travolta when they duetted in *Grease.* In 1974, though I didn't want to admit it to myself, she was dressed for anything but success.

Olivia was just about to meet her Waterloo, and I couldn't bear it. It was 6 April, the venue was the Dome in Brighton, the presenter was Katie Boyle, and Greece was making its debut with bazouki music of little distinction. But none of that is important now. What was important, then as now and disturbingly so for me, was that there was another frisson, a far from pleasurable one, going around me that matched the frisson that was going through the Brighton audience. Something big was going to happen and it wasn't going to start in Olivia's nightie.

The multiple frissons were unleashed by a rock 'n' roll-style number. There were wo-wo-wos from the vocals, and a doo-wopping sax that did the fills in the rock 'n' rolling chorus. There was even a bingy-bongy piano playing descending chords. In other words, this was just what the British pop world, fascinated as it was with rock 'n' roll revivalism at the time thanks to Roy Wood and Wizzard, Suzy Quatro and Mud, wanted to hear. Worse, it was what the rest of Europe wanted to hear as well.

The Swedish assault on Brighton had been well planned. It was led by two rock stars, Björn Ulvaeus, singer and songwriter from The Hootenanny Singers, and his keyboard-playing friend Benny Andersson from The Hep Stars, who were known as the Swedish Beatles, if only in Stockholm. Benny had the beard, Björn had the permanent smile. They were joined by Agnetha Fältskog and Benny's girlfriend, the Norwegian-born Anni-Frid 'Frida' Lyngstad. Neither of the women had beards, but Agnetha could be immediately distinguished from Frida because she had blonde hair. What's more she would later cause outrage from Glasgow to Granada by waving her bottom, tightly swathed in satin, at audiences whose number included a fair few pre-pubescents. Frida, so far as I could understand, would not have stooped to that kind of thing. Together they were Abba and they had a song that everybody could understand. It was about love and took Napoleon's doomed battle as a metaphor. On that night in Brighton, the band's conductor Sven-Olof Walldoff was dressed as Napoleon, and Björn and Benny wore vaguely militaristic tunics made from silk which made the historical allusion very clear indeed. Agnetha and Frida wore silky outfits, too, and made Olivia's winceyette number look as dowdy as it was.

The song's lyrics went not a little like this:

My, my!
At Waterloo, Napoleon did surrender
Wo yeah!
And I have met my destiny in quite a similar way
The history book on the shelf is always repeating itself.

Was the history book on the shelf always repeating itself? Was it really? It seemed, rather, that the history book of the Eurovision Song Contest, that big book in which words like Ding-Ding-a-Dong and Boom-Bang-a-Bang had been used all too liberally, would have to be thrown away since its powers of prediction had been shockingly overstated.

I climbed the stairs to bed that night with a heavy heart. The television programme, all four hours of it, was only half over. All the songs had been performed and now all that Brighton, and indeed Europe, awaited was the tantalising farrago of the scoring system to pronounce the winner. Often this part of the programme has been a capricious affair in which national resentments have come to the fore and as a result so have some truly terrible songs (Iceland, for instance, has been one of the countries least likely to vote for Britain, no doubt because of lingering anger over the Cod War), but not that night. I lay under the covers with my ITT radio jammed against one still disbelieving ear until Katie invited Abba to perform their winning song once more. Only then was it officially all over. Wo yeah.

The only consolation for this misguided patriot, but I could not have known it then, was that the most successful song ever in the Eurovision Contest was British. 'Save Your Kisses For Me' by Brotherhood of Man won the most points of any entry in the contest from 1956 onwards. It scored 164 points in 1976, though, intriguingly, it only beat Catherine Ferry's second-place song, 'Un, Deux, Trois' by 10.4 per cent of the vote. No, it was Italy's long-forgotten 1964 winner 'Non Ho L'Eta' by Gigliola Cinquetti that was the most overwhelming victory, triumphing with a lead of 65.3 per cent of the vote over second-place Briton, Matt Monro and his delightful song 'I Love the Little Things'. Monro, with 17 votes, couldn't compete with Cinquetti's 49. Now Matt is all but forgotten. But as Abba so eloquently put it in their later song, 'The Winner Takes It All', obscurity was the fate of losers:

I've played all my cards
And that is what you've done too.
Nothing more to say
No more ace to play.
The winner takes it all
The loser standing small.
Beside the victory
That's our destiny.

Amazing, isn't it, that the best known and arguably best Eurovision winner, the five-million selling 'Waterloo' by Abba, only had a 25 per cent lead over 'Si', the second-place entry by Gigliola Cinquetti (hoping to repeat her decade-old triumph). Isn't it?

With the exception of Abba's 'Waterloo', the Eurovision Song Contest hasn't sustained the interest of millions of television viewers by means of its music. Heavens, no. After all, for much of its history, the contest has been dominated by songs with silly titles and lyrical sentiments so trite that they made me want to invade Luxembourg and really explain things to their songwriters. The silly titles started in 1967 with the Netherlands entry, 'Ringe Ding'. The next year, Spain won with 'La La La', which expresses the profundity of the Eurovision project in three syllables. Lulu obviously thought she knew which way the contest was going (into the single currency of Eurogibberish) and offered 'Boom Bang-a-Bang' in 1969. Her reward was a four-way tie for first place.

Apart from 'Ding-dinge Dong' by Teach-In in 1975, 'Boom Boom Boomerang' (Lulu should have sued) in 1977, and the 1984 Swedish triumph 'Diggi-Loo Diggi-Ley', though, the titles haven't been quite so bingy-bongy-boo as memory serves. In recent years, the silliest title has been 'Yodel in the Canyon of Love', but this entry with its (one hopes) unintended cunnilingus subtext, was thankfully deemed unsuitable to represent the UK in 1997.

But the sentiments have been mostly banal. Consider Dana's 'All Kinds of Everything', which set Ireland on its path to trans-continental song contest domination back in 1970. The lyric was not unadjacent to the following:

Flutter-byes and butterflies
All types of goo –
All kinds of everything
Remind me of you.

But the song's very semantic emptiness made it the perfect open text – endlessly interpretable to anyone with a smattering of English, symptomatic of the European dream in all its meaninglessness. For Dana's sentiments *were* meaningless: in such an imaginative world, where undifferentiated everything can remind you of something, nothing would serve just as well. Dana had to win.

All too rarely has there been a real song about serious issues. Typically, if scandalously, Kikki Danielson's 1985 Swedish entry was beaten into third place, even though this was a serious feminist number called 'Bra Vibrationer'. Forget about strange sanitary towels with holes cut out so the blue liquid could pour straight through. Women wanted something more than that. 'What do we want?' 'Vibrating bras!' 'When do we want them?' 'As soon as they've been invented, please!' That was the cry of Kikki and her sisters, wasn't it? What's that you say? It doesn't mean that in English? Apparently, Bra Vibrationer means Good Vibrations. Very boring.

Maybe viewers' interest in the Eurovision Song Contest has been sustained by the clothes, since they form an abject history of sartorial mistakes (like haute couture fashion shows but, ultimately, less tragic). In 1969, for example, Lulu, the Glaswegian belter, wore gold boots and black velvet hot pants on to which had been sewn a matching bib. I also dimly recall two appliquéd butterflies on breast and hip (you'll never get into the Freeman's catalogue dressed like that, young lady). Later came Olivia Newton-John's aforementioned tribute to the adaptability of winceyette and Abba's four-part hymn to the virtues of multi-coloured satin. And who could forget the Brotherhood of Man's winning ensemble – clingy nylon shirts over the blokes' beer guts and berets over carefully teased hair for the women? And who will ever be able to erase from their cultural memory that moment when Jay and Cheryl of Buck's Fizz tore away their ra-ra skirts mid-routine in 1981? Not me, by thunder, not me. As late as 1988, Céline Dion wore a drop-waisted puffball skirt paired with a double-breasted naval jacket (what were you thinking of Céline?) when the Canadian sang the Swiss winning entry 'Ne Partez Sans Moi'.

Yes, yes, all very interesting. But the real reason people watch the Eurovision Song Contest is not because of music or clothes, but because of the scoring process, which takes nearly two hours of TV airtime each year. During it, all pretensions to European unity can be set aside, and we can root for whatever rubbish carries our national standard. The long-time Eurovision presenter Terry Wogan contended: 'I love the Eurovision Song Contest for its magnificent foolishness, its grand illusion that it brings together the diverse peoples and cultures of Europe on one great wing of song, when all it makes manifest is how far apart everybody is.'

Magnificent foolishness, yes. So much more worthy an impulse for taking an interest in a competition than patriotism. Foolishness always stands the test of time; patriotism never. In any event, as I learned in 1974, patriotism is often even further misplaced because many of the contest's best artists have not been nationals of the countries they have represented. Céline, Olivia, to name but two. Nana Mouskouri, subsequently a Greek politician, sang for Luxembourg, as did her fellow Greek Vicky Leandros. Gina G sang for Britain (in one of the greatest travesties of the contest in recent years, her 'Ooh Aah . . . Just a Little Bit' was beaten into eighth place by some wet Celtic blah whose name eludes me) even though, like Olivia, she was Australian. And as for Katrina Leskanich, the woman who fronted Katrina and the Waves when they won for Britain in 1997 with 'Love Shine a Light', she was American, though resident in East Anglia.

The scoring system works like this. Each country gives 12 votes to its favourite song (clearly a country cannot vote for its own entry – that would be silly), 10 to the second favourite, 8, 7, 6, 5, 4, 3, 2, 1 to the next eight. Nobody gives many votes to Iceland, and there is an international conspiracy that prevents either Hungary or Romania winning anything. These are the basic rules.

As a result the Eurovision Song Contest delays a hard core of trivia-obsessed nutcases for four hours each year. Perhaps the continuing success of Eurovision among viewers is symptomatic of a decadent continent's slide into cultural oblivion, our values fatally distorted by exposure to Cliff Richard and Johnny Logan's insipid oeuvres. Or maybe, instead, Eurovision is symbolic of the sophisticated sublimation of intra-European conflict into pointless contests of which *International It's a Knockout* is the other leading example.

★

THERE WERE A LOT OF BRUISED KNEES IN BOURNEMOUTH THAT NIGHT

Pointless contests, magnificent foolishness. And television has enshrined these twin virtues in quiz and games shows. Which is quite proper, since the medium of television itself sometimes wades neck deep in pointlessness.

How vividly I remember that night in Bournemouth in 1979. It was a night when Stuart Hall, Eddie Waring and the rest of the *It's a Knockout* crew had come to town. As a direct result, there were a lot of bruised knees in that corner of England that evening. With legs tied together, teams had to hop up and down a ramp, negotiating damp patches which made them fall over, while carrying a tarpaulin of water which they were to tip into a cylinder. The team who had the most water in their cylinder would go to the next round in Switzerland. In 1979, it was the people who invented games rather than the participants who apparently needed to take drug tests.

The grim-faced St John Ambulance crew sat huddled in their thermals, ready to tend to swellings and minor dislocations, not really entering into the spirit of the thing. There was some sort of job creation scheme going on at the overstaffed scoreboard.

Arun's four girls and boys had slipped over at least three times, but managed to make it to the cylinder, where, unaccountably, they tipped the water on to the grass. Arun's cheerleaders, four boisterous bathing beauties (colour-coded shower caps and one-piece bloomers), stopped bouncing for a moment. 'Ho, ho, dear me, that is what you call chagrin on the faces of the Arun team,' said Stuart Hall.

Nothing could stop Stuart Hall being cheerful. He would have made a lousy war correspondent. He was forever putting his arm round surly Arthur and inquiring after the score with a beam on his face. Unfortunately, the director was in a foul mood.

Whenever Hall hymned Bournemouth ('That's the scene in front of the pier in the sun'), we would cut to boys and girls in woolly hats and scarves, or an unsmiling couple, husband in Russian fur hat, wife with anorak hood drawstring pulled tight. This was, after all, July.

The games rarely made any sense and Hall's explanations only made matters worse. They could not have been intended to help participant or viewer. 'You've got a guy here who's going to go up a slope with balloon and he's going to give it to his mate and you've got to go like dynamite.' I was very confused. How would they know when to stop?

The best games in *It's a Knockout* always involved water or foam. Admittedly, there was one in which a woman bouncing on a trampoline with a tennis racket had to dodge flying packets of flour, and perhaps hit one with a forearm smash, but that looked less like a game and more like an accident waiting to happen. The crunch game, as far as one could tell, involved PE teachers in short shorts writhing in foam while carrying footballs and wearing clowns' feet. The contestants on *It's a Knockout* weren't so much prepared to make fools of themselves in front of millions, but insisted on their right to do so.

When the first version of it was broadcast between 1966 and 1982, *It's a Knockout* sometimes felt like compulsory fun. The new series, which began in the summer of 1999, did not command such clout – partly because it is shown on Channel 5, but also because it is hosted by Keith Chegwin who is, clearly, no Stuart Hall. But watching repeats from the seventies seems like glimpsing a happier, less self-conscious world. *Ask the Family* it wasn't. Nor *Countdown*. Nor, for that matter, *Mastermind*. No, it didn't tax your brains at all. But it did look like the competitors were having more fun than Magnus Magnusson's guests.

*

ONE EVENING AT ROCHDALE TOWN HALL

'In Greek mythology, which name meaning round eye was given to gigantic beings each of which had a single eye in the middle of its forehead?'

'Centaur?'

No, you fool. No, no, no!

'No. Cyclops.'

'Which term, coined by John Ruskin, describes the attribution of human emotions to inanimate nature?'

'Anthropomorphism?'

No! Obviously not! No!

'No. The pathetic fallacy.'

'What is the name given to the thick, insulating layer of fat which lies beneath the skin of whales and other sea mammals?'

Hold on, it's –

'Blubber.'

Blubber, yes. Of course.

'In the theatre, who's referred to as the angel of the production?'

The what? The *angel*? In the *theatre*?

'Erm, someone who backs it?'

'Correct.'

What was that? Someone who whats it?

'In 480 BC, Leonidas and his Spartan troops died heroically while defending which pass from the invading Persians?'

Now, I know this. Lesbos. No. Euphrates. No. Bannockburn. No –

'Thermopylae.'

'Correct.'

'In mathematics, what name is given to the longest cord in a circle?'

Hold on. The longest cord in a circle. Now if you've got a circle which would be the longest –

'Diameter.'

Who is winning?

Sshh!

'Correct.'

'According to Virgil, when Aeneas descended into the Underworld, what gift did he have to take with him?'

No idea. Not one.

Wine?

'A lamb?'

'No. A golden bough.'

Oh, that's interesting. That would explain the Frazer book.

The what?

The Frazer book. You know, *The Golden Bough.*

Sshh!

'Which queen was the last of Egypt's Ptolemaic dynasty who committed suicide in 30 BC?'

Cleopatra. Cleopatra. Cleopatra!

Cleopatra.

'Cleopatra.'

'Correct.'

See.

Sssh!

'Which Stuart king on his deathbed reportedly apologised for taking an unconscionable time dying?'

Oh that's interesting. Who could that have been?

I don't know, one or the other. Charles I or Charles II. Wasn't there a James?

What a funny thing to say when you're dying!

'Charles II.'

'Correct.'

A TAX ON STUPIDITY

By contrast with *Mastermind*, the National Lottery really is a tax on stupidity. Not just the stupidity of those who buy tickets, but the rest of us who are prepared to see our licence fees spent on *National Lottery Live!* the most lucrative game show on British television, broadcast on BBC1. We're paying for free advertising for Camelot's dodgy products, for celebrities to plug their new albums and films, for one of the worst pieces of programming that the BBC has ever broadcast.

At least on commercial channels they have ad breaks for this sort of thing. At least on the shopping channels, everyone knows the deal: you're going to get the hard sell and, in the unlikely event you see anything you'd want to buy (that darling figurine for your radiator shelf, a home gym bigger than most people's homes), then you choose to make the purchase. On BBC1 we're entitled to expect better, but it's getting worse: we have two Lottery draws a week, more balls on the BBC than ever before.

When the midweek Lottery draw began in 1997, BBC1 obliged the Lottery company Camelot by offering lots of TV hoopla for its new product. Carol Vorderman, the woman doomed to be billed by the tabloids as 'TV brainbox' and who, to my mind, had a hitherto unimpeachable career arranging the vowels and consonants and completing quite tricky sums on *Countdown*, described how to arrange your marks on a Lottery ticket to minimise the risk of sharing the jackpot. Intriguingly, in the weeks when the jackpot had not been won, marks tended to be bunched at the top or bottom; in the weeks when the jackpot was shared, the winning combination of marks usually formed a nice trellis pattern. But the problem with this sort of advice is that it can be self-defeating – every lemon and her husband would be bunching their marks if they took Carol's tip. Also, it lured viewers into believing that through their skill and judgement they could increase the chance of winning a bigger sum of money. But that is nonsense. Through skill, judgement and not a little book learning, you might win *Countdown* or *Mastermind* but not the National Lottery.

Carol Smillie, the show's host, interviewed some past Lottery winners, all of whom seemed boringly normal. It would have been more fun surely to have interviewed Wayne and Waynetta Slob, the couple who had spent their dole money on scratch cards until that fateful day when they won. They spent their winnings on a top-of-the-range lavatory in the living room and a pizza delivery firm, complete with moped, in the adjoining kitchen. 'So, what's the secret of your success,' Carol Smillie would ask. 'Bunching or trellis?' Waynetta, furious at such intrusive questioning, would fix her with a blank stare as she sat on her customised toilet, and reply: 'I am having a fag.' Now that's what I call class.

But we weren't being encouraged only to buy Lottery tickets. 'The album we're bringing out on 10 March, but I'm not here to talk about that,' said Michael Ball after his grisly mauling of a *West Side Story* classic. There was an obliging clip from the awful-looking film *Extreme Measures* starring guest Hugh Grant. And the Spice Girls were able to plug their new single.

Even as entertainment the half-hour show was lamentable. This show had what showbiz producers call top-drawer guests. But if you have the Spice Girls on a show, what a waste to have them read badly from autocues about the five 'good causes' to which Lottery money goes. I would have had them miming to backing tapes, making suggestive remarks about oral sex to a blushing Hugh Grant and generally behaving badly.

Grant at least had the grace to look thoroughly embarrassed. This grim appearance, after all, was part of his career rehabilitation after that thing he did or had done to him down in La-La Land. But he behaved as sulkily as if he was doing community service. It was a shame he didn't have time to change out of his gardening clothes before he appeared on the show. 'Why is it the Americans are so keen to see more British talent?' asked Smillie, alluding surely to acting rather than sexual indiscretions. 'Well,' mused Grant after a reflective pause. 'No one knows.' Tell it like is, Hugh, my man!

And then the moment we had all been waiting for. The studio audience started howling again; after all, this had been billed as 'All the excitement of Saturday on a Wednesday,' whatever that meant. Now it was time to push the buttons on Lancelot and get those balls rolling, Hugh. 'Very exciting. Can't wait,' he said. Instead of magnificent foolishness, I thought, just foolishness; instead of winning pointlessness, big prizes; instead of scholarship, stupidity. Instead of television that at least attempts to inform, educate or entertain the innocent, *National Lottery Live!*

CHAPTER 4

1976: Mrs Slocombe's Pussy

A NATION OF SHOPKEEPERS

I was thirteen when I first saw *Are You Being Served?* and my tender sensibilities, dancing on the borderline between childhood and adolescence, were shocked. How could a British sitcom broadcast on BBC1 refer to Mrs Slocombe's pussy? It broke a code of silence. A woman's genitals should not be referred to in public, especially not on prime-time television before the 9 o'clock watershed, and certainly not on the channel that had broadcast the Queen's coronation.

There was a very special upset for me in Mrs Slocombe's weekly pussy-naming, not least because, at thirteen, female sexuality was to me a much more secret world than the male's; it was tucked away in the girls' changing rooms and never really discussed in public, even though its primal force occasionally filled the air. Perhaps I was jealous of girls for their changing bodies and the mastery they seemed to have over those changes. In public, boys attempted to break the power of women by joking about girls' breasts or legs, or by expressing a commanding lust for them; only a very few would go further and talk about the mysteries that lay between girls' legs.

Mrs Slocombe's pussy changed all that. I felt betrayed, particularly by the laughter of the studio audience which was noticeably more hysterical when Mollie Sugden put on her common northern voice and told Miss Brahms: 'Oooh, I had terrible trouble with my pussy last night, you know.' They were laughing at a middle-aged woman's sex, which seemed to me to be a new territory for television comedy: busty young trollops were a staple, as were sexless spinsters; but a middle-aged woman who had functioning sexual organs – what was funny about that? It was funny surely, because it dissolved that secret source of female power into a double entendre.

Most of those laughs seemed to me to come from middle-aged women, Mrs Slocombe's contemporaries, rising enthusiastically high above male grunts. But what were they laughing at? The intrinsic hilarity of the double entendre? Surely not. The release prompted by a breach in sitcom etiquette, the hilarity produced by transcending some taboo? Perhaps. I fancy that it was also a loud outbreak of protective laughter at themselves: after all, if you're going to face a comedic roughing up, best to get your laughter in quick and loudest. But, of course, it's a strategy that doesn't work: laugh hard at a joke and someone will want to tell it again, and again, and again. So it was with Mrs Slocombe's pussy.

Are You Being Served? was replete with these kinds of devices, I felt, and so it came to typify for me a very British tendency to cruelty. Not just because every one of its characters was a mess of a human being, whose failings we loved to dissect week after week, but because that mess and cruelty was for once reflected back on its audience, that mass audience of British people whose sense of national identity was deepened by exposure to this programme as to any royal ceremonial narrated by Richard Dimbleby or Raymond Baxter. Why? Because it was quickly apparent to me that, maybe unintentionally, David Croft and Jeremy Lloyd had created a metaphor for Britain.

Grace Brothers was Britain, a disunited kingdom that had started crumbling during the war and, against all the odds, against all the laws of physics and of good taste, still kept going, supplying a dwindling bunch of customers with things that they surely could not want. In John Osborne's fifties play *The Entertainer*, an earlier comic evocation of Britain's decline, the veteran music hall star Archie Rice exhorted his audience: 'Don't clap too hard – it's a very old building.' Grace Brothers was an old building too, but that didn't stop *Are You Being Served*'s audience clapping and laughing like irresponsible subjects of a once great kingdom, clapping and laughing at their own downfall.

This was a shop that time had forgotten, that carried on regardless, heedless that the world was changing outside. If it had come in smellyvision, Grace Brothers would have smelled like Albert Steptoe's used bath water. Like the Shopping Channel nowadays, the mens- and womenswear departments of Grace Brothers stocked things that nobody in their right minds would seriously consider buying. It was staffed by women and men who didn't like outsiders encroaching on their space. They didn't like their leaders much either, especially Mr Cuthbert Rumbold, who was a jug-eared incompetent of a manager, ill suited to take over the reins of power from Young Mr Grace who, even though he was aged at least 120, would never push off this mortal coil and had a libido which would shame young bucks ninety years his junior. Young Mr Grace ruled Grace Brothers thanks to feudal deference, which was just as well, since nobody had seen him do a scrap of work in his life. 'You've all done very well' – that was his catchphrase, as he doddered through the third floor with an implausible filly on his arm, airily, *royally* even, waving as every British king and queen has always done.

Worse than not liking the customers or their bosses, though, the staff of Grace Brothers didn't like each other much. Admittedly, Mr Lucas sometimes went on a date with Miss Brahms but her contempt for him was, for once, of the kind that could not be construed as playing hard to get. No, she thought, he was a sleazy twerp with reptilian eyes and a horrible synthetic car coat, and she was right.

Metaphors of Britain's decline have been a dime a dozen in the post-war years. Typical in its clumsy obviousness was Lindsay Anderson's 1982 film *Britannia Hospital*, in which the chaotic, run-down hospital awaited a royal visit to mark its 500th anniversary. By contrast, *Are You Being Served*'s unwitting metaphor was particularly fecund, perhaps because it was unwitting. Its very unintentional quality made it prescient: how could Croft and Lloyd have known, if they had conceived the drama as metaphor, that, as the 1980s began, a shopkeeper's daughter called Margaret Thatcher and her monetarist henchman Geoffrey Howe would set about shrinking Britain's manufacturing base to the size of a pin and thus make the country's economy more and more dependent on its service sector?

How could Thatcher think Britain could ever thrive as a service economy? Britons hate other people so much that they would hardly want to spend time pandering to them, still less making them feel good about themselves. Being snide to them, yes, feeding them foul food and brown water with grit in the bottom instead of proper coffee, yes; but serving them? Serving was what the rest of the world should do for us. We used to have an empire, you know!

If only Thatcher and Howe had known their sitcom history, they would have realised theirs was a bad idea, that Britain's service sector could never do the business required of it, that some other economic miracle must be considered. Invading France and confiscating their cheeses until they agreed to pay us a huge annual fee which would enable Britons to sit around in singlets watching daytime TV. That would have been an achievable and certainly popular political goal. In *Fawlty Towers*, the service was so bad that even the food inspector was presented with a rat when offered water biscuits for his cheese. This was not a country in which people served, or at least served other people, and never, heavens no, with good grace. In *Are You Being Served?*, the store was increasingly a front for pantomime turns, more and more frequently visited by the TV audience before or after opening hours when its staff could indulge their proper vocation – playing among themselves to no discernible economic benefit. In one episode, for instance, based around the theme of a sales drive, the total takings were 32p and only that much because Mr Grainger had deigned to sell a customer a pair of socks. For the rest of the day, the staff spent their time dressing up in German national dress, drinking Rhine wine and rhythmically slapping each other in the time-honoured manner of Teutonic dancing. Are You Being Served? Hardly.

If Grace Brothers was a metaphor for Britain, this was a Britain where men of almost any age (from Mr Lucas's twentysomething to Young Mr Grace's onehundredandtwentysomething) were always trying to cop a feel as though it was their birthright, where women were pneumatic dollies or sex-starved harridans, where gay men were sad sacks doomed to lead domestic lives of deceit and degradation. This was a Britain intolerant of difference, uncomfortable with outsiders and resentful of insiders. I came to hate *Are You Being Served?* with a passion since I realised the unbearable, and unintended, truth of its critique.

The first episode of *Are You Being Served?* I saw was broadcast on 8 April 1976. The episode was called 'No Sale' and began in the style to which I was to become accustomed. The till chinged, the electric bass played a descending line, the reassuringly bland signature tune started and the show began. 'First floor perfumery, stationery and leather goods,' announced a woman's voice in rhythm with the music. 'Wigs and haberdashery. Kitchenware and food. Going up!' It was the same every week; everything was in its place, everything was orderly and so a nation of shopkeepers could comfortably sit back to watch a notion of shopkeepers make a mockery of their chosen profession. Even though younger shoppers, like me, in the mid-seventies wouldn't know a haberdashery if it kneeled down in front of them and measured their inside legs. What did one purchase at a haberdashery? Haberdashes perhaps?

The third floor of Grace Brothers was laid out before us like a stage. Characters made their entrances from the two lifts and swept down the stairs to their appointed places. By April 1976, Miss Brahms, Mrs Slocombe and Mr Humphries in particular had refined their entrances so perfectly that they didn't have to say anything to reduce the studio audience to welcoming whoops. The show had been running for three years and so the audience knew what to expect, knew, perhaps, when they should laugh. Miss Brahms tottered to her work station in something ludicrously tight, Mrs Slocombe staggered from the lift, yellow hair a go-go, legs akimbo after some mishap on the way to work, and Mr Humphries – how *did* Mr Humphries get from the lift to the menswear department every morning? What verb would be appropriate to account for his entrance? It isn't a $64,000 question. Mr Humphries minced.

Like Larry Grayson, that other seventies TV homosexual, Mr Humphries minced forward across the stage towards the camera as middle-aged women screamed their laughter and men, I suspect, smiled narrowly. That dapper old queen whose wrist was always limp, and who forever standing on the balls of his feet, could have minced for England. He couldn't even walk straight. In the episode in which the Grace Brothers staff were required to wear lederhosen to help sell German goods, Mr Humphries wore the shortest shorts in tight leather and boots that looked at least three sizes too small. He could not but mince. In my fancy, in every episode Mr Humphries was compelled by a sadistic but cunning director to wear constricting German shorts under his three-piece suit and was required to wear small shoes that forced him to walk ridiculously. Like foot-bound Chinese women, John Inman must have suffered for his art, the poor love.

In the 'No Sale' episode, Young Mr Grace had decided that his department store should open half an hour earlier at 8.30 a.m., and everybody arrived for work thoroughly discomfited. Captain Peacock was the first to appear. Though the Captain was unimpeachably attired as ever, he was cross because he had not yet breakfasted. 'I thought Mrs Peacock made breakfast,' said Mr Rumbold. 'Not at 0600 hours,' rejoined the testy Captain. 'I woke her up and she turned over and murmured something that sounded remarkably like "Get knotted!"'

Get knotted. What a fantastic expression. Nobody outside a seventies British sitcom ever said 'Get knotted'. Try waking up the person in your bed at some unholy hour and asking for breakfast and it's a safe bet that they will say many things, but not one of them will be 'Get knotted'.

There are things that people say only on television, and 'Get knotted' is only one of them. For instance, there was once an episode of *The Avengers* in which Patrick Macnee told Diana Rigg that he would approach his quarry like 'a cat in carpet slippers'. What he meant by this, I feel sure, is that he would be very, very quiet indeed. But this is a nonsense. I don't know if you've ever put a cat in carpet slippers and implored it to creep up on something (perhaps you could try that when you've finished this chapter), but the result is hardly a byword for stealth or silence. And yet, *The Avengers* was filled with such absurdities as these. In fact, they were the chief reasons for watching the programme. To be an aberrant decoder is sometimes the only way to get value for your licence fee or for the long, long, otherwise unjustifiable hours spent watching television.

Similarly, the puerile masquerade of seventies non-swearing was worth watching because it was deliciously nonsensical. In the seventies, no matter how angry a character got, they rarely transcended the unwritten lexicon of permissible oaths. True,

George A. Cooper, who played Billy Liar's dad in the sitcom spin-off from Keith Waterhouse's play, swore all the time. But he was the exception that proved the rule. As we sat in our living room watching the Fisher family in theirs, the Jeffries family would keep a scrupulous account of the number of times Mr Fisher senior would say 'bloody' during a half-hour episode. Some weeks it was more than thirty. But his monomaniacal swearing made him barmy, a living room loony driven to verbal excess by the madness of the times, like Alf Garnett but less political.

Otherwise there was very little swearing. At HM Prison Slade, Norman Stanley Fletcher, no matter how angry he got with Mr Mackay or Lennie Godber, only expressed himself with the words 'Naff off!' Even in something as edgy and contemptible as the racial-tension sitcom *Love Thy Neighbour*, where white called black 'Sambo' and black called white 'Honky', the angriest words ever spoken were 'Flaming Nora.' 'Flaming Nora!' Jack Smethurst's racist white proletarian socialist would exclaim when confounded yet again by Rudolph T. Walker's aspirant black Tory. 'Flaming Nora!' Smethurst would shout, because he couldn't say on television what such a man would say in real life. *Coronation Street*'s Jack Duckworth had recourse to the same expression whenever his wife sent him down to the cellar to bring up another barrel of Newton and Ridley's ale. 'Flaming Nora, Vera!' he would moan rhythmically as he descended the steps into the Rovers cellar. Though he could have said worse.

I would hear more swearing in my fifteen-minute playground scamper in the mornings after milk at Alder Coppice Primary School, and consequently television thus inhabited a neutered realm where the vulgar language one heard in the street, the playground or the office hardly ever contaminated what one heard on-screen. At primary school, too, we talked about sex, but on television it could only be acknowledged through the moralising filter of double entendres. Mrs Slocombe's pussy was the most reckless. Reckless because middle-aged women weren't supposed to have sex, or if they did, a clean-minded British television audience didn't want to think about that over its gammon and chips, thank you very much. The only way the *Are You Being Served?* scriptwriters seemed able to deal with this was by making it axiomatic within the series that she never had sex, that she was a stereotypically sexually frustrated harridan. They had created the Pandora's Box of Mrs Slocombe's sexuality; now it was their responsibility to keep a lid on it.

The next member of Grace Brothers' staff made their entrance. A tight black leather biker's outfit capped by a helmet descended the stairs. 'Can I help you, sir?' said Captain Peacock. The helmet came off and Miss Brahms shook her blonde hair at him. She shook her hair and then he was a she. Sexual confusion – that staple joke of post-war British life ever since men grew hair over their ears. Men of Captain Peacock's generation and demeanour were always mistaking women for men and, more often, vice versa. Eric Morecambe frequently made the same comic mistake as Captain Peacock, but, then, as Eric always slept in the same bed as Ernie, noisily munching an apple as his long-time companion rattled more purple prose into his portable type-writer – as lovable and sexless as Laurel and Hardy who had shared the same bed, too, and without any hint of homosexual desire – gender roles existed chiefly to be mined for gags.

More engaging, though, was Miss Brahms's face, mascaraed into a semblance of allure but, with a lower jaw firmly set and lips turned upwards only against their will. Like Pauline Quirke's Chigwellian Sharon Theodopolopoudos in *Birds of a Feather*, with her exaggeratedly inverted U of a mouth, Miss Brahms was a type, arguably the prototype for the Essex girl stereotype (work with me) – the set of the jaw expressing the supposed fact that she was a bit thick, the blonde hair and the short skirt, the blank eyes suggesting that she was the kind of woman whom it would be unwise to cross.

It's been an exquisite torture watching Wendy Richard grow old on screen, studying her as she mutated from dollybird in *Are You Being Served?* to ruined widow in *EastEnders*. I often imagine Miss Brahms of *Are You Being Served?* and Pauline Fowler of *EastEnders* are the same person. It's hard not to do this when you watch television. It's hard to stop your imagination transcending the limits of the programmes you watch, just as the actors themselves flit between dramas.

Television plays hurtful tricks on people who watch it long enough. It doesn't step outside time, but accentuates its effects and brings them into unbearable close-up. When *Are You Being Served?* was repeated again in the late nineties, suddenly the two Wendy Richards were juxtaposed, one selling lingerie, the other a sullen lounge lizard, nursing a tepid half in the Queen Vic. I looked at her face and time travelled, backwards and forwards: in her young face I could see the features hardening; in the old I could see the lost potential, sexiness isomorphised into bitterness.

Her first incarnation on *EastEnders* was too shocking, though. How could Miss Brahms marry Arthur Fowler, a man who was played by Bill Treacher, who looked as though he'd stepped from another era. Treacher, that bluff East Ender with roses in his cheeks and a haircut that time forgot, looked like nothing so much as John Mills's chum in *This Happy Breed*, a heart of oak in a body thwarted by its ration-book diet of powdered eggs and spam fritters, a noble chap to be sure and just the sort of fellow you'd want around to while away the hours over cards in the Anderson shelter, but not, oh God no, not the sort of geezer who could have pulled Miss Brahms to a soundtrack of Barry White in a club out Romford way.

Mrs Slocombe was the next to arrive on the Grace Brothers' shop floor, as ever staggering down the stairs, and looking as though she had been dragged through a hedge backwards and then pushed back through it forwards for good measure. She'd arrived in the sidecar of Miss Brahms's current beau and her coiffure had suffered terrible punishment as a result. It was so bent it looked like the hairstyle adopted by Douglas Hurd's rubber puppet in *Spitting Image* – a hairdo swirled to a point like an ice cream cornet. All it needed was a Flake stuck in the top and a squirt of raspberry sauce.

'When you said he was a TT rider, I thought you meant he didn't drink,' said Mrs Slocombe. 'It's going to cost me a fortune at Madame Beryl's to get this knocked back into shape.' She would get her hair done at a place called that. As a result the pretentiousness of Mrs Slocombe's aspirations would be punctured by the reality of getting her rug rethought by a woman whose professional nomenclature was as culturally conflicted as her best customer's psyche.

Her hair was out of kilter and her knickers were in a twist. 'There won't be any customers you know,' she told Mr Rumbold. 'And what it's doing to my domestic arrangements. Having a bath at six o'clock in the morning played havoc with my pussy.'

There was a pause here, while the audience considered Mrs Slocombe's pussy. By 1976, the audience had been given pause to reflect on Mrs Slocombe's pussy on a weekly basis. It had become as much part of the show's ritual as the title music and the concluding credits. Perhaps the rest of the audience visualised the scene, as I did then, as I do now. A lonely, sex-starved woman on the wrong side of forty at best, lying in a bath of lukewarm water as a raw, steel-grey English morning kept its counsel outside, her pubic hair drifting longingly to the greasy surface, abjectly; the slow, scrupulous process of getting ready for work – applying the make-up, putting on the matching skirt, waistcoat and frilly blouse, dealing with her beehive – and the irksome business of work itself still ahead of her. She was as on the shelf, as thoroughly neglected, as the unbecoming Westphalian-made bustenhalters that lay pristine and unworn on Grace Brothers' lingerie department shelves. How could we have made you like this, Mrs Slocombe? How could we have done this to you?

Maybe nobody imagined the scene as I did. But I couldn't do otherwise: I was, after all, shocked that the word 'pussy' could be used even as a double entendre. How could a show aimed at a mass audience – not the late-night crowd of liberal deviants and twisted avant gardists who would later make Channel 4 their own, no, but mums and dads in Cwmbran, Cumbernauld and Coventry – draw attention to a woman's vagina and her sexuality, while in the next breath restoring us to the furry familiarity of the world of pet cats? Usually, double entendres were puerile things, the sort of chancy remarks that would prompt Dick Emery's cross-dressing parody of a floozie to reply: 'Oooh you are awful. But I like you!' But this double entendre was of a different quality, the shock of its explicitness related to the vitriol of its contempt for a middle-aged woman's frustrated sexual ambitions.

For Mrs Slocombe was sex-starved. Later in the episode, she and Miss Brahms conspiratorially discussed an evening the latter had spent at the pub. Miss Brahms had been accosted by a bloke in an open-necked shirt with a hairy chest and big muscles. 'Just a minute,' said Mrs Slocombe, her frilly front a-quiver. 'How old was this man?' 'Oh, he must have been forty if he was a day.' 'Oh quite young, really,' said the predator, not as choosy as she might once have been. What was the audience laughing at? The older woman hoping to pick up the younger's cast-offs? Miss Brahms went on: 'I was wearing my skin-tight jeans. You know, the ones with a patch just there.' (At this point, she patted her right buttock.) ' "Blimey," he says, "There's a stitch going" and he grabs hold and won't let go.'

'Oh, imagine!' said Mrs Slocombe in her posh, affronted voice. 'Go on,' she added, in her northern, down-and-dirty voice, that was always played off the former to satirical effect.

'I ordered a large gin and tonic with a lot of ice, put it on his bill and poured it down the front of his trousers,' said Miss Brahms. Here was the icy composure of the young woman with sexual capital to spare.

'Don't some men take terrible liberties?' asked Mrs Slocombe poshly. 'Where exactly is this pub?' she inquired in her vulgar northern accent.

Mrs Slocombe, though, wasn't always thus. In the German Week episode, she recalled her hatred for the Hun. 'I haven't forgotten being flung flat on my back by a land mine on Clapham Common, and the German air force was responsible,' she disclosed. 'All the other times she was flat on her back the American air force was responsible,' chimed Mr Lucas. The whole air force? Like the old gag about the woman who has only had sex three times (once with Terry, once with Harry, and once with the The Royal Fusiliers), this joke, courtesy of scriptwriters Lloyd and Croft, relied on a woman's sexual appetite being oppressively endless. Perhaps Lloyd and Croft were, as many British men seem to be, threatened by this possibility and so implied that such women are laughably loose as a result. In this case, though, there was a twist: Mrs Slocombe had aged to the point where she couldn't get any sexual gratification (this itself relies on the misogynist notion that women become sexually less appealing as they age, and do so more quickly than men) and yet was constantly tantalised and punished for her earlier excess by having to work in close proximity to a woman so sexually attractive that she could afford to ice the genitals of those men she rejected. Mrs Slocombe, with her icy genitals (what does her surname suggest if not that?), could not afford to do the same to any man. She couldn't afford not to fancy anyone. She was desperate for sex, any sex.

After the comic pause, Mrs Slocombe added: 'He sleeps in the airing cupboard and the gurgling of the tank woke him up.' Oh, of course, *that* pussy, the *male* pussy of legend. 'All that dirty stuff you were thinking about a sexually frustrated woman in her bath? Well, that was your dirty mind,' the script all but said. 'You sick, sick people.' And yet, why was this double entendre repeated week after week, long after the sexual reading of her allusion had been comically confounded shortly after the first time it was mentioned? For two reasons. First, because *Are You Being Served?*, like many long-running British sitcoms and dramas, appealed to its audience partly because of its soothing ritual: the same jokes each week, like the same signature tune, the same credit sequence ('You have been watching . . .' that purported guarantee of sameness and of quality throughout British sitcoms of the seventies, underwriting what we had just seen). Second, because, if you want to keep a woman down, you must put her down again and again and again.

In any case, it wasn't Mrs Slocombe's pubic hair that was the show's visual focus. No. It was the frightful thing on her head, courtesy of Madame Beryl. As the writers and directors grew more confident in their creations' celebrity, the more ready they became to collapse them into pantomime figures. Thus, Mrs Slocombe's wig was often yellow in later episodes, a shrieking signifier to the audience that she was a farcical character, a sign that it was safe to laugh, that it was right to whoop, permissible to enjoy oneself. This was of a piece with the tendency towards fancy-dress farce and musical interludes. It wasn't exactly a shift from Pinter to pantomime, to be sure, but it is true that the subtlety of *Are You Being Served?* (such as it was) became less and less noticeable as the show became more and more part of the cultural fabric of our blighted nation.

But the yellow peril of Mrs Slocombe's hairdo caused a problem for the dynamic of the show. If there was any creative tension in *Are You Being Served?*, it was that there was only room for one pantomime dame. To solve the problem, the candidates alternated. In the 'No Sale' episode, it was not Mrs Slocombe's turn, and so it was Mr Humphries'. He came on, last to enter and first in our hearts. Just as Mrs Slocombe was the sexually thwarted battleaxe, punished for being a woman that men could no longer regard as desirable, so Mr Humphries was a pert camp poppet, whose sexuality the writers would barely allow us to imagine. By contrast with Mrs Slocombe, whose bath-time frustrations and longings leapt to my mind, Mr Humphries' sexuality was to be imagined not at all, but instead shrouded in seediness and a desperately abject jauntiness.

He came on wearing a sailor's hat, a greatcoat and a kit bag. As fast as you could say 'Hello, sailor! Fill your pipe with rough shag?' the audience had begun to applaud his fairy footfalls across the shop floor. He had, he declared, just hitched back from a party in Newcastle-upon-Tyne in this sailor's outfit. At one point during the journey, though it's not clear why, his hat band had read 'Kiss me quick!'

'I bet you meet a lot of nice girls that way,' said Mrs Slocombe with the naivety that only a comic stereotype can bring to the analysis of a difficult situation.

'I did,' said the garrulous sailor. 'Not to mention a roving reporter, a trendy bishop, a stringvestite and a dustman with a very interesting tale to tell.' With that, he swung his kit bag over his camp shoulder and minced, as was his wont, to his work station.

Now hold on for just one second. Let us consider this taxonomy of Mr Humphries' weekend companions. A reporter – no doubt to expose shady shenanigans of the kind in which Mr Humphries, we are to suppose, has been involved, and for which, one day, unless society has lost all semblance of righteous moral fervour, he will be exposed and punished in a Sunday tabloid. A *roving* reporter, at that, roving to imply, no doubt, all kinds of sexual licence. A trendy bishop – well, there's one of those in every bunch of bananas, isn't there? We all know those clergymen and their choirboys, don't we? Eat your heart out, Socrates! The dustman, too, a man professionally engaged in dealing with human waste, thus temperamentally equipped to hang out with sleazy queens on a sordid weekend of unmentionable doings. True, all this was very subtle and implicit, and as a result, no doubt, John Inman, who played Mr Humphries, could, as indeed he did, deny that his character was gay. This was a noble stand for John Inman to take: after all, Mr Humphries had been outed by gay groups in the seventies only to have his character impugned for its theatrical campness. It was only right for Inman to 'in' Mr Humphries. Perhaps he could have gone on to 'in' other men – George Michael, Ian McKellen, Ron Davies. Back into the closet the lot of you! That means you, Peter Tatchell!

And what is a stringvestite when it's at home? Is it a man? A woman? Or simply a fashion error masquerading as a lifestyle choice? String vests may have a certain cachet among some misguided strata of British society, but they do not, surely, feature in the well-dressed homosexual's wardrobe. Or indeed in the wardrobe of the worst-dressed homosexual in this Queen's realm. No, the string vest represents something else: a parody of perversity, a mockery by straight men of homosexuality which is forever in their minds intrinsically connected with fetishism. To make fetishism ridiculous and thus to deprive it of its subversive power, they clothe it in daftness, in string vests or Kiss-me-quick hats. Like a leather-clad spanking madam in fluffy carpet slippers, it's less threatening that way. There is, as there was in Mrs Slocombe's double entendres, fear in this ingenious humour. Oh, heavens, yes it is ingenious! It takes wit to create laughs from such a fearful, hateful, handful of dust.

But hang on a second. There was a phone call for Mr Humphries. It was his mother on the line. A shame, but we could only hear his end of the conversation. 'Of course, I'm still your little boy. No I haven't changed, not all that much. Well, I can't help it if I'm popular, can I? That reminds me, if a man rings up with a Scottish accent, you're the cleaner and you've never heard of me. What do you mean, there's someone coming up the garden path in a kilt? Lock the door and hide in the cupboard.

Whatever you do don't open the door unless you see a young policeman carrying a rolled umbrella, and if I can borrow a helmet from the toy department, that'll be me!' Ah, poor Mrs Humphries to have such a boy! To have to play the game of deceit to keep him safe from the rapacious kiltocracy of Scottish homosexuals. Kilts are suggestive things for such scriptwriters to introduce at such a point. They imply, to sassenachs who can only imagine what kind of naughtiness goes on beneath the sporran, a world of sexual licence and degradation. And only imply: the scriptwriters would never get their hands, or their audience's minds, dirty with the real fears that lay behind their tartan symbolism.

In another world, we would have heard Mrs Humphries' side of the conversation. But the likes of her are regularly silenced. Mothers and wives are often the disappeared of television. David Croft and Jimmy Perry created the most memorable, the most frightening in Mrs Mainwaring in *Dad's Army*. In one episode, the platoon gathered in the Mainwarings' drawing room for a buffet. Mrs Mainwaring was supposed to make an appearance, which sent a chill throughout the assembled company. Corporal Jones looked as though one of his 'fuzzy-wuzzies' from the Boer War had captured his bayonet and shoved it where the sun doesn't shine. 'They don't like it up 'em, sir!' We heard Mrs Mainwaring crossing the floor upstairs – these were not the feet of an Englishwoman, but of a burly Wagnerian heroine, or perhaps a languorous elephant who could crush her husband like a bunch of dry kindling. Fear shone from every male face, but thankfully for them, Mrs Mainwaring never came downstairs and so we could only imagine the horror that was Captain Mainwaring's spouse. This is a common TV device: in *Minder*, for instance, we never see 'Er Indoors, that is to say Arthur Daley's wife; in *Frasier* we never see the whippet-thin wife of Niles Crane, and here, the humorous descriptions of Maris's slightness flourish in the rich soil of her absence. All this is thoroughly misogynistic, no doubt, but what is striking is the power that is accorded to

Mrs Mainwaring, the very opposite of Mrs Slocombe's impotence. Men must either laugh at themselves and their fear of women (as they do with Mrs Mainwaring); or make women powerless and laughable (as they do with Mrs Slocombe).

But enough of this. It was time for lunch. A horrible lunch, to be sure, in the Grace Brothers canteen, since this was Britain and this was a department store catering for a demographic with one foot in the grave – like Dunn and Co, that one-time dash of habers to dapper granddads, but less with it, daddio. So no wonder the canteen dessert was vile. 'How's your Queen's Pudding?' asked Miss Brahms. 'It doesn't quite live up to its promise,' replied Mrs Slocombe, fluttering her eyelashes so much that they looked in danger of affixing themselves to her hair. 'Oh I don't know,' said Mr Lucas. 'It promised to be awful and it's disgusting.' Then Mr Lucas, for the first and last time in his life, initiated a philosophical inquiry: 'What is custard?' Good question and yet one which we don't have the space to do justice to here, save to remark that it was clearly not what rested solidly on Mr Lucas's pudding.

And yet, I loved this scene. It was here, at last, that the staff had some chance for camaraderie, to set aside this pretence that they were there to sell things to those intrusive interlopers called shoppers and instead to do what they were best at and moan freely. It was only in these scenes that Grace Brothers became for me a place where human beings worked.

When I watched the 'No Sale' episode of *Are You Being Served?* again recently, nearly a quarter of a century after it was first broadcast, I remembered, as if realising for the first time, how much I hated the programme. The BBC was repeating some old episodes of the series now presented as classic comedy. In the late nineties, the show was loved by a new audience who saw the contradictions that upset me so much in 1976 as merely laughable hang-ups from a distant era. Mrs Slocombe's pussy now no longer had the power to shock. We live, after all, in a

TV world where swearing is common, where Julian Clary can just about disturb us with a reference to fisting and Norman Lamont, but otherwise the ubiquity of shock tactics on television and elsewhere has stopped us from being shocked. The mincing of Mr Humphries and Mrs Slocombe's pussy had become sanctified, part of a national television history.

I HATE NERYS HUGHES

As I grew up, I came to think that British TV comedy was cruel and conservative. Britons seemed to love to take pleasure in other people's misfortune. We were never happier than when we were laughing at camcorder pratfalling on *You've Been Framed.* But that was only cruel comedy at its most basic. At a much more sophisticated level, Ray Galton and Alan Simpson made careers from aspirant comic characters who could not escape their ruts: Hancock, despite the Noël Coward smoking jacket and intellectual pretensions, was doomed to remain baffled on the first page of Bertrand Russell; Harold Steptoe, for all his bourgeois dreams, was fated to live in a rag and bone shop. In John Cleese and Connie Booth's *Fawlty Towers*, Basil would never succeed in freeing the hotel from riff-raff or eluding his wife's arriviste vulgarity. In John Sullivan's *Only Fools and Horses*, Del Boy Trotter could never pull the scam that would buy him a one-way ticket out of Peckham. We couldn't help but laugh at other people's suffering.

But this suffering was also conservative. These characters would never escape their existential lots, or move freely from one class to another. They were stuck. I imagined that these characters were popular because they reflected the frustration of those who couldn't escape their lives either.

In Britain, even the most radical-seeming sitcom writers or TV comedians have often been very conservative. Even the likes of Carla Lane and Billy Connolly, people who you wouldn't automatically regard as hateful, have been painfully reactionary in their comedy. Consider, for instance, Carla Lane's *The Liver Birds*.

It started, way back in 1969, like this.

What's got four legs, walks peculiar?
Talks with all the choicest words?
What's got four arms, loves to grab yer?
Answer is two Liver birds.

Those were the days. Two oestrogen-charged chicks with more loon pants than sense, bent on pulling all the gear guys on Merseyside. That, at least was what the riddle that formed the lyric to the title sequence song of *The Liver Birds* indicated. And then there was the pick-up exchange that was spoken over the closing credits: 'Eh – you dancin'?' said the bloke. 'You askin'?' said the bird. 'I'm askin'.' 'I'm dancin'.' What cool. What sass. Or at least what passed for it in the late sixties and early seventies.

They sounded a right pair of goers, Beryl and Sandra. Just like the presenters of *The Girlie Show* more than a quarter of a century later, or just like Anna in *This Life*, but with more self-esteem and more colourful wardrobes. They were girls who just wanted to have fun in dodgy clobber. But, in between the intro and outro patters, something happened. These ballsy babes mutated into florally-frocked fluffheads, staggering across their flat in clogs, waiting for Mr Right to come and make their lives worthwhile. Waiting. Never initiating.

Sandra (the posh, bosomy one, whose slender role was crushed into nothing by the shocking ineptitude of Nerys Hughes's acting), was trying to pull John Nettles, whose lithe charms were undermined by the fact that he didn't seem able to do up the buttons on his shirt. A problem he shared with many men of that era.

She had bought a sugar bowl. That was the comic premise

of the first episode. The aim was to surround lithe John with domestic objects and so turn his mind to conjugal felicity. And thus to lure him into proposing to Sandra. Even for that grisly, gauche time, Sandra's approach seemed a mite indirect.

There was once a song by Half Man Half Biscuit called 'I Hate Nerys Hughes'. Only when I watched the first episode of *The Liver Birds* could I really appreciate the profundity of that sentiment.

Beryl (the skinny, common one, whose slender role was fleshed out by the RSC-trained talents of Polly James) was not impressed. 'Does he not know that we dip our spoons straight in the bag?' Carla Lane, who was responsible for this low-level banter (there wasn't a punchline worth the name from beginning to end of this half hour), always seemed to find domestic incompetence intrinsically hilarious. One thinks of Wendy Craig's kitchen klutziness in *Butterflies* (also by Carla Lane) – the source of husband Geoffrey Palmer's middle-aged disappointment and so many lame jokes – but not, naturally, while one has one's strength. Women were weak, neurotic, incompetent. At least if one took Carla Lane seriously.

Then Mollie Sugden (for it was she) came on. Here she was Sandra's mother, but substantially the same character as Mrs Slocombe, a grim-faced battleaxe with two accents. She was accompanied by her useless lump of a husband. They had spent thirty years together on the same sofa, looking in opposite directions, and they were reprising that scene now for Sandra and Beryl, in order to show that it was necessary that they should start divorce proceedings. True, her husband was a gormless bull of a spouse. But what were the grounds for divorce? I imagined that one ground was insufficient laughter. And another was his talon-like toenails. Things like that can make even the best marriage lose its lustre.

The humorous irony of this scene was of the kind that could have been grasped by a backward three-year-old: just as Sandra looked to her parents to supply a role model of wedded bliss, mum and dad proposed to split.

When I saw this episode of *The Liver Birds* again, it seemed much more shockingly reactionary and joke-lite than memory served. But we were younger then, dafter, more impressionable. But no more, no more. Now, women on television are depicted as tough cookies who need a man like a fish needs a trouser press.

Or are they? Around the same time I saw this re-run, I also saw *The Girlie Show*. It was billed as the show 'where girls are girls and boys are nervous', but the reality was that the girls hosting it were nervous and the boys who seemed to make up the overwhelming majority of the studio audience were boys, salivating over 'supermodel' Rachel Williams.

Not for nothing were the first words of the title sequence 'Hello, boys' – this was Wonderbra entertainment at best, and at worst something that wouldn't delay an intellectually challenged goldfish. It was hosted by two rather diffident women who bore little relation to the oestrogen-charged babes promised by the pre-programme hype. Like the Liver Birds, they promised female autonomy, but delivered male dependency. I switched over from Channel 4 to BBC2. There, The Boys Show, otherwise known as *Fantasy Football*, was coming to a close. Veteran West Bromwich Albion striker, Jeff Astle, was, for reasons that have never become clear to me, dressed in a cowherd's smock, and was singing 'Girls Just Wanna Have Fun'. They may wanna, Jeff, but over on Channel 4, it didn't look like they were.

There is an argument that a show where women can express their sexuality and treat men as sex objects is empowering. But when so much of *The Girlie Show* consisted of men bulging in their designer underwear – the first edition had a report on the furore around Calvin Klein ads in the US, followed by a piece about some men who work in that misnomer, a 'fun pub' – there was a danger that the most committed feminist in the audience, even if she had spent the evening on a course of mind-contracting drugs, would feel bored rather than empowered.

DOWN THE PERSONHOLE WITH BILLY CONNOLLY

If women want to be empowered, they shouldn't look to Billy Connolly for inspiration. While much British comedy has since grown up from the days when Mrs Slocombe's pussy and the Liver Birds held sway over confused women and insecure men alike, Connolly carries on regardless.

Connolly's putative humour consists of pandering to the most dunderheaded prejudices. In his 1996 series, *Billy Connolly's World Tour of Australia*, for instance, there was a sequence from his stand-up routine in which he developed this theme. 'Political correctness isn't down to politicians – it's down to social workers. It's their fault that there are things in the street called personhole covers. It isn't a fucking personhole cover: it's a manhole cover. It covers a hole that a man goes down to work in the sewerage department of the city. When women show an overwhelming desire to be covered up to their necks in shit then we can change the name of it. Until then it's a fucking manhole cover!'

But political correctness isn't a term invented by social workers; rather, it is one that is consistently invoked to defend everything from telling anti-Irish jokes to the notion that Benny Hill was a comic genius. More importantly, Connolly's joke was based on a false premise, the repetition of which legitimises that falsehood for the thick people in his audiences: there are no such things as personhole covers and, even if there were, social workers would have no jurisdiction over what they were called. Just as there were never any plans by Labour councils to change the colour of bin bags from black so as not to offend ethnic minorities. Just as there was no EC directive to make horny-handed British fishermen wear effete hairnets on their boats for hygiene reasons. And yet for the bigoted, the sexist and the thick – the male whoops and whistles that greeted this gag when he told it at Sydney Opera House surely came from such people – the elevation of this kind of untruth into a comedy was welcome. Perhaps it was because Connolly did his apprenticeship as a shipyard welder in the all-male Govan shipyards that he felt the need to play the boys-only proletarian mystique card. Women have as much – and as little – desire to stand up to their necks in shit.

And then there was another gag, selected as a highlight from his stand-up show to pad out his travel programme. 'I saw a policeman on television in Britain,' began Connolly. 'He was the chief guy, the head bummer. Big fat Masonic bore. Right. Fat arsehole couldnae point to a street let alone police it. He says: "We're declaring a war on drugs. We're going to get drugs off the street." This is the prick who can't even get drugs out of prison! Look in any prison and they're doing drugs and shagging each other.' This was a comedy of hate, the twisted reasoning of the lynch mob: smear the victim with filth and blame them for smelling bad. What's more, the police don't have jurisdiction over prisons – so again his joke was based on a false premise.

For me, watching this twenty years after I first became acquainted with Mrs Slocombe's pussy and its repressive power, Connolly's routine was amazing. Here was a guy who, in his baggy pyjama-like trousers and hippie beard, looked like nothing so much as the Dude from *The Big Lebowski*, an ex-hippie with blameless views on most things, the beard of a Creedence Clearwater Revival fan and a leisure time composed chiefly from acid flashbacks. But Connolly, as soon as he opened his mouth, disclosed that he was no grown-up flower child, but a reactionary comedian more poisonous than the scriptwriters of *Are You Being Served?* could dream up – more poisonous because he looked the opposite of what he was.

In the intervening two decades, most British comedy had moved on from the comedy of hate. True, Bernard Manning packs them in and Roy 'Chubby' Brown is popular, but TV audiences have become less ready to laugh in cosy conspiracy with sexists and other hate-mongers. Except, that is, for Connolly, the last emperor of a dying dynasty – a comedian, thankfully, with no heirs and just as many graces.

WHO'S GROOMING THE BADGERS FOR THE BADGER PARADE?

But while Billy Connolly's brand of British humour seems to have one foot in the grave and the other one poised to join it, there is a different kind of comedy that has been consistently popular and shows no signs of dying out. It's a strand of TV humour that does not alienate me, that does not make me ashamed to be British. The British also enjoy absurdity in their TV comedy and I like them for that. Take *Monty Python*'s fish slapping dance. Two men in pith helmets stood on a canal tow-path slapping each other's faces with fish in time to music. Then, as the music climaxed, one of them produced a huge, probably plastic, fish and thwacked the other so hard with it that he fell into the canal. Why is that funny? Who knows? Who cares? And who cares to explain, since to account for such comedy's talent to amuse would be to kill it off.

In the late nineties, the same has been true of Harry Hill, whose humour is the full *Monty Python*, absurd and inexplicably funny. How can we account for his appeal? And why should we?

Harry Hill's nan was a confused woman. She thought the contents of a Cornflakes box were a jigsaw puzzle of a hen. So many orangey pieces, no edges and all of them seem to be part of the beak.

It got worse. 'Who's the white man who crouches in the corner of the bathroom?' Nana Hill asked her grandson. 'The white man with the black hat. You lift the black hat and put the effluent inside, pull his arm and he roars his approval. Who is that?' 'You should know – you married him,' replied Harry. I could try and account for why this joke is funny, but that would kill it.

Now look here, if you're reading this, who's grooming the badgers for the badger parade? Nobody, that's who. The man who is the controller of Channel 4 insisted that Harry Hill keeps the badgers for the second series in late 1998 because he found them very funny indeed.

I say 'man', but he was in fact, if his appearance on *Harry Hill* was anything to go by, a ventriloquist's dummy with a disproportionately large desk and a wife who didn't find the comedy shows he broadcast funny at all. Despite his insistence that the badgers stay, he didn't seem to have noticed that in every episode of the first series there was no parade because of the badgers' militancy.

And, true to form, there was trouble with those badgers again. 'You've tried it on once too often, you pink-skinned toff,' Gareth Southgate badger told Harry Hill. 'Yeah, you should have played me from the start,' said Michael Owen badger. The badger finale, like the badger parades of yesteryear, looked set to be a debacle.

Trying to make sense of Harry Hill is like trying to make a jigsaw out of Cornflakes. The result is very orange and crunchy. Even the dummy who runs Channel 4 could not explain the show's appeal: at the end of the first episode of the second series, he was seen sitting and laughing on a sofa before asking: 'What the hell was all that about?'

Indeed. The same question used to come to my mind at the end of *Vic Reeves' Big Night Out*. The show went through a weekly ritual. Vic would come on singing a popular song from the time (this was the early 1990s, so Jesus Jones's 'International Bright Young Things' was among them). He would then sit at his desk, introduce his assistant Les and show him first a bunch of chives and then a spirit level. Les was afraid of chives, you see, though he could not but raise a smile when he saw a spirit level.

And so it went on: a series of intrinsically meaningless turns that gained a semblance of significance through weekly repetition. Rather like *The Fast Show*, which only became comprehensible and thus funny by the fourth episode of a series when we understood the characters and had memorised their catchphrases. But repetition isn't enough to make Harry Hill or Vic Reeves funny. Oh, no. What media studies types would doubtless call 'the deployment of the prosaic in an absurdist context' is also important.

Consider the song sung by Vic Reeves' and Bob Mortimer's Irish singing duo, Mulligan and O'Hare, in their later series *The Smell of Reeves and Mortimer*:

My Rose has left me,
I'm in a mood.
She's gone to Kenya
With the bloke from Allied Carpets.
She wasn't immunised
That's a legal requirement!
She's increasingly slapdash
Since we bought that new hearthrug.

Here we can see that much of the comedy resides in the juxtaposition of the traditional tropes of the romantic ballad with the domestic triteness inherent in the purchase of floor coverings. If we wanted to think about it at all.

It's similar on Harry Hill. One week he had veteran socialist balladeer, Billy Bragg, on to sing novelty songs:

Aga do do do
Push pineapple
Shake the tree

and the impassioned historical materialist did so with a conviction usually reserved for songs of a greater import. Harry Hill also invited Little and Large on to sing Pet Shop Boys' songs, and the juxtaposition of those jaded showbiz stars with the satirical bile of Neil Tennant's lyrics proved irresistible. Syd and Eddie gave it loads. 'I've got the looks,' sang Syd, implausibly. 'I've got the brains,' rejoined Large with little conviction. 'Let's make lots of money,' they chorused.

Enough of this. Harry Hill was back after these turns to hymn that lovely invention which he carried on his back. 'The knapsack – where better to put your knap?' he eulogised. Good point. His knapsack was so big that it proved a useful weapon in knocking encroaching sunbathers off his collection of sun loungers. Hurrah for the knapsack, then – not only useful for storing knap, but also a good means of securing one's personal beach space in the adverse conditions imposed by the modern world.

But absurdity is sometimes not enough. Absurdity plus repetition is often what makes Hill's strange world funny. And in this, Harry Hill, like Vic Reeves, like Harry Enfield, is showing a sensitivity to the history of British comedy. For, if British people like anything, they like something that is familiar, something that is reassuring and something that they can repeat in public – whether it is in the school playground or in the office.

*

WHERE'S ME WASHBOARD?

Arthur Atkinson's music hall routine was always the same. He'd walk on to the stage, point at a member of the audience and say: 'Have you seen it?' He'd then cross the stage and point at someone else: 'Have *you* seen it? Eh?' Then he'd walk centre stage and ask everybody: 'Where's me washboard? Eh? Where's me washboard?' Then he'd point with his left hand under his right arm to the place, one felt sure, where his washboard should be but wasn't.

'Where's me washboard' was Arthur Atkinson's catchphrase and its very mention was enough to send his audiences into hysterics. It was typical of the austerities of post-war Britain: then even the gags were probably rationed. In any event, they were certainly about as funny as a speech by Herbert Morrison to a Labour conference.

As it went on, Atkinson's routine delved deeper into meaninglessness. Anyone who laughed particularly hard would be singled out for ridicule. 'What you larfin' at, eh? I've seen you wrapping presents when it's nobody's birthday.' Even more insinuatingly he would add: 'I've seen you *wrapping presents* when it's nobody's birthday.' It didn't make any sense at all, but the audience was laughing again.

And yet, the point of catchphrases, those staples of British comedy, is that they aren't intrinsically funny. They only become so thanks to context and repetition. Dick Emery's 'You are awful, but I like you!' meant nothing unless said by his brassy blonde character, each and every week of the series. Similarly, the smutty double entendre of John Inman's 'I'm free' wasn't suggestive until it was fitted into a context of proverbial homosexual promiscuity.

The catchphrase, after all, is a fixture in an otherwise protean world of television comedy. Punchlines may have changed from week to week, from joke to joke, but the catchphrase was something solid, something dependable, something like *Monty Python*'s parrot sketch that you could repeat in front of your friends.

Bruce Forsyth knew this better than anyone else: after all, *The Generation Game*, which he hosted during its heyday between 1971 and 1978, consisted of little but catchphrases, a weekly script that barely changed. It started with the call and response of Brucie's opening gambit to the audience: 'Nice to see you. To see you?' 'Nice!' bawled the audience in unison. Then Brucie breezed through a landscape whose only signposts were other catchphrases. 'Give us a twirl, Anthea!' 'The scores on the doors!' 'Let's have a look at the old scoreboard!' 'What's on the conveyor belt tonight?' and 'Didn't she do well?' They were regular friends, as much as the cuddly toy that would always trundle by on the conveyor belt.

In the seventies, it seemed that a light entertainment show on television was not complete without a clutch of catchphrases. *Dad's Army* was the leading example – Captain Mainwaring's denunciation of Private Pike as a 'Stupid boy'; Sergeant Wilson's 'Would you mind awfully falling in?'; Private Frazer's 'We're doomed!'; Corporal Jones's 'Don't panic' all gave us handles to understand the speaker's character. Morecambe and Wise preferred the old-style call and response of 'What do you think of the show so far?' 'Rubbish!' – a catchphrase that only became funny after repetition. Imagine: if 'Rubbish!' was said once, the response would have just sounded rude; when it was repeated it became an engaging game. Then, and perhaps now, there was a delight in the infantile repetition of formulas that became more and more hilarious as time went on, as new contexts were found for old phrases. For instance, quiz show host Magnus Magnusson probably never thought that 'I've started so I'll finish' would become a coital jibe.

It may have seemed that the catchphrase died in the

mid-eighties, and, like Mrs Slocombe's pussy, would only have a spectral second life for new viewers slightly baffled at its original appeal. By then we had evolved beyond the comforting comedy of repeated formulas, where familiarity bred content. Hadn't we? No: by the end of the eighties, Harry Enfield had appropriated that history with a character whose name was a catchphrase – Loadsamoney – and later with Smashie and Nicey's introduction to the greatest hit of Messrs Bachman, Turner and Overdrive, 'Let's rock!' Suddenly, the catchphrase was no longer soothing, but capable of being viciously satirical – attacking eighties greed and Radio 1's rich, erm, cultural heritage.

Some of the writers who worked for Enfield wrote for Vic Reeves and *The Fast Show*, where the catchphrase mutated into its latest post-modern incarnations. *Vic Reeves's Big Night Out* was pitted with them, not least the weekly section in which Vic would ask the audience: 'What do we say when we see the Man with the Stick?' 'What's on the end of the stick, Vic?' the audience would reply, as obediently and as barmily as the fans of Bruce Forsyth and Morecambe and Wise had done twenty years earlier. Later, in Vic Reeves' and Bob Mortimer's cod-game show, *Shooting Stars*, came the apparently meaningless cries of 'Uvavu' and 'Eranu', and the exhortation to lure the 'dove from above'. *Shooting Stars* was as formulaic and as catchphrase-determined as *The Generation Game*. The comedy of reassurance, still, but with a self-conscious, ironic twist that Bruce Forsyth would never have dreamed of.

The same was true of *The Fast Show*, which supplied many of the catchphrases you heard around the playground, offices and, latterly, TV advertisements, in Britain. 'Scorchio!', 'Suits you, sir', 'Which was nice', 'And I was very, *very* drunk', 'Does my bum look big in this?' None of these cherished phrases meant anything in its own right but gained context and thus comedy through repetition.

The chief writers and performers of *The Fast Show*, Charlie

Higson and Paul Whitehouse, appreciated the historical role of the catchphrase in British comedy. The aforementioned Arthur Atkinson typified this: he wasn't a real music hall comedian, but a parody of one performed by Whitehouse on the show – complete with a baffling array of catchphrases. This sketch-based comedy programme, with thirty routines in as many minutes, gave viewers not just a catchphrase but a regular variation on that theme. Thus, in the second series there was a sketch called Jesse's Diets, in which a filthy country oik came out of his hut to tell the camera: 'This week, I have been mostly eating . . . taramasalata.' In the third series, over the caption 'Jesse's Fashion Tips', Jesse emerged from his shed covered, one suspected, with cow pats and with string holding up his hideously stained trousers, and said: 'This season, I will be mostly wearing . . . Dolce e Gabbana.'

The Fast Show was not above parodying its obsession with catchphrases. In one show, there was a self-satirising sketch featuring Colin Hunt, the office irritant. He wore a bulldog clip on his nose and asked a colleague: 'Did you see it last night? Brilliant, wasn't it?' Then he started to repeat what he had seen on the TV the previous evening: 'I'm a alien! I'm a alien! . . . Then there was a new character, Mr Pork! Where's the pork? Hello, have you got the pork? Oooh, porka!' 'Didn't see it, Colin,' said his colleague. 'What? Not even Sports Car Freak or the Turnip Family? Bonjour Mr Turnip?' Colin was obviously completely bonkers – just the kind of person who would recite catchphrases from *The Fast Show* in public. Intriguingly, it wasn't Higson and Whitehouse who were satirising their own work here, but someone who watched the show: the sketch was sent in and Higson and Whitehouse liked it because it sent up *The Fast Show* and *Fast Show* bores.

★

A NEW BUFF FOR THE OLD HELMET

Twenty years after I first saw *Are You Being Served?* I saw Ben Elton's sitcom *The Thin Blue Line*, and in 1996, at least, I thought it was the most culturally significant programme on television. Even though it was a ruin at the end of the British sitcom cul-de-sac, even though it was a conservative show set in a necessarily conservative institution – a British police station. Even though, like *Are You Being Served?*, it was broadcast on BBC1 and teemed with comic stereotypes and smutty double entendres.

But *The Thin Blue Line* engaged me, not least because it was written by Ben Elton, whose stand-up routines during the eighties often consisted of politically-committed smut, and whose sitcoms (*The Young Ones* and *Blackadder*) were among the best in the eighties. Elton's stand-up struggle was to make us laugh at people's twiddly bits irrespective of their race, gender or creed, but because of their size, shape and all-round naughtiness. Instead of laughing from cruelty or fear, we were to laugh warmly, as part of a Britain gently coming to terms with its multicultural ethos, with strong women, with sexual ambiguity, without hate.

The Thin Blue Line was often funny because it deliberately satirised the golden age of British comic stereotyping. It was like a critique of *Are You Being Served*? faxed in by a subversive fan of the show. Instead of the saucy bird, the implausible queen, the putatively ordinary lecherous chap, the straight-backed colonel and the off-the-peg battleaxe, Elton created several other tokenistic characters who gently subverted the British sitcom and played with smut self-consciously. The most successful creation was Constable Kevin Goody: could it be an accident that this preposterously camp PC had an unfeasibly large helmet? Please. He recalled all those pouffy stereotypes of the seventies sitcom. He waved his hands in the neurotically effete way of John Inman, and his mincing was an eloquent homage to the golden days of TV homophobia. In one episode, a documentary crew came to make a film about the police station where Goody worked. He prepared for his close-up with a new hairdo and a theatrical queeniness: 'I'm going out a constable,' he said as he minced back from the men's toilet, 'but I'm coming back a star.' He had to be gay. But, no. The joke was that Goody was straight: he pushed all our gay buttons, twitched with all the gay TV tics, and yet still lusted unrequitedly after WPC Maggie Habib.

The key problem of *The Thin Blue Line*, though, was that the two black characters were likeable but dull. This is often the fate of black TV characters when they appear in an overwhelmingly white milieu: black characters can bore for England, in *EastEnders* and in *The Thin Blue Line*. This is a dreary form of subversion: TV viewers have to witness tediously virtuous characters from ethnic minorities until the racists in the audience realise that black people are not all drug dealers or short changers.

Thus, Rudolph T. Walker played a slightly simple Guyanan desk sergeant in *The Thin Blue Line*; the flip-side of the character he played in the seventies. Bill Reynolds, the true-blue Tory of *Love Thy Neighbour*, who would call his racist next door neighbour 'snowflake' and 'honky' after he had been abused as 'nig-nog' and 'sambo'. But there was no scope for the comedy of hate, that staple of British sitcoms for so many years, in *The Thin Blue Line*.

The only safe object of ridicule was Inspector Fowler. Rowan Atkinson's character, like PC Goody's, was one with historical sitcom precedent – he was a repressed, too-orderly suburbanite, like Richard Briers in *Ever Decreasing Circles*, and possessed, one felt sure, a vast collection of bicycle clips. And yet, as distinct from the presentation of PC Goody, this comic stereotype was not subverted. It was safe to laugh, in Ben Elton's worldview, at this character. For instance, Inspector Fowler recalled his humiliation on the *Antiques Roadshow*: 'When I slapped my family jewels on the table all they did was laugh.' The straight suburbanite and his unwitting double entendres. Classic stuff.

But Ben Elton's critique of the seventies British sitcoms wasn't popular and didn't make it to a third series. Maybe the time for the subversion of all those stereotypes had passed. Perhaps we have moved on, become less hate-filled, less afraid of difference, less sexually repressed. Laugh? I nearly had a non-threatening, revisionist chuckle.

CHAPTER 5

1981: Sebastian Flyte's Teddy Bear

BRIDESHEAD REVISITED REVISITED

Jeremy Irons, who played Charles Ryder, narrated a lyrical introduction as the camera slid languorously across college after sunburnt college: 'Oxford in those days was still a city of aquatint. When the chestnut was in flower and the bells rang out high and clear over the gables and cupolas, she exhaled the soft airs of centuries of youth.' By the time I got there, the soft heirs of centuries of inbreeding had been exhaled over Oxford, withering flowers and vying with the bells. In Oxford at that time, all England's public school-educated youth was on noisy fire and silken dalliance on their backs lay.

I hated *Brideshead Revisited* when it was first broadcast in 1981. I so thoroughly misunderstood the adaptation of Evelyn Waugh's novel that I thought it was about contempt when really it was about love and loss.

But who could blame me for that? I'd arrived in Oxford in the same year as *Brideshead Revisited* was shown on television and found it the coldest place on earth, cliquey and more class-ridden than anywhere I'd been in my life. I'd returned to England from my gap year in the United States, where warm people had befriended me and found my accent entrancing. By contrast, Oxford seemed to be a student city that detested the outside world and even many of the students who lived and worked there, especially those with provincial accents. I have a memory of sitting at dinner in hall on my first evening in college at Oxford and asking someone to pass me a glass down the long table. My flat 'a's upset someone, and in the long, long silence that followed I waited for a response. 'Pass a glass?' said someone eventually, mocking a northern accent. 'You mean Parse a glarse.' No one sent a glass down the table to me. Thoroughly gauche in my late teens, I didn't know how to deal with this snobbery.

Later that term, during a tutorial, I asked my tutor to tell me how to pronounce Kant. 'Do I pronounce it Kant or Karnt?' I asked. This seemed such an important question then that its answer might well yield the first principle of philosophy. 'Oh, it's Karnt,' said my tutor, not unkindly, but authoritatively and yet wrongly.

John Mortimer's adaptation of the novel for Granada seemed to be in league with these mispronunciations and the class criticism they implied. After all, when Sebastian Flyte (played by Anthony Andrews) came back from church one morning, he told Charles that he had been to 'marse'. Surely nobody in the known world spoke with such long 'a's, even *extremely* snooty Catholics? This seemed emblematic of the alienation I felt: I would never be a member of this club; I would never parse. I felt furious as well as unworthy. This was the time and the place for a neutron bomb, not at all for an adaptation of a historical novel that, unwittingly, had set in train its own nostalgia industry. But this was England, where nostalgia was and is more powerful than bombs. Before the adaptation of *Brideshead Revisited* finished on television, there were Brideshead Undergraduate Guided Tours of Oxford, led by well-spoken young men with floppy hair, creased linen jackets and tasteful ties. The tourists couldn't get enough of them. Waugh would have hated the commodification of his lament, which, for me, is a nice revenge. Now there are *Inspector Morse* tours of Oxford, too, conducted by people who know how to show viewers the sights of Oxford they have savoured on television. Television won't leave this city alone while Oxford keeps its beauty intact.

The rest of the first episode didn't endear me to the Oxford in which I then lived nor to Evelyn Waugh, whose novels, I decided in a fit of unsustained resolve, I would never read. I was oblivious to the tenderness and love that coursed through the programme, and instead saw everything in it as an affront to me, an insult that was confirmed by the coldness I felt from most of my fellow students and even from working-class people whose jobs were bound up with serving us.

Charles Ryder first bumped into Sebastian Flyte at the barber's. Sebastian was leaving, carrying his large teddy bear. Charles's friend, who had accompanied him to have his hair cut, was revolted, but the barber was enchanted. And Charles, too, was preparing himself to be captivated. 'That was Lord Sebastian Flyte, a most *amusing* young gentleman,' said the barber, unctuously removing the young men's coats before showing them to their chairs. 'He's the Marquis of Marchmain's second boy. His brother, the Earl of Marchmain, went down last term. He was very different.' Flyte, said the barber, warming to his theme, had not wanted a haircut, but had come instead for 'a hair brush for his teddy bear. It had to have very firm bristles, not to brush him with but to threaten him with a spanking when he was sulky. He bought a very nice one with an ivory back. He's going to have Aloysius engraved on the back. That's the teddy bear's name.'

I loathed this speech. 'Too much information, you deferential throwback!' I shouted at the screen. And yet, I overstated the barber's deference and this made me misunderstand, crucially, Waugh's novel. The barber wasn't only deferential (though he was surely that, since such an attitude was common among tradespeople in cities such as Oxford in the interwar years), but he was also, and overwhelmingly, charmed by Flyte, the golden boy with his adorable eccentricities – the lightness of him, his beauty. To all of this I was oblivious. Instead, I felt only contempt: the contempt of Sebastian Flyte for those who were not part of his charmed and charming circle; and the contempt of the barber for those who spoke with flat vowels and had set aside their teddy bears along with Andy Pandy several decades before. And I felt resentful contempt of my own, for Sebastian and his deferential barber.

I have never been able to waft commandingly into a basement barber's with a camel coat over my shoulders, igniting smiles and happiness, to buy something frivolous. There was a time while I was an undergraduate when I had the double crown at the top of my forehead permed, true, but that was hardly a gesture of supreme decadence, nor did it win the admiration of crabby barbers or, indeed, anyone else. Instead, while I was at university I got my hair cut silently, studied hard, drank bitterly and got the Midland Red coach home, walked across dark allotments and into a bright place where people were pleased to see me. It was only fifty-six miles away and yet I crossed so many barriers to arrive and to leave. How could the country I lived in be so divided, even then, and how could the barriers be so close to home?

When Sebastian next appeared before Charles he was drunk. He was standing before Charles's open ground floor window in the quad, poised to throw up through the window and nearly over Charles's feet. He threw up, wiped his mouth and then, mustering the thinnest of smiles, disappeared into the night with his rowdy friends. In the morning, Charles's scout (cleaner, servant, personal policeman, moral coach, confidant, all-round flunkey), cleaned up the vomit (Did it not occur to Charles to clean it up himself? How could he bear to sleep with that stench in his rooms overnight, particularly as he had now closed the windows?). He then picked up the five shillings left there for his trouble, and told Charles that he shouldn't drink so much. By the time Charles had returned from his lectures that same morning, though, the room was filled with flowers, along with an apologetic note from Sebastian. The scout, played by Bill Owen, was even now arranging the last of the bouquets. 'A most amusing young gentleman, sir,' he said, warmly. 'I'm sure it's a pleasure to clean up after him!'

Again, this would never happen to me. It would never be a pleasure for anyone, still less a total stranger, to clean up my sick. No landlord would escort me to the door of his pub, wipe his face with a bar towel and then tell his friends: 'That Lord Stuart half drowned me with his own vomit. What a young wag he is, to be sure!'

Most of the friends I cultivated at Oxford were state-school pupils revolted by this dynamic which we saw on screen and which we thought was transposed into reality. From this culture of deference, though, we received no bounty since it was not offered to us. Still less, had we been accorded such deference, could we have stooped charmingly to pick it up with the grace of a Sebastian Flyte or the diffidence of a Charles Ryder. We had neither the skills, nor the temperament. This dynamic was a curious legacy from an earlier, more exclusive era that had to be stamped out; it was part of what, in the past, had kept the likes of us out. Most of us, obviously enough, took *Jude the Obscure* as our text: Jude's had been the fate of our ancestors – to build the walls that kept us out. Now, though, we were inside the walls and it would be different – if only we didn't have to contend with working-class Judases conspiring against us. Or so it then seemed.

For many of us, after all, attending university felt as though it was a huge responsibility both to ourselves and to the generations before us who never dreamed of studying at a college, least of all at Oxford. Few of our parents had reached any form of tertiary education. My father had though, as his thirties turned into forties, studied for a production engineering degree at Aston University. In the front room, which was off-limits to his children, my father had wrestled with mathematics and metallurgy, while I sat in the other room watching *Andy Pandy*, *Dad's Army* or the 1970 World Cup. Then he went to lectures where he sat amid long-haired youngsters with whom he had next to nothing in common. It wasn't, so far as I could judge, a time of strawberries and punting; he never had occasion to buy a hairbrush with which to admonish his recalcitrant teddy bear.

When I learned I'd won a place to Oxford, I phoned my dad at work and remember him being really touched in a way that I'd not experienced before. 'You're cleverer than all of us,' he said fondly, a remark that has danced happily around my head ever since. But I also took that remark as a responsibility: my cleverness, if that's what it was, shouldn't be thrown away when I went to Oxford. None of my forbears had had the chance to exhibit their cleverness or anything else at such a place, and so the weight of their exclusion lay heavy on my shoulders. I remember crying sentimental tears a few years later in 1987 when I watched on television Neil Kinnock's party political broadcast. It was part of the same shockingly misguided presidential-style campaign that included the Sheffield rally, so I was prepared to be disgusted. But Kinnock asked why were he and Glenys the first people from their respective families in a thousand generations to go to university? Why? Because between Sebastian Flyte's days and theirs and indeed mine, egalitarian governments had established free education for all children and set up the ladder for us to climb as well as the safety net to break our fall. We could climb up the ladder belatedly, but if only we shook off our mental chains like water. Working-class men who said things like 'Lord Sebastian, such an *amusing* young man' – they would never get their feet on the first rungs. They were holding themselves down, and they were making things more difficult for us. They made me and my friends angry, and yet we didn't know what to do with that anger, except to sit sullen in barbers' chairs. And we *were* sullen, but not only because we were holding back our anger. We all wanted to be other than we were, to be as confident and self-assured in the world as many of the public school-educated boys and girls around us. Instead, we were awkward and seething – which didn't encourage scouts, barbers or anyone to speak well of us.

We were recognised by our lack of poise, by our uncertainty. These are the words, at least, of Richard Hoggart in *The Uses of Literacy*, where he writes about the 'uprooted and the anxious', the scholarship boys who leave their homes, first, spiritually, through reading and education, then physically, by going away to college. They were the first to leave their societies, their classes, and they never really belonged anywhere again. By contrast, Sebastian Flyte in the barber's, in the quad, at the lunch party, at mass, belonged everywhere – the world was his and he was comfortable with the arrangement. Who wouldn't be?

Hoggart writes: 'I am chiefly concerned with those who are self-conscious and yet not self-aware in any full sense, who are as a result, uncertain, dissatisfied, and gnawed by self-doubt. Sometimes they lack will, though they have intelligence, and "it takes will to cross this waste". More often perhaps, though they have as much will as the majority, they have not sufficient to resolve the complex tensions which their uprooting, the peculiar problems of their particular domestic settings, and the uncertainties common to the time create.' I stood not long ago in a bookshop reading these words in tears, because they were about me – too much about me for comfort when I studied at Oxford. (Tears again but, ultimately, as the ABC song taught me in the early eighties, tears are not enough.) I've always wanted those three years back so I could live them well, to live them wilfully and to cross the waste that much of that time was for me. I would have walked around with a teddy bear, or a real bear on a chain, or a lobster on a leash, and bought all three tailored silk pyjamas to wear when we went out in public. I would have carried my burden more lightly, not been overcome by a spirit of seriousness and of shame.

There was another scene in *Brideshead*, that only now can I cherish – because the spirit of seriousness has taken flight from me, hopefully for good. Charles's cousin Jasper breaks off from his final exams to chide him about his now-hedonistic lifestyle. He dresses down Charles for his new flashy clothes, his profligacy, his choice of friends, his drinking. Charles smiles, reaches into a cupboard and produces a bottle of champagne which he proceeds to open while he defends himself: 'I usually have a glass of champagne about this time. Will you join me?' There was drinking for me at Oxford but none of it had these lighthearted and insolent qualities. I wish everything I had done there had had such cheerful insolence.

The characters with whom Charles initially made friends were academic pedants, one step up from proletarian scholars, those common people who were never given the chance to flourish in our sight. As for the proletarian scholars of twenties Oxford, we never got to see their kind.

Perhaps now I'm getting nearer to why I hated *Brideshead* at the time and why I still feel uneasy about the drama, even though now I understand Waugh's novel. It is because the adaptation and the book never give a chance to any other way of being at Oxford than that of Sebastian and his coterie. Near the beginning, Charles divides Oxford students into three classes – the flamboyant aesthetes (like Sebastian, like camp, reptilian Anthony Blanche), the proletarian scholars (those we don't see, whose characterisation is so thin that not one appears, even in the novel) and those like his first friends and like his first undergraduate self, third-way academics in embryo, who appear as stereotypes rather than flesh and blood individuals.

I felt tyrannised by this taxonomy, since in 1981 I regarded it as still being true. There were privileged aesthetes who lived with beauty, and the rest of us, who did not. But there was a fundamental difference between Charles's times at Oxford and my own – the flamboyant aesthetes of my day were copyists from whatever old Oxonian texts they could get their hands on, but, as they re-enacted these novels, they lost the books' charm. There were putative Zuleika Dobsons, acting out the adventures of the eponymous heroine of Max Beerbohm's 1911 novel in which a dazzling beauty visits Oxford and is responsible for a mass suicide among the students. And why not? There was in 1981 a dining society called The Dobson Society which was women-only except for the male guests who were required to throw themselves into the river during Eights Week for the privilege. There was another called The Northey, which was named after Nancy Mitford's young femme fatale.

But most dining societies were all male or male-dominated. The Knights of Marchmain, for instance, those gallant cavaliers by name and by activity loyal to the aristocratic ethos of *Brideshead Revisited*, as a post-dinner feat, would choose a woman to whom they would present red roses, chocolates and a Marchmain cocktail. That they were not often in a fit state to perform this task was evinced by the fact that one of them skewered both feet on the gates of University College after delivering a cocktail to a lucky, lucky woman. Just before I arrived, The Assassins Dining Society had received national newspaper publicity: Nigel Dempster exposed their attempt to destroy the topically-named Thatcher's restaurant in Thame after a boozy dinner. And there were others. The Prince Albrecht Society was a gathering of those who believed that HRH Prince Albrecht of Bavaria was the heir to the Stuart dynasty and thus had, they argued, a legitimate claim to the British throne. The Piers Gaveston Society memorialised Edward II's catamite and, though their drunken evenings were reportedly most like a sweaty sixth form disco, their decadent aura of sodomy and tainted Catholicism wafted through Oxford like incense. The Scruton Society, named after the Conservative philosopher Roger Scruton, would meet to discuss such questions as 'dealing with the lower orders', though after their evenings, few of them would be able to deal with undressing for bed. The Straight Line Society consisted of men who would, after their alcoholic dinners, put two pins in a map of central Oxford, and walk the route indicated – over roofs, through houses, bushes, theatres, concerts and philosophy lectures. They would walk over books, over my face, down through the basement barber's where men permed my hair silently, up over gables and cupolas, through my nightmares, through the orchestras playing at the Sheldonian Theatre, through libraries, lectures, poetry readings, football matches. On and on until they had finished marching.

In such a context, when Charles was invited to a select luncheon in Sebastian's rooms, I was ready to be disgusted at the spectacle. I could take in none of the atmosphere of kindness, nor the beauty of the meal – nor, really, could I develop a proper understanding of the exclusivity that is necessary for their kindness to be kind or their beauty beautiful – and so no powerful class analysis of the scene at all, just resentment. They started with plovers' eggs and champagne, and had moved on to Lobster Newburg when the last guest arrived. This guest was Anthony Blanche – poised, certain, catty Anthony – who, during the meal, memorably, or at least memorably to me, referred to one woman as a drab. I'd never heard that adjective become a noun before and immediately feared that I was such a noun myself – a graceless, flat-vowelled drab. I knew too that I would become all verb if Anthony were to turn his cattiness on me: I would blanche, I would quail and, maybe in that season, I would have plovered – plovered my head deep into my feathers and plovered away on thin, wading bird's legs.

Later in the meal, Blanche went to the balcony of Sebastian's rooms and recited a section of *The Waste Land* through a megaphone down through the heavily scented summer breeze to returning rowers below:

He, the young man carbuncular, arrives
A small house agent's clerk, with one bold stare,
One of the low on whom assurance sits
As a silk hat on a Bradford millionaire.
The time is now propitious, as he guesses,
The meal is ended, she is bored and tired,
Endeavours to engage her in caresses
Which still are unreproved, if undesired.

Unwepwoved and unwepwovable, Blanche, with his lisp the mark of the effete aesthete outsider, unleashed a flurry of 'w's over the balcony. And then he came to the conclusion:

Bestows one final patronising kiss,
And gropes his way, finding the stairs unlit . . .

Blanche was tossing fragments of Eliot's already fragmentary poem from the balcony to the quad lawn where his inferiors smilingly took in his recital, without comprehension. But the recital was about them, they were the low on whom assurance sat as a silk hat on a Bradford millionaire. Perhaps like the small house agent's clerk, they were awkward in their assurance; or perhaps like a Bradford millionaire they were lower-class kids who, while they were at Oxford were parvenus who could have their moment of silk hattery, before the time came for other hats to be put on – City bowlers, small house agent's clerk's trilbies – the headgear of working men. By contrast, Blanche was one of the high on whom assurance sat properly like a silk top hat upon a flamboyant aesthete.

And the low had their degraded lives – that was what Blanche was trumpeting through his megaphone – but it was a degradation, unlike his, without charm or brio. It was one bound up with rape, ugliness and boredom, and ended with the clerk descending from a typist's bedroom, where some foulness had been committed, down dark stairs back to the oblivion where he – venal, cruel, unkind, all-too-earthly man – belonged.

His poetry still exploding, barely audibly, still less comprehensibly, on the low below, Blanche returned into Sebastian's rooms in search perhaps of more lobster and Cointreau, his one final patronising quotation bestowed on the air where it sat fatly for a moment, wepwovingly, before it plummeted down.

In *Brideshead*, there was no other story than that of decadents and of aesthetes and their self-righteous nostalgia for another age. Just as the TV adaptation of *Brideshead* was inspiring a nostalgia for an exclusive age that had died and been reborn in these corpses, I was bringing my hope to Oxford to be born. And the midwives of my hope were Anthony Blanche's pale imitators.

When I saw *Brideshead Revisited* again in 1998, I felt strongly the words spoken by Captain Charles Ryder in the opening scene of the adaptation, lying awake in his military bunk to find himself thirty-nine and loveless. 'Something within me, long sickening, had died,' he says. And so it was with me, but what had been sickening in me was not a nostalgia for a charmed youth, still less a thwarted passion for a Catholic heiress, but a self-destructive bitterness for Oxford that I've outgrown. Now I am more healthy and stronger, only overtaken by a sense of loss for three years in time that could have been happier, had I had the will, had I not been so embroiled with a resentment for the *Brideshead* ethos, a resentment which Nietzsche describes thus: 'The noble man lives in trust and openness with himself, the man of *ressentiment* is neither upright nor naive nor honest and straightforward with himself. His soul squints.' I insisted to myself that I would watch *Brideshead* without squinting.

When I revisited *Brideshead Revisited* in 1998, I saw love and loss, and in the early episodes, a sort of kindness, which occasionally touched me. In the opening scene, for instance, Captain Charles Ryder failed to stop one of his men, Hooper, having his hair cut under the orders of a brutish colonel. The colonel considered Hooper's hair to be too long and so charged someone to deal with it. It recalled an officially inspired rape, a vulgar affair, a scene unfit to be seen by lords or teddy bears, from which Ryder walked languidly away. In Hooper's world, this was what happened: an unwilling soldier crudely hacked at his hair with scissors not designed for the task; in the other world to which Hooper is not privy, teddy bears get better treatment.

Afterwards, no one took it upon themselves to console Hooper for this brutality. He was an unpopular officer, one who didn't properly belong anywhere, but who was uprooted and anxious everywhere. Only later did Ryder make a point of apologising to Hooper. This was very well dramatised in the adaptation. In the book, the apology was merely reported, thus:

'It's not the sort of thing that usually happens in this regiment,' I said.

'Oh, no hard feelings,' said Hooper. 'I can take a bit of sport.'

In the TV adaptation, by contrast, this exchange took place with a lovely rhythm. After the incident, Hooper and his men were marching from the camp. Ryder wheeled into step with Hooper and offered him the apology. The rhythm was lovely because the marching came to symbolise the onward march of history in which Waugh and his Ryder have no faith; the rhythm of the marching men was countered briefly by Ryder's gentility, his voice the last breath of proper kindness from a fast disappearing world.

And yet, now, Ryder's kindness is hard for me to tolerate. The velvet of Ryder's gentility, after all, concealed the iron of his class hostility, his expression of Evelyn Waugh's loathing for the Hoopers of this world – the anxious and the uprooted. For

Hooper *was* uprooted – thrown into the army with little understanding of how it worked; so comprehensively out of joint with his post (he was a platoon commander and Ryder's subordinate officer) that he addressed the men who were contemptuous of him by their first names, and yet received no compensating solidarity from the officers around him since he was not one of their clarse; so much a wafer-thin character that he can be presented as a thoroughgoing professional incompetent without the viewer or the reader wondering why. We knew next to nothing about Hooper, except that he was Charles Ryder's lustreless symbol of the Youth of England. He only existed in relation to Ryder's, and by extension Waugh's, lugubrious loathing for what the future held. But I at least wanted Hooper to become more than just Waugh's symbol. I wanted him to have a lustre all of his own. I should have made *Brideshead Revisited* a trilogy – the extant novel would have been flanked by a prequel about Hooper's early years and the sequel would have been called *Hooper: The Radiant Years*.

The Hooper who existed in *Brideshead Revisited*, though, bore all the weight of Waugh's opprobrium. At the end of the TV series, as in the novel, Ryder rounded on Hooper in his thoughts. He was reflecting on the beauty of Brideshead, its august history, and its destruction by soldiers billeted in the house. 'The builders did not know the uses to which their work would descend; they made a new house with the stones of the old castle; year by year, generation after generation, they enriched and extended it; year by year the great harvest of timber grew to ripeness; until, in the sudden frost, came the age of Hooper; the place was desolate and the work all brought to nothing; *Quomodo sedet sola civitas*. Vanity of vanities, all is vanity.'

Poor Hooper to have had to bear all this. 'He was a sallow youth, with hair combed back, without parting, from his forehead, and a flat, Midland accent,' reported Ryder early on. Poor Hooper, poor Stuart. Pictures of me at the time show me to have my hair combed back, without parting, from my forehead. Memories of the time show me to have had a flat, Midland accent that would never quite parse muster in Oxonian society, to my initial incredulity and continuing anger.

Perhaps it was good that Hooper did not take Charles's kindness, but instead played down the significance of the incident. Ryder's gesture to Hooper was only one of politeness, of good form; it showed his breeding, not his empathy for or understanding of the affront to Hooper. Hooper may have been Waugh's unfeeling symbol of the rise of cultural materialism, his index of the shabbiness of Britain to come, but I would have comforted him with a better quality than Ryder could have attempted. Better than that, I wouldn't have allowed a public school twit of a colonel to order that his hair be cut; unlike Ryder, who seemed incapable of even protesting against the incident, I would have rebelled in the name of Hooper. The likes of Hooper and his ancestors have suffered too much, unimagined by Waugh, and out of anger, and kindness, I would not have let the latest Hooper suffer another moment's indignity at the hands of someone who had not suffered enough.

The rest of *Brideshead* has many such episodes of kindness that did not revolt me so. One, in particular, stayed with me. After the luncheon, Sebastian and Charles were the only ones left in the room. Sebastian suggested they go to the Botanical Gardens to look at the ivy. As they walked through the gardens, arm in arm, I took this, perhaps against the grain of the director's or indeed the author's intentions, as a gesture of tenderness and of consolation in a cruel world. No wonder Charles loved Sebastian and chose his world, above the cold ones that surrounded him at Oxford. I, too, would have liked someone to take me by the arm and show me the ivy.

That tender love recalled Charles's reflection years later on that meeting with reproving Jasper. As Jasper left Charles's room, Jeremy Irons' languorous narration as the older, disaffected

Charles Ryder, began: 'Now I could have matched his gamecock maturity. I could have told him that to know and to love another human being is the root of all wisdom.' And I know now that it is.

But hatred has its place, too. Once my parents came to see me for the day and I took them on a walk around Oxford. We wound up standing at the side of the lake at Worcester College. Across the lake from us and inaccessible was a group of young flamboyant aesthetes, drunk on Pimm's. The men wore boaters and blazers, the women summer dresses. It could have been a lovely scene for my parents to see, an English idyll, a costume drama as winningly fanciful as *Brideshead Revisited* or *Inspector Morse*. But it didn't belong to my parents or to me. It was ruined. 'Oh, look at those common people over there,' yelled one to his friends, in a deliberately affected bray. My mother's face was furious, and my father's revolted: the likes of them still didn't belong here. We walked away, back to a café where there weren't many students. Now, I wish I had dived into that lake, swum across and killed them with an ivory-backed hairbrush, stuffed teddy bears into their mouths. That's how I should have left Oxford – with blood on the blazers and boaters floating on the lake.

TEA AND CRUMPET

In the 1995 adaptation of *Pride and Prejudice*, we saw Mr Darcy in a long shot riding straight-backed through a landscaped park to his ancestral seat. What a posture! What a pasture! He could have been Sebastian Flyte's nineteenth-century ancestor, but for the fact that Darcy could not – heavens, no – have been a Catholic. He looked effortlessly elegant, a man perfectly in tune with the curve of his horse and the curves of the countryside thanks to his well-filled britches and his landscaped hairdo. Today, he might well spend most of his gate receipts on an interesting drug habit and be abusive to those who had paid good money to picnic at lakeside seats, but then he was a soul who was integrated into his surroundings, happy with his lot and his plot. He didn't need a teddy bear as a comforter.

Or did he? We then cut to a close-up of Darcy, and read a different story. He was sweating after his long ride, his brow troubled by something or other, the burden of his social role weighing heavy on his shoulders, the poor lamb. How could that brow be soothed and that tension washed away? Darcy climbed down from his horse, handed the reins to an underling, removed his coat and plunged into the lake in the grounds of his Derbyshire home. We saw him swimming underwater and then saw him climb out, his white shirt clinging to his chest. It may have been a soothing swim for Darcy, but not for anyone watching who had more than an academic interest in the effect of damp shirt on white bosom. What would Elizabeth and her relatives the Gardiners, who were being shown round Pemberley at the time, make of this appearance? After all, Lizzy was already confused by the conflicting images of Darcy she had built up in her mind – the proud, arrogant Darcy of the Netherfield ball, and now the smiling Darcy she had seen in the portrait hanging at Pemberley.

How would she react to this new, wet Darcy who emerged from the lake, as sensual as could be and as proto-Byronic as possible? With 'Hold my bonnet, Aunt Gardiner. I'm going to get myself a piece of that!' perhaps? In Andrew Davies's BBC adaptation of Jane Austen's novel, this would not have been inconceivable.

There was no such swimming scene in Jane Austen's novel. Andrew Davies added this to the story, just as he had added many other scenes (the Netherfield ball, the newly-married couples driving away from the church), in order to give us a better understanding of the characters. That at least was what

Davies said in interviews. In the BBC book, *The Making of Pride and Prejudice*, Davies told his interviewer: 'In almost any version of Jane Austen I have seen, everyone seems terrifically stiff and buttoned up the whole time; you get no sense that they are living, breathing, feeling people inside. So I thought, "What do they do in their spare time?" and decided to show them going riding and shooting and fencing. Darcy goes swimming at one point and it's partly a way of showing him as a real human being.'

Partly. But also it is a scene which helped with the sexing of *Pride and Prejudice*, that fitted well alongside its parade of women's bosoms pointing at unfeasible angles and achingly exciting shots of men's thighs astride panting horses. Davies, too, made Miss Elizabeth Bennet not just mentally active, but physically so, too. We saw her running through the fields, her dress muddy, her cheeks aflame, her bosom heaving, to Netherfield, and into Darcy's sight. In the novel, Darcy would admire 'the brilliancy which exercise had given to her complexion'. But Davies saw this as a legitimate extension of a character who is, in the novel, often to be found running out of rooms and going for rambles in the countryside. 'I'm not sure how far people will agree with me on this,' said Davies, 'but almost I think this is a coded way of Jane Austen telling us that she's got lots of sexual energy. This is probably what appeals to Darcy, unconsciously at any rate, who is used to some very artificial females. Here's a natural one, who runs around, gets her feet muddy, says what she thinks and it turns him on!' He went further in his interview with the *Daily Telegraph*: 'It's quite obvious that she would be wonderful in bed.'

Is it? Nothing in the novel suggests anything about Elizabeth Bennet's sexual abilities. Nor does even Davies's adaptation. When I watched it, I was intrigued by Miss Bennet's bosom, as I was with Becky Sharp's in Davies's 1998 adaptation of Thackeray's *Vanity Fair*. Bras, I knew, worked on the same principle as the suspension bridge. So did the TV adaptations of great

British novels: once up, they could support any freight that anyone cared to thrust into our view.

How very different all this was from the BBC costume dramas that I watched on Sunday evenings when I was a boy. Once, we had tea and crumpet without a hint of double entendres. Double entendres were reserved for any other night of the week but Sunday. They were reserved for sitcoms or for Larry Grayson's accomplished stewardship of *The Generation Game* in the late seventies. On Sunday evenings, instead, we gathered before our screens to worship English literature; some may have tuned in earlier to worship before *Songs of Praise*, but in my childhood household, at least, that was the time for preparing toast and dripping, celery sticks and little cakes for tea. English literature, in this context, meant crinolines and top hats, murky London streets and healthy rural rides, characters who spoke proper rather than like what they did in the celebrated plays of Mr Ernest Wise. English literature, too, meant tastefully sublimated sexuality and interesting discussions about money. *Brideshead* just about squeezed into this schema, but Sunday evening on BBC1 was perfectly suited for Austen. On television, English literature whisked us back to a past where everything was nicer and, preferably, the unhappy lot of common people didn't interrupt the fine sentiments. That was why adaptations of Dickens were so troublesome to me: there were too many gap-toothed harridans, too many foul old dads who weren't there for comic relief, too many of Hooper's and my down-trodden ancestors for comfort. No wonder, then, that I marginalised Dickens into silliness: his novels teemed with Mr Threegses and Mistress Wiggleses – daft names that undid the seriousness of his social critique. The Brontës and Thomas Hardy were too troublesome for Sunday evening worship, as well: there was too much wayward passion in those writers for their stories to be made into proper, chaste TV dramas at this holy time.

On British television, *Pride and Prejudice* was the ideal Sunday evening entertainment. An English teacher at my sixth form college had told us at the outset of our studies that Jane Austen was a genius even though she told the same story again and again. He had underwritten her safe appeal, and underwrote too, just in time, Fay Weldon's 1980 adaptation. Weldon had her sex and money, but hardly the kind that Davies later injected into his adaptation. In Weldon's version, David Rentoul's Darcy did not dive into the lake to demonstrate his character's seething manliness; instead, in the long silences in which Elizabeth expected him to speak, he held his mouth open in a sort of pout and then his tongue would fall from the roof of his mouth, sensually. The Chancellor of the Exchequer, Gordon Brown, does the same thing when he pauses halfway through sentences and the effect is lascivious, only less self-consciously so. Elsewhere, though, Lydia Bennet's moral laxity was conveyed chiefly by means of harnessing her embonpoint and thrusting it into a trajectory unfeasible for 1813 or indeed any later age, just as it was when Julia Sawalha had her breasts pushed up and together in the same role fifteen years later. Spillingly implausible bosoms always spell shamefully lax morals in televised English literature, whatever else may change.

For me in 1980, Weldon's version was a wonderful adaptation, as hilarious as the book and faithful to its formidable speeches. 'In such cases as this, it is, I believe, the established mode to express a sense of obligation for the sentiments avowed, however unequally they may be returned.' Thus said Miss Bennet as she rebuffed Mr Darcy's first, hateful proposal. Such delicious circumlocution! Such English *sang-froid*! Such brightness of spirit and of intelligence!

No other nation's literary figures could speak like Austen's heroes and heroines. Even if Britain, at the end of the 20th century, had no empire and was not a place of propriety, decency and courtesy, we could, through watching adaptations of Jane Austen, imagine a time when all was well, even if this milieu was as contrived as Camberwick Green. Even if the British soldiers in dress uniform who came to woo the sillier Bennet girls resembled those of Pippin Fort. It may have been just as fictional as anything that happened in Trumptonshire, it may have been as pointlessly ritualistic as anything that goes on involving soldiers around Buckingham Palace, but it was just as socially useful and nostalgically suggestive.

Only a year before going to Oxford, I saw this adaptation with a patriot's eye: what a wonderful heritage we enjoyed, I thought, us Britons – united by television adaptations such as these. Only a year later, that patriotism was damaged by the shock of Oxford. For once, nostalgia wasn't stronger than bombs. My nostalgia for a better Britain, for a time that was better for never having existed, had been blown up. Once, I had jumped aboard a Wellsian time machine, back to the Edwardian era where *Camberwick Green*'s Dr Mopp drove unimpeded through the country lanes of England under the summer sun to fulfil his duties. Once, too, I had gone back in time to hear English properly spoken by Darcy and Miss Bennet as he made his second proposal to her. Once I had enjoyed this *Camberwick Green* for grown-ups.

But then I had watched *Brideshead Revisited*, and it ached with a nostalgia that I could never feel, since it was a lament for a world in which Hooper and Jeffries did not yet exist.

When I watched the 1995 adaptation of *Pride and Prejudice*, as a result, I was suspicious. Costume dramas in my post-*Brideshead* world were dubious, and repaid more attention than I had given them before. In *Brideshead* I saw old clothes and old postures, under which a political critique had been smuggled in – and one that had devastating implications for me. In the case of *Pride and Prejudice* in 1995, I was presented with a better-ordered, more desirable world than even Jane Austen dared imagine. *The Making of Pride and Prejudice* shows that the costume designers, make-up artists, wig experts, musicians and set designers strove to make the adaptation more authentic than the original novel – as if their true worship is to the times in which the book was set rather than the novel itself. In Austen's novel there is little about interiors and costume; and yet, on screen, the clothes, the hair-styles, the interiors of English country houses in 1813 are meticulously created. Mr Bennet, for instance, often wore a banyan coat, a kind of long dressing gown: 'I found a picture for Mr Bennet I really liked,' said costume designer Dinah Collin. 'He's not interested in going out and about in society, and so he wears a lot of velvets to be comfortable at home. We gave him spectacles and the banyan, a garment rather like a long dressing gown worn at home for warmth and comfort.' Here, as elsewhere, the adaptation created a visual image of a character – out of necessity, in one sense, because a character had to look definite and thus affront the sense of those readers who had created the character in their mind's eye. There is always that kind of necessary brutality when a novel is adapted for the television. This is partly because of the dictates of making a TV drama: you have to show *something* on screen.

But this everyday brutality was overlaid with another, special violence: instead of a faithful depiction of England in 1813, we saw an England that was more pristine, a fresh, well-scrubbed milieu in which we would all want to live. The most interesting criticism of the series came from Aileen Ribeiro, head of History of Dress at the Courtauld Institute. 'It all looks too crisp,' she told the *Guardian* in 1995. 'They'll go into a great deal of accuracy. They'll cut patterns from original garments, but we have a kind of vision of the past predicated on portraits and visual images and the way we imagine people moved and stood and walked, and the late 20th century is just so antipathetic to this notion. The faces are wrong – they're just too healthy – and everything looks too much like a fashion shoot, even if they try to slightly artificially distress them. The total bare look, the well-scrubbed, shining look – an actress couldn't cope with this. There's always the sense of 1990s make-up, even if it's infinitesimally put on.' In 1813, women (or the kind of women who would have populated Austen's novels) paradoxically, had to embrace a make-up free aesthetic, even though they were so unhealthy-looking that they might have looked better with some on; while in the 1990s, the much healthier actresses who depicted these women, and who were much less in need of make-up in order to achieve this well-scrubbed, shining ideal, wore make-up to look authentic, to look part of a glowing past. Authenticity, if that's what it was, had to be appealing. In fact, it wasn't authenticity that the make-up artists were striving for but a more attractive simulation of that authenticity – something inauthentic as a result, but better for that. The clothes, the hair, the dances, the make-up were all better than accurate depictions of what it was like in England in 1813, but to be completely successful simulations they had to affect to be accurate, authentic, faithful. Similarly, the interiors of the stately homes – Pemberley, Longbourn, Rosings – were pristine. For Ribeiro, too little account was taken of the unfashionable, the imperfect and the mismatched accretions of furniture and decoration. 'Sometimes it's like looking at a National Trust thing, frozen on screen – and life isn't like that,' said Ribeiro. 'It's much more grey, isn't it?'

But grey was not a colour in the palette of those who wanted to paint a better, brighter past. Everything must shine in this golden age of heritage. We had to be spared those moments that I had often experienced when wandering on the wrong side of the ropes at a stately home, those moments when I saw the rudimentariness of the toilet facilities in times gone by, the ugliness of the rooms, the laughable inadequacy of the libraries, or the uncomfortableness of the poorly-upholstered furniture.

Instead, we were given a falsified past, meticulously created in the name of authenticity. In this context, *The Making of Pride and Prejudice*, the explanatory book, was a wonderful part of the heritage industry that protected us from the horror or even the workaday ugliness of the real past, just like the Admiral Nelson boxer shorts or the World War One-style lighters that I could have bought from the Past Times catalogue.

But what of the sex? Andrew Davies had toasted his own crumpet for tea time. Perhaps this was just a cynical response to fears that the Sunday evening BBC costume drama, the sort of thing that is supposed to justify the licence fee, seemed to be doomed in the early nineties. In 1993, the TV writer Alan Plater predicted that if Andrew Davies's earlier adaptation of George Eliot's *Middlemarch* did not succeed, it might go the way of *The Woodentops*. In the event, *Middlemarch* was a success and the novel became a bestseller – a success that Eliot never lived to enjoy. Despite this, perhaps sex was necessary to keep our interest in our national literature. And who better than Andrew Davies to achieve this, the man who routinely uncover the smouldering passion that lurks in our primmest classics?

Ultimately the sexing of *Pride and Prejudice*, though, was all trussed-up foreplay with no consummation. Darcy's bosom heaved, and so did Lizzy's, but they were never pressed together. It was still an English heritage kind of sex, with all the oozings and writhings and nasty stains airbrushed out. Sex in 1813, if Sunday night English literature was anything to go by, was healthy, fresh and well-scrubbed. It would never have done for Andrew Davies to have written a bedroom scene for Darcy and Miss Bennet, no matter what other liberties he took with the story. It would have tampered with the trajectory of her embonpoint too much, ruined the authenticity of his sideburns. For the sake of English literature, and for the sake of not sullying a non-existent past, I would never find out if that Bennet girl was wonderful in bed.

CHAPTER 6

1982: Jack Duckworth's glasses

REVELATION ON THE INNER RING ROAD

I first saw *Brookside* on Channel 4's opening night, 2 November 1982. It wasn't the best programme on the night – that was a then rare screening of *Sunset Boulevard.* But *Brookside* was the most important: the Britain I knew was ready for its close up and, thanks to Phil Redmond, *Brookside* was going to provide it. Like the street where I had been raised, Brookside Close was a cul-de-sac made up of nice new houses. The front lawns ran down to the pavement, cars sat in the sun on their driveways, and by the street sign on the corner there was an attractive arrangement of little shrubs, just as there was in my street.

The first episode started with the titles rolling by as the camera took us from the familiar, grand landmarks of Liverpool's waterfront, to the two cathedrals near to the secular icons of the two football grounds, and then out of the city along busy dual carriageways into the suburbs, to West Derby and finally to peaceful, leafy Brookside Close itself. You could shoot a similar sequence tracing a journey from Birmingham's city centre, from St Philip's Cathedral, down through the Bull Ring surmounted by the

Rotunda, down into Sparkbrook, up into Sparkhill and along the Stratford Road to the cul-de-sac where my family lived.

In 1982 I was grateful for *Brookside*. For the first time, here was a TV programme set in a street that I could recognise. Until then, the two commanding soap operas were *Coronation Street* and *Crossroads*. The former looked to me as though it was filmed in an earlier time and bore no relation to Britain in the seventies or eighties, no matter how cherishable its characters were. Like the brass band title music, this seemed to be entertainment for another age or at least for another demographic. Until the mid-nineties purge of pensioners from *Coronation Street*, to my mind Weatherfield was England's equivalent of Florida, a place where old people congregated to talk about things that bore little relation to the lives of young people such as myself.

As for *Crossroads*, it may have been set in Birmingham, the city I knew best and cared about most of any in the world, but it had been refashioned as an unrecognisable place. True, there was some cunning in that Crossroads Motel was located in a suburb called King's Oak, a mixture of Selly Oak and King's Heath (or King's Norton), but otherwise it bore no relation to the real Birmingham or indeed the real world in general. This wasn't just because of the amateurishness of the acting or the ludicrousness of the wobbly sets (both satirised viciously and perfectly justifiably by Victoria Wood in her Acorn Antiques sketches; and by the 1979 Radio Rentals video recorder advertisement: 'It can take 16 episodes of *Crossroads* (if you can!)'). Admittedly, Amy Turtle, the common Brummie troll of a gossip who worked at the motel, had a name which sounded as unappealing as the Gravelly Hill Interchange (a.k.a. Spaghetti Junction), but otherwise I didn't recognise the show's setting. Rather, *Crossroads* was set in a fantasy land, just off the Alcester Road. Meg Richardson and her nauseating, squeaky-clean family ran the motel as their feudal domain: anyone with a semblance of a Brummie accent was under Meg's mules. Even before I was properly politicised, I hoped that Shughie McFee, the Scottish chef, would whip off his oversized chef's hat, distribute his kitchen knives among the cut-throat Brummie Bolsheviks and take Meg and her degenerate family off to some Ekaterinburg in Warwickshire where they would be ruthlessly despatched.

The revolution never came and *Crossroads* carried on from 1964 to 1988 with a grasp on reality only slightly more slender than that of my bloody fantasies. Typical was the eleven-month pregnancy of Meg's daughter Jill, who was played by Jane Rossington. Rossington became pregnant at the same time as the character (scriptwriters, even on *Crossroads*, could be uncannily perceptive about some things), but soon after had a miscarriage. Producer Jack Barton told Jane Rossington that the viewers' response to her character's pregnancy was good, so good in fact that he wondered if she would mind being padded up on the show to make it look as though she was still pregnant. She agreed, but two months later became pregnant again. Her pregnancy continued until Jane Rossington's bump became a baby. Jill Richardson, as a result, was pregnant for eleven months – the gestation period of another species, the soap opera star, whose natural history is very different from ours. Typically, hardly anyone noticed: but then no one ever watched *Crossroads* for its close resemblance to real life.

As I grew up I hungered for something on television or at the cinema that was like the school life I knew. But when I was young that hope didn't seem as though it would ever be fulfilled. In the early seventies, the only schools I saw on television were either in *Tom Brown's School Days* or in *Whack-O!*, Frank Muir and Denis Norden's sitcom from the late fifties which was anachronistically revived in a series of new episodes in 1971. But at these schools, the boys, and they were only boys, spoke with alien accents and the teachers wore mortar boards and carried canes. They bore no relation to my experiences. Imagine, then, what a relief it was when *Grange Hill* was first shown in 1978, just as I was studying for my O levels. Here, for once, were schoolkids I could recognise, not the swots of *Top of the Form* or the science geeks of *Young Scientist of the Year*, but real kids. I could tell they were real kids because they looked uncomfortable in their school uniforms. Their ties were big and knotted clumsily, their blazers often torn and ill-fitting, and their language was the stuff I heard in the playgrounds. For too long, school dramas on TV seemed to be written by ex-RAF chaps who had used their heads too freely while playing the Eton Wall Game in their youths, if you catch my drift. I didn't understand the banter in *Whack-O!* or *Tom Brown* – should I be speaking this way to my friends? 'What-ho, Binkie! Time for tuck, what?' Not in the state schools of the West Midlands of the 1970s.

The kids at Grange Hill Comprehensive, Tucker Jenkins, Trisha Yates, Benny Green, Suzanne Ross, even Samuel 'Zammo' McGuire, all looked like kids I knew, and, even though they had London accents, spoke in a vernacular I understood. Zammo, like Damon Grant's gormless mate Gizzmo in *Brookside*, even had a nickname like my mates: I had a friend called Mushas, some just about comprehensible mutation of his surname Marsh; another was called Perky, a bastardisation of his Percival surname. I was called Jaffa-Cakes and sometimes Joe. Like my schoolfriends, the kids in *Grange Hill* did not have jolly japes, wizard wheezes or looked as though they would know what a tuck shop was. Instead, they bought chips on the way home, just as I did, were out of control, as we often were, insulted teachers, and were embroiled in truancy, bullying, smoking, shoplifting, drug taking, having sex, supporting disappointing football teams, hating David Cassidy, loving David Cassidy and being protective of our protractors. *Grange Hill* even looked like my experiences: to make the programme look more convincing to its children's audience, kids'-height camera angles were used.

In the early seventies, Ken Loach's *Kes* came close to at least looking like my schools, but I'd been taken to see that film on a school trip to the Sedgley Clifton cinema and, as a result, it was the official version, endorsed by liberal teachers. For that reason, it could not take its rightful place in my heart. I could not love *Kes*, even though in the film Brian Glover uncannily captured the dysfunctional loathsomeness of many a games master when he acted out his footballing fantasies by beating a team of small boys. Glover's performance had such resonance that, years later, when I saw him playing God in the Mystery Plays at the Lyceum Theatre in London, I couldn't resist trying to affectionately pat his bald head as he rose past my seat in the cradle of a fork lift truck towards heaven.

The Birmingham-set crime series *Gangsters* came closer than *Kes* could to winning a place in my heart, partly because it was about criminals and so couldn't be part of a school curriculum. But mostly because it was set in Birmingham and so, for once, I saw somewhere I recognised on television. Once on *Gangsters*, there was a car chase that ended in the multi-storey car park opposite the Bull Ring on St Martin's Queensway. That was the car park where we would go when we went shopping. Mum and Dad would hold our hands as we went down in the urine-smelling lift, and walk us through the dank underpass below the Inner Ring Road towards the heady delights of Corporation Street. But *Gangsters* wasn't at all realistic: the story was about an ex-SAS man called John Kline who managed a nightclub called The Maverick. This job put him into close contact with the city's underworld which, despite all I knew of the happy tedium that was Birmingham, teemed with exciting groups – illegal immigration rackets, fast-handed Chinese triads, prostitution rings, drug pushers and, above all, men with sideburns so commodious that, by rights, they should have attracted the attentions of the West Midlands Serious Crimes Squad, or maybe just the West Midlands Trivial Crimes Squad. *Gangsters* made Birmingham seamily glamorous between 1975 and 1978, at least I thought it did, like the Little Italy of Scorsese's *Mean Streets* or Jean-Pierre Melville's *Le Samourai*, films which I would see only a few years later. Down these mean underpasses, a man must go – that was maverick John Kline's beat. In reality, nobody had ever tinged Birmingham with glamour.

Otherwise the Birmingham I knew only flashed briefly on screen. I didn't much care for the TV adaptation of David Lodge's novel *Nice Work* in the late eighties, even though I liked the leads: Warren Clarke, who played Wilcox, the Brummie managing director of Pringle's engineering firm, and Haydn Gwynne, who played Dr Robyn Penrose, temporary lecturer in English and a devotee, like me, of semiotic materialism. I fancied her rotten. But Lodge's Rummidge, that reductive simulacrum of Birmingham, was too obviously a conceit for his fictional games. Lodge put a disclaimer at the start of his novel: 'Perhaps I should explain, for people who have not been there before, that Rummidge is an imaginary city, with imaginary universities and imaginary factories, inhabited by imaginary people, which occupies, for the purposes of fiction, the space where Birmingham is to be found on maps of the so-called real world.' But I wasn't buying that: this was a distortion, a Disraelian two-nations novel whose criss-crossing pathways had been trodden across my all-too-real Birmingham.

The only scene I liked in *Nice Work* was the last one. Dr Penrose has been educated in the ways of business, and Wilcox has been given a thorough grounding in the joys of non-penetrative sex and high-brow literature (although, he confesses, he will never finish George Eliot's *Daniel Deronda*). The dramatisation ended with their differences mutually respected, and Wilcox in his big MD's saloon driving around the Inner Ring Road as Randy Crawford belts out something wonderful from the world of popular culture and thus beyond Dr Penrose's ken, on the car stereo. The reason I loved the scene was that Wilcox was laughing, laughing harder and harder as his car drove on and the music got louder and the camera pulled back to leave him in long-shot with Randy's voice still up close and personal, and his car spooling seemingly endlessly around the loop of the Inner Ring Road, before the final credits rolled. What I wanted from the television drama wasn't realism, still less the schematic drama of Lodge's imaginary Rummidge, but a positive image: Wilcox driving around the city I loved, having learned something, but not enough, about the outside world from his cultured semiotician. And yet he was happy in his lot, his circular fast lane.

Empire Road, the first black British soap opera, which was set in Handsworth, Birmingham and ran only for a couple of years in the late seventies, carried a load as heavy as the one which I, probably improperly, foisted onto *Nice Work*. From its Matumbi theme tune to the huge Victorian houses now occupied by black and Asian Brummies, this was a recognisable milieu too, and I felt pride that the soap was being played out in Handsworth, when it could have been set in so many other English cities; and disappointment when it didn't quite succeed. And yet, perhaps, the reason it failed was that the burden of hope proved too much: Norman Beaton, in particular, had to carry such a heavy load of black Britons' expectations, in a similar way to the ones which have settled on comedian Lenny Henry, the acceptable face of black Britain in TV entertainment for nearly two decades. *Empire Road* was a soap opera that hoped for racial harmony: in its final episode, Marcus, from a Caribbean family, married Ranjanaa Kapoor, and the programme ended with hopes for an end to inter-racial tension. Perhaps *Empire Road*, filled, like the old British Empire, with many different ethnic groups, could live together in harmony at close quarters. But it was too hopeful: six years later, Handsworth and Lozells were torn apart by riots, as were many other British inner cities with large black populations that same year.

★

THE VIEW FROM UNDER THE PATIO SLABS

Brookside, by contrast, declared from the start that it wouldn't be upbeat or hopeful. Instead, it was going to be really real. The houses of Brookside Close weren't facades and were used for the interior shots. In this, the soap is very different from *Coronation Street*, where the real brick terrace is only used for exterior shots, and interior footage is filmed in the nearby studio. *Brookside* even looked like real life: the lighting was so muted that it looked like the steel-grey of a Merseyside afternoon was lighting the kitchen-sink drama inside. True, this was a phoney realism: in fact, 2.5 kilowatt lamps were placed on hydraulic lifts to simulate daylight downstairs or upstairs in the Close's houses. Yes, but it looked real to me, and that was what mattered – to give us the shock of recognition. The makers of *Brookside* hoped to reflect the real world in a way unimaginable to the producers of *Coronation Street* or *Crossroads*. '*Brookside*,' said the Official Companion book published in 1987, 'portrays the way we really are – human beings trying to make ends meet; men and women looking for security in an increasingly insecure world; young people asking for nothing more than a job; ordinary people with a spirit and a sense of humour which is no greater or less than that possessed by those who live in Glasgow or Newcastle or Birmingham – even London.'

I read those lines now and have very mixed feelings about them: I have a tear in my eye and yet a sneer on my lips. A tear, because the eighties, especially the early eighties, were a miserable time for British people who didn't share the prevailing Thatcherite vision, and so anything that depicted something of what it was like to suck on the fuzzy end of the lollipop during that time (be it 'Yosser's Tale' from Alan Bleasdale's *The Boys from the Black Stuff* or Bobby Grant's shop steward in *Brookside*, agonising over the threats to his members) was welcome and all the more important because it was so rare. And yet a sneer, too, since *Brookside* never represented the way we really were. There's sentimentality in those lines, which repulses me now, even though I was tempted by this feelgood pretence of a radical political agenda. Any projection of a single mood onto a group of people will flatten the differences between individuals and is likely to be sentimental. Young people have never, en masse, asked for nothing more than a job. When I was a young person I wanted much more than that: I wanted fame, an output of literature to make Tolstoy blush, an interesting drug habit and quick success as lead guitarist for the Dumb Waiters. (None of this seems to have happened yet, but, by thunder, the Dumb Waiters' potential will be realised. Oh yes, it will.) Just a job? I was built for better things than just a job, and so, I suspect, were many of the working-class kids who were my contemporaries. And what of these twin sentimentalised pseudo-responses to the vicissitudes of the eighties, 'spirit and a sense of humour'? Most of the people I knew who suffered unemployment or any kind of reverse brought about by the Conservatives' management of the economy met those with anger and, sometimes, wretchedness. Spirit and senses of humour are supposed to be our responses to times of adversity, but in reality sufferers are hardly ever so stereotypically stoic. But this attitude of *Brookside*'s producers was writ large through many of the storylines. *Brookside* was a blessed relief when it hit the screens in 1982, but the preachiness that the above quotation discloses, its appropriation of controversial social issues of the day made it seem opportunistic and ultimately unreal. *Brookside*, throughout the eighties, claimed to be relevant to the problems of modern Britain. And, in the context of that time, it was. Before *EastEnders* began in 1985 and until *Coronation Street* reinvented itself in the early 1990s, no soap other than *Brookside* dealt with issues such as rape, unemployment, the black economy, industrial strife, with anything like the seriousness that they demanded.

But this made *Brookside* relevant, never realistic. There were two big differences between the street where I lived and Brookside Close. One, the neighbours on my street didn't talk to each other as much as those in *Brookside*, not least because they didn't have to further the plot, but also because society is never as communal as it is depicted in soaps: for the most part life goes on behind closed doors. Where the camera can't intrude – that is where the camera wants to be.

The second difference is that reality isn't very exciting, whereas *Brookside*, at its best, was very exciting indeed. For all the time I lived in my cul-de-sac, and for years afterwards, there was never a siege in our street; nobody killed their husband and buried them under the patio; a house was not taken over by a religious cult; gangland thugs did not beat up men down our way; men did not drive their cars across neighbours' lawns; nobody, so far as I knew, had incestuous sex; there was no woman who plunged to her death from scaffolding with her baby in her arms. I remember once there was some talk because a neighbour had an after-dark table tennis tournament, the garden ringed with fairy lights and resounding to excited cheers and jeers, but otherwise nothing much happened where I lived. None of the football-mad boys down my street got a trial, as Damon Grant did in *Brookside*, to play for Torquay United. Perhaps there was a lesbian kiss, perhaps there was a gay son, perhaps a husband did rape his wife, perhaps some daughter was going cold turkey in a little bedroom with the curtains drawn, but these things could only have taken place behind closed doors, these secrets could only with great difficulty have found their way into public consciousness. Reality is a much more tedious, recalcitrant beast than was ever dreamed of in Phil Redmond's philosophy for *Brookside*. His was a vision that pretended what we were seeing was reality, while really we were watching TV drama.

In the nineties, *Brookside* became even more sensational, as it filled more air time with thinner, but noisier storylines. 'Inflation has set in,' said Jimmy McGovern, who wrote for *Brookside* during the eighties before moving on to write *Cracker* and *Priest*. 'The *Street* used to be immune to it but even there writers are losing faith in the actors, and the actors are losing faith in the characters. So people have to place great faith in the stories. But that's when inflation sets in because one story has to top another.'

Typical of the inflationary way *Brookside* dealt with a good story was Beth and Mandy Jordache's murder trial in the mid-nineties. It could have been great drama. Beth and Mandy stood accused of murdering Trevor, an incestuous rapist of a husband, and burying him under the patio slabs, but the opportunity for a moving story was squandered, partly because the courtroom drama was screened over five consecutive nights. Gone was the weaving of storylines that makes the texture of soap opera so alluring, and instead each episode was exclusively concerned with the court case. But for anyone who had watched the earlier episodes, this was a pointless drama of reiteration. We knew all about the beatings Mandy had taken from her husband Trevor, how Beth had been raped and beaten by her father, how the younger daughter Rachel was in denial about her own rape. We knew how Mandy and Beth had been driven to kill Trevor and bury his body under the patio, how they had dug it up again to take off his ring and put it on the body of a dead tramp. We heard these details as the briefs opened their cases, as they cross-examined the witnesses, as they made their closing arguments, as the judge summed up. It was a drama for the hard of understanding.

All of this must have come across very drearily to viewers not familiar with *Brookside*. Visually, it resembled nothing so much as *Crown Court*, that seventies lunchtime drama series which demonstrated the rich potential of the British courtroom as stage. Unfortunately, ever since our screens have been saturated by more sophisticated court-based drama, from *LA Law* to every other Hollywood thriller, so the presentation of the Jordache trial was as dated as it was dramatically lame. What's more, in *Crown Court* each case was decided in half an hour. We had invested two and a half hours in the Jordache trial – a whole week! – and we still had to wait to find out if they were going down.

Brookside had only once before tried the five-nights-a-week special, a few months earlier when Trevor's body was discovered under the slabs, and then as with the courtroom drama it was thin stuff, an unwelcome trend, leaving fans feeling cheated by what came across as an exercise in ratings manipulation. Yes, there were two well-judged performances in the witness box from Sandra Maitland and Anna Friel as Mandy the weak and Beth the strong. We were also treated to a delightful dumb show as the camera made its regular trips along the front row of the public gallery, past Mick and Bing, the neighbourly voyeurs, past Brenna, Trevor's sister, a green-eyed queen of misplaced loyalty, past Rachel, the sullen teenager in her Sunday best, to solid Sinbad, the saint who loved Mandy no matter what. But it wasn't enough to fill the longueurs.

The courtroom episodes were particularly disappointing because *Brookside* had traditionally excelled during its key dramatic moments – the siege, Sheila's rape, Barry and Terry getting beaten up by Tommy McArdle's hoods, Sue tumbling with her baby from the scaffolding. Traditionally, too, it was superbly written: I still laugh out loud whenever I think of Barry Grant's Scouse *sang-froid* when, held hostage by a gang of cultist Christians and subject to their dystopian ravings, he asked: 'What is it with you Man United fans?'

But, a week later, *Brookside* was back in the saddle. The previous week had felt like a life sentence, but by the following Tuesday Mandy and Beth Jordache, who had suffered twenty years of mental and physical abuse in the soap opera, were jailed for filing Trevor under P for patio. This episode at least was high-octane soap opera, condensing recrimination, forgiveness, bitter tears, even a ludicrously schematic wedding into the last ten minutes before Mandy was sentenced to life imprisonment for murder and Beth to five years for conspiracy to murder. Only Brenna let a twisted smile play around her lips as the verdicts were announced.

Behind the drama there was more than a hint of legal polemic. One juror, convinced that Mandy and Beth would have to be convicted with the law as it stands, added: 'The law has failed these women. Because they were too frightened to act at the moment of extreme provocation it assumes it was a pre-meditated killing.' The remark was a clear reference to the defence of provocation in such cases which was then under review. *Brookside*, as in its earliest days, had pretensions to be at the cutting edge of a social issue.

In this way the Jordache pair transcended their soap opera status. Mandy and Beth's convictions became symbolic of the way in which women who fight back against domestic violence are treated in British courts. Sara Thornton has been in jail since 1989 for stabbing her violent husband to death. Kiranjit Ahluwalia served three years of a life sentence for killing her brutal husband while he slept, but was released in 1992 after a campaign by women's groups. Mandy Jordache was the first depiction of such a woman on television, drawing attention to a moral dilemma which feminist campaigners felt was ill-resolved by the courts.

At the time, women's groups announced they were pleased that the makers of *Brookside* had opted for guilty verdicts. To such groups, the storyline showed the audience how dreadful the law was. But here, as at other times when *Brookside* leapt on to its moral high horse, realism had been sacrificed in favour of making a proselytising drama. True, the storyline was not completely didactic, which was just as well since when art does so it becomes dreary. Indeed the writers were keenly aware that the story had great dramatic potential. Dramatically, the guilty verdicts in *Brookside* offered lots of scope. If the Jordaches had been acquitted, all that viewers would have been promised was a wedding between Mandy and her window cleaner beau, Sinbad. As a result of their conviction, instead, I remember cheerfully expecting tearful visits, a prison baby, nuptials in the nick and the inevitable appeals. Not to mention the 'Free the Brookside Two' T-shirts and the Jordache range of patio furniture. But I never quite expected that Beth would die in jail, releasing Anna Friel from the soap and onto the covers of men's magazines.

Brookside had married exciting plot developments with a storyline that had social relevance. At least it did not seem like a dubious attempt to drive up ratings. Subsequent storylines in *Brookside*, though, have seemed thoroughly cynical, notably the handling of the incestuous relationship between Georgia Simpson and her brother Nat.

DALLAS WITH DUNG

It was rather different on *Emmerdale*, which never had pretensions to be grittily realistic, but was, initially at least, enervatingly pastoral. Then some dunderhead gave it a makeover to render the soap as over-inflated and suspect as *Brookside* became in the late 1990s. From 1972 until the present there have been lambs gambolling in the opening credits. But it must have been a relief to the actors who played some of the original characters – Annie Sugden, farmer's wife and obligatory soap matriarch, and Amos Brearly, proud-sideburned scion of Dales and puller of pints in the Woolpack – that they were not around to witness the decline of a programme which once had the English banality and restraint of *Brief Encounter*, into something which Les Dawson rightly called '*Dallas* with dung'.

During the seventies and early eighties it was a rustic idyll; in the mid-eighties, characters were as likely to roll in the hay as bale it. By 1989, when the show's title was shortened from *Emmerdale Farm* to *Emmerdale*, many viewers were as revolted by the sexing up of the show as *Archers* listeners would be nearly a decade later. In a Christmas 1993 special, a plane crashed into the village of Beckindale – a sensational storyline that alienated many of the soap's fans.

Subsequently, the soap became further puffed up. The hour-long 2,000th episode special in 1996 was typical. It wasn't the nice lesbians who were the problem. No, Zoe and Emma were blameless role models, corrupted only by the Sodom and Gomorrah around them. Everywhere you looked in this hour-long special, there was some tawdry scene being enacted. There was posh Kim Tate, her sunbed tan spilling out of a bathrobe, come to seduce callow Dave; slimy antiques dealer Eric Pollard snogging a policewoman, while her husband fumed in the Montego outside; rivals fighting over the memory of their dead lover outside the coroner's court.

Zoe, the Jane Herriot of this dale, had to face the advances of crudely-drawn chauvinist Farmer Adlington. It was a storyline that was so clearly signposted that if one of the protagonists had said to camera, ''appen tha' knows how this 'un 'll turn out?' the whole viewing population would have replied: ''appen'. While Emma was at a do, receiving an award for her preposterous Harrogate tapas bar, The Red Pepper, Adlington had lured Zoe to his barn on the pretext that one of his animals was sick. Then he attempted to rape her. 'I know you're one of them,' he advised. 'And you know why don't yer? Because you've never had a proper man seeing to yer.'

Even more crude were the comedy commoners, the Dingles, who made their opposite numbers in *Coronation Street*, the Duckworths, seem a trifle snooty. Like the Duckworths and like the Brummie plebs over whom Meg Richardson and David Hunter used to lord it in *Crossroads*, they were there to be laughed at, or to muse pathetically on their fate at the bottom of the heap.

In this episode, Nellie Dingle, the doyenne of rustic white trash, was trying to get her no-good son Butch to do some work: 'I want this pigsty that clean that you can eat dinner off the floor.' No doubt baffled by this demand, Butch retired to the cottage roof with a six-pack to contemplate life's bitter mystery, while Nellie looked for him. 'If you've gone to that boozer, I'll geld yer,' she quipped.

Through this ruined landscape wandered Seth Armstrong, once the grumpy old cuss of the Woolpack, the oik with the ludicrous moustache whose chief function in happier days was to be patronised by Henry Wilks. In the mid-nineties he had mutated into a fond old man uttering homespun philosophy through that same moustache, a sethsayer who deserved a fee from the tourist board for his contribution to rural mythology. He was a relic of a kinder age who had seen more than he bargained for during his declining years: the Lockerbie-style plane crash, the subplots about child abuse, nuclear protesters, village vigilantes, and the endless infidelities – the whole attention-grabbing paraphernalia of the modern soap. A once charming rural idyll, *Emmerdale* had become a moral cesspit. But perhaps we the audience are to blame: after all, the producers are only trying to give us what we want, to boost ratings through sensationalism.

WHERE 10 DOWNING STREET IS MADE OF FIBREGLASS

Nonetheless, *Emmerdale* still kept a corner of its heart pickled for those who wanted its rusticity untrammelled by modern developments, if only in its opening credits. But by marginalising its rusticity thus, *Emmerdale*'s producers showed a disregard for what people want from their televisual Yorkshire. Yorkshire has been a county given over to nostalgia for a kinder, easier, more rural age – at least on TV. *All Creatures Great And Small*, the adaptation of James Herriot's novels about a rural vet, ran from 1978 to 1990 and was set, like *Emmerdale*, in the Yorkshire Dales; *Heartbeat*, the TV series about a copper patrolling the North Yorkshire Moors was set in 1964 but broadcast from the early 1990s onwards; *Last of the Summer Wine*, that near-death experience masquerading as a sitcom, declined to put both feet in the grave and instead filled our screens with northern pastoral for more than a quarter of a century.

But if you're unsated by watching such nostalgic, Yorkshire-based dramas on TV, you can visit the places where the programmes are set. This is TV tourism, as heritage-based and fantasy-filled as visiting Castle Howard or Chatsworth, or as watching *Pride and Prejudice*, and thus as much part of an Englishman's birthright as any other part of the nostalgia industry that booms in this once green and pleasant land. Even if *Emmerdale* has become perverted with tapas bars and wife-swapping, you can still visit the village setting of the drama to get a restoration of one's fantasy notions about what the soap, and by extension Britain, could and should be like. You can still find Beckindale pristine in the village of Esholt, near Bradford. You can't have a pint in the Woolpack, but you can look around the village, visit Kathy's Diner and nose around Home Farm as part of the Emmerdale Experience. You can visit *Last of the Summer Wine* country, too. If *EastEnders* and *Brookside* got their acts together, there could be tours of Albert Square, tourist knees-ups in the Vic and re-enactments of the siege at number 7 Brookside Close. Instead you have to go to the relevant Web pages to get virtual tours of both.

Perhaps it isn't such a good idea for TV programmes to have tours, since viewers already mistake what they see on television for reality, and encouraging them to visit the sets can only compound this. For instance, Bill Podmore, once producer of *Coronation Street*, recalled that in the sixties fans of the *Street* were so keen to see the facade of *Coronation Street* that they would risk being hit by trains as they passed through a railway goods yard so they could climb onto a viaduct and look down on the set.

Podmore wrote: 'I have no doubt many of those sightseers expected to discover the stars of their favourite programme living there permanently, and probably thought we just came along with our cameras on Mondays and Wednesdays to catch up on the everyday story of their lives. So often a character such as Hilda would be called on to wait behind the front door of her supposedly cosy little home, when in fact she was standing with teeth chattering and a freezing wind tugging at her skirt. Annie Walker complained her mouth was often so frozen, she had the greatest difficulty in speaking her lines.'

This fake terrace was enough to fool some of the people some of the time. But the original *Coronation Street* terrace, when the soap started in 1960, wasn't even an outdoor facade but a flimsy affair, constructed in whatever indoor space the studios would allow. Pavement and road were painted on the floor, and the set was contained within measurements so small that the writers had to take care that no one episode included houses at both ends. All the scenes had either to be set next to the Rovers Return or at the end of the Street with the corner shop.

In 1982, the Queen opened the newly-built Coronation Street, lovingly constructed from reclaimed Salford brick, and now more solid than ever. As *Coronation Street* got older it became more realistic – even as it passed into television mythology and thus could have been expected to become increasingly fantastical.

But what is reality? And to what extent does television drama supply it? And more importantly, why are there now three Rovers Returns in Manchester?

In 1988, Granada opened Coronation Street to the public, or rather it opened the street where the exterior shots are filmed to the public. Instead of scaling walls or risking being run over by trains, fans are now paying tourists. But still the confusion between reality and television persists. As they wander down Coronation Street, nobody can resist looking through letterboxes. Everyone becomes nosy here, hoping to see the Websters' horrible home in the raw, or even Kevin and Sally Webster themselves, but all are disappointed, since the interiors aren't used for filming. When I visited and looked through the Websters' letterbox all I could see was dust and some bits of wood. To make matters more complicated, not all the exterior shots of Coronation Street are filmed in this terrace either: for instance, Frisky the cat, who nestles under the eaves in the opening credits, was shot doing so in a Bolton terrace and the film was edited into the real *Coronation Street* footage.

In keeping with this semiotic multiplication, the Granada Studios tour has two Rovers Returns. One is merely a frontage for photo-opportunities, and for exterior shots. The other is a smaller simulation of the studio interior, where you can buy a drink, a pint of Newton and Ridley's, though that isn't the name of the brewers who make the real beer. There's a third Rovers Return, of course, where they actually film the stuff, but that isn't part of the Studios tour so you don't get to see that. This is a hall of mirrors, where nothing is real and appearance itself is no reliable guide. At least, that's what I told Michelle, the guide. But she seemed unimpressed.

Michelle, who forcefully declined to answer my pressing plot questions about bedhopping characters, ushered a group of us into the *Coronation Street* Experience. Just off the Street itself, this consists, incredibly strangely, of a rotating floor – like that of a bad seventies disco – overlaid with cobbles and crush barriers and thus redolent to me of Accrington Stanley Football Club's terraces in the late sixties. When the floor turns, visitors standing on the terraces are moved to face a succession of TV screens that tell some of the *Street*'s stories. There's Martha Longhurst, Ena Sharples and Minnie Caldwell sitting conspiratorially in the snug! Bet Lynch sliding into a lake in a Rover 2000 as Fred Gee looks on despairingly! There's evil Alan Bradley plunging under a Blackpool tram!

Despite the laboriousness of the concept and the snapshot brevity of this trip down memory lane by means of a turning terrace, the *Coronation Street* Experience was undeniably moving. There was one clip of Hilda Ogden, the comedy commoner, folding away Stan's glasses and silently putting them in their case for the last time. It was the early eighties. Stan was dead (admittedly after a tragi-comic sequence of episodes in which Stan was ill upstairs while all the world knew that he was not coming down again, since the actor who played him, Bernard Youens, had pre-deceased him by a few months), and for once Hilda was given her moment of dignity, touching our hearts with her grief. There wasn't a dry eye on the terrace – until somebody's mobile phone went off, anachronistically.

Tourists do strange things on the Granada Studios tour. John Churnside, a former Coal Board engineer who has been working as a tour guide and actor at Granada since the tour opened, said: 'I don't know if you remember, but Des Barnes [the *Street*'s Geordie bookie] once planted a money tree in his front garden. As I took the tour round the Street, people were throwing money under the tree.' The same sort of people, no doubt, who used to send Bill Tarmey (who plays Jack Duckworth) money to repair his glasses. Jack and Vera Duckworth had replaced Stan and Hilda as comedy commoners; as befitting Jack's lack of status, he pulled pints at the Rovers with one hinge of his glasses held together with tape.

If you lean over the gate to the Duckworths' back yard to see if there are any birds in Jack's pigeon loft (there aren't), you'll see that the gate is marked with graffiti. Joe Paterson, another tour guide who worked for Granada Studios for more than a decade told me: 'Some of the graffiti is real, some of it is put there by kids on the tour. It's impossible to tell which is which.' 'Real' here means applied by artists on the set; 'real' in other words, means fake. And yet it is fake graffiti that is more real than real graffiti would be, since it is seen by more people and thus holds its position in the world vigorously.

The philosophers Jean Baudrillard and Umberto Eco have written extensively about this phenomenon, the putative copy that transcends and even obliterates the original, but neither would be prepared for the semiotically dizzying experience of the Granada Studios tour. Fakery is the tour's true theme – Orson Welles would have loved it. On the backstage tour, you walk down a fake Downing Street, where you have to elbow aside families standing on the steps of Number 10 to get your own picture taken. This is a very odd thing to do, since all of us, unless we are very peculiar indeed, will try to pass off our photos as shots of the Downing Street in Westminster. Won't we? Maybe not. Roman, our guide, said: 'If you want to take a photo, do. Ours is better than the real one anyway.' Well said, Roman: this Number 10 may be made of fibreglass, and may have had its proudest moment in the adaptation of a Jeffrey Archer novel (how it must have suffered, poor thing!), but, by all that is Elsie Tanner, for northern tourists this photo-opportunity is much cheaper than one involving a return fare to Euston.

There's a Baker Street frontage, too, which is clearly much better than the one down south. In fact there isn't one down south; the modern Baker Street is more famous now as the headquarters of Marks and Spencer, and even though Baker Street Tube station has platforms decorated with Robin Jacques' illustrations to Conan Doyle's Sherlock Holmes stories, Holmes's flat at 221B Baker Street is not, because it cannot be, treated with the respect that it receives in Manchester. Sherlock's Baker Street never existed and there was never a 221B outside Conan Doyle's literary imagination. Fictional reality here is trumped, is made more real, by real fakery. I would have told Roman this, but when he saw me approaching he pretended to be talking to someone else.

Across the street from Granada Studios is the Victoria and Albert Hotel, which recognises its status as part of the TV fantasy land of this quarter of Manchester. Holmes and Watson also have their hooks in this place, too. There is a Sherlock Holmes restaurant – to tie in with the Granada TV series rather than the Conan Doyle books. The restaurant adjoins Watson's bar, with its tables of bubbling chemicals and sofas of babbling businessmen, and both are simulacra – putative copies of Edwardian rooms that transcend their originals and in so doing even obliterate the originals. And, indeed the V&A hotel, each of whose rooms is named after a television programme, is a 150-year-old warehouse that was opportunistically converted into a hotel when the Granada Studios tour opened in 1988.

The V&A doesn't embrace this mixture of TV fantasy land and archival funfair with as much enthusiasm as it might, though, not least because this is a five-star hotel with an upgrade policy for those who want slippers and baskets of fresh fruit added to the rich but nonetheless standard mix of trouser presses and hermetically-sealed shower caps, rather than a temporary home for telly addicts. As a result, you can't order wigs, gowns and gavels to act out your penal system fantasies behind the closed doors of the Crown Court suite. And you can't order Sweep and Soo from room service so that you can play puppets with your poppet in the Sooty suite. If this was a TV-themed hotel in the US you could do just that. If this was America, you could probably arrange to be awoken by a real-life psychopathic killer in the Cracker suite.

The Granada Studios tour, which has attracted more than five million visitors since 1988, doesn't just imitate the past; it affects to define the future. To mark its tenth anniversary in 1998, for instance, a futuristic white-knuckle ride called Skytrack opened, the first solocoaster, no less, towering above the Street. A warning sign said: 'Please secure or remove all loose items such as bags, spectacles, contact lenses, hats, footwear, clothes etc.' Not the sort of ride that would have appealed to Percy Sugden or Ena Sharples, then: cap, hairnet, stout, glasses, false teeth – they'd have all gone west as Skytrack plummeted pell-mell towards a semblance of oblivion. Now that's the kind of hyperreal simulacrum I'd have paid good money to watch.

SO MANY GOOD STORIES UNDER ONE ROOF

We don't want to see reality on television. That is too boring. We want to see its titillating imitation. Nowhere is this more true than in the mushrooming of docusoaps, that defining trend of late-nineties British television. Admittedly, these are not a radical new development – *The Family* was doing something similar a quarter of a century earlier. But one can understand the temptation to tap into this rich seam: no actors, no scripts, no narrators, cheap to produce and compelling to watch. The frisson of realism, too, is a key part in docusoaps' appeal – even if that frisson is based on a delusion. In reality, docusoaps privilege the self-regarding, the larger-than-life, those who don't mind making fools of themselves for the camera.

Once it seemed that the only stumbling block to the continued success of docusoaps was that the supply of patsies would dry up. But, given the pressures on documentary makers to produce cheap, glossy entertainment, they will be out there, hunting for subjects for their real-life dramas, for years to come. Not just that, but those who star in such programmes are likely to become celebrities. As Jeremy Beadle used to warn at the end of each *You've Been Framed* package of camcorder pratfallery: 'Who knows, next week the star of the show could be you.'

Sometimes, the fly-on-the-wall documentary maker wants their subjects to forget that the camera is there. That way they will be less able to perform and cultivate their own celebrity, that way they will be more likely to make fools of themselves without realising they are doing so for a mass audience. Digital Hi-8 technology makes cameras less obtrusive, improves the quality of images, reduces by as much as tenfold the costs of location work, and makes editing easier.

It was Peter Watson's 1974 fly-on-the-wall documentary series *The Family* which, without high technology, but arguably with base motives, first laid bare the intimate lives of a real British family, the Wilkins of Reading. For twelve weeks this was an unmissable soap, all the more so because it was real life – or so it seemed – unfolding before us. There were only two scenes the film-makers weren't allowed to capture: the Wilkins going to the toilet or making love. In a memorable exchange in 1988, Margaret Wilkins asked Watson: 'Why did you choose us?' 'Because you were just an ordinary, close-knit family who cared about each other,' replied Watson. 'Rubbish,' said Mrs Wilkins. 'You couldn't believe you'd found so many good stories under one roof.' Four years after the documentary was broadcast, Mr and Mrs Wilkins divorced. But Mrs Wilkins was perceptive. It's rarely reality that the documentary makers want to represent; like news journalists, they want good stories with bizarre twists and larger-than-life characters. If they shed any light on reality, it's merely a welcome bonus.

During the eighties and nineties, the trend for fly-on-the-wall documentaries developed with a programme about Queens' College, Cambridge, and Channel 4's portrait of Northwood Golf Club, whose committee resigned after they were depicted as sexist suburban snobs. The BBC countered with *Fishing Party* about four risible rich chaps – one of whom was fined after he was filmed shooting a seagull. The common appeal of these programmes was that they encouraged viewers to laugh at the foibles of the posh people who populated them. As for buffoonery, former England football manager, Graham Taylor, hardly had his reputation enhanced by the fly-on-the-touchline revelations of his rich command of Anglo-Saxon vernacular.

But it was *Sylvania Waters*, Paul Watson's 12-part docusoap about a rich Australian family shown on BBC1 in 1993 that arguably unleashed the flood of docusoaps in the mid-to-late nineties. The Baker–Donaher family were the flip side of the Wilkins of Reading: different hemispheres, different social class. Eight years after the soap opera *Neighbours* began, which had made suburban Melbourne seem so appealing, *Sylvania Waters* purported to show the real suburban Australia. Many Australians didn't like it, and the family was criticised there for their brashness, bigotry, hard drinking and smoking. Unlike glamorous, unimpeachable Scott and Charlene in *Neighbours* (played by Jason Donovan and Kylie Minogue), the Baker–Donahers were hardly good role models for Australians. Noeline Baker and Laurie Donaher were proud of the hard-working way they had earned their money and were determined to enjoy their lives to the full. The intra-family rows, especially between Noeline and her son Michael, and daughter-in law Dione's pregnancy, were staples of the the series, which was was narrated by the teenage son, Michael. If this was real Australia, Australians didn't want to recognise the fact, but everybody wanted to watch it. More likely, this wasn't real Australia, but instead confirmed stereotypes Australians loathed.

What was a trickle of docusoaps has since become a flood. *Airport*, *The Shop*, *The House*, *Lakesiders*, *The Cruise* – the addiction to pseudo-reality prevails. Add to these camcorder entertainments purporting to capture real life in the raw on film – *Police! Camera! Action!*, *Weddings From Hell*, *Neighbours At War*, *You've Been Framed* – and you have a picture of a nation of viewers that loves to watch real people making fools of themselves on television.

What intrigues me about programmes like *You've Been Framed* is their bad faith. The pratfalls are never fatal. There was once a programme called *And They Walked Away*, a magazine of near-fatal motor sports crashes, which could be passed off as acceptable because the racers who walked or crawled from the wreckage lived to be interviewed and so give their implicit imprimatur to the otherwise purely intrusive spectacles of them being cut from cars or spinning through the air. But what is entertaining here is the sight of someone else's misfortune. That said, there will never be a motor sports video clip show called *And They Didn't Walk Away*, for then such voyeurism becomes indefensible, becomes a sickness. Or maybe watching such near-death experiences is itself symptomatic of a sickness.

Speed, death, broken glass, twisted metal – maybe we're not so very far removed from the perverted protagonists of David Cronenberg's film *Crash*: we get our kicks watching crashes on Route 66. It's sad that, unlike the characters of *Crash*, we have to pretend that car chases are not titillating.

Something similar happens when we watch fly-on-the-wall documentaries, but with such putative slice-of-life programmes the narrator doesn't overtly reassure us; rather, the programme looks like it's real life, raw and true, and all the more edifying for that. But this is a delusion: instead, the instant stars of the Adelphi Hotel, Liverpool, who were the subjects of the BBC docusoap, *Hotel*, for example, played up for our delectation at the behest of exploitative documentarists. The result was a mutually-degrading spectacle that fed our appetite for making others look stupid.

And no wonder: the formats are cheap, often exquisitely if basely entertaining and, unlike the soap operas which they increasingly resemble, this seems to be real life, even though in the show real life is edited for entertainment value and producers focus on those who are most likely to perform for the camera. One of the results of this docusoap trend has been that several performers have used the series in which they appear to become celebrities. *The Cruise*, for instance, was the making of Jane

McDonald. Before the series began, the thirty-six-year-old cabaret singer was thinking of giving up her career, which had revolved around club dates in the North, to get married. But, thanks to the exposure she received on *The Cruise*, which was watched regularly by 12 million viewers in the summer of 1998, she became nationally known – so popular in fact that when she got married, 10 million viewers tuned into her one-off wedding special programme. But it didn't end there: shortly afterwards, her album topped the charts and went on to sell 100,000 copies. Later in the year, she performed a four-month stint at Blackpool Opera House. Once, it had seemed that those who starred in docusoaps were patsies who could only be exploited and humiliated by having their foibles broadcast to millions; but subsequently, thanks to the likes of Jane McDonald, the exploitation is the other way round.

THE SOAP OPERA HOUSE

Quality of access has become a touchstone for fly-on-the-wall documentary makers; the better a film-maker is at inveigling himself or herself behind closed doors, the better, the more revealing and thus, it seems to follow, the more realistic the final film will be. Ingratiation. Duplicity. These are the chief skills a modern documentary maker needs, as Michael Waldman showed when he made *The House*, a docu-soap about the workings of the Royal Opera House in the mid-nineties.

Waldman talked himself and his camera crew into situations in which access was usually denied. Again and again he slipped unnoticed into the woodwork when a particularly revealing meeting was taking place, and, as a result, he got, or thought he got, closer to the truth, closer to reality. Where some soaps, such as *Brookside*, have found their touchstones of reality in relevance to contemporary society, film-makers such as Waldman have found reality in revelation. True, he may not have been in the toilet with a diva or between two opera-singing lovers in bed, but if there was a revealing story between the sheets, Waldman would have been there with his camera crew.

And one can see what happens when a film-maker fails to get behind closed doors. Paul Beriff's 1996 series *Astronauts* was supposed to be the inside story on NASA's finest, the first time that a documentary crew had been allowed to film astronauts as they prepared for a mission. But Beriff elicited little more than NASA PR speak from the crew of the Endeavour space shuttle, Flight STS72, even though he had spent more than a year with them building up a rapport. Viewers are not interested in these difficulties: we are now so conditioned to expect that an observational documentary will get under the skin of its subjects, that the failure of a film-maker to do so looks like professional incompetence.

Michael Waldman said: 'One is persuading people, often against their better judgment, that there is more to be gained than lost from appearing. What you see is the consequence of my refusing to allow the door to be closed in my face three times a day.' This is true of all the documentaries he has made, from *Queens' College Cambridge*, the 1982 series which showed the quad squad in all their varied repulsiveness, to the two-part series about the behind-the-scenes work on the Olympic Games in Atlanta. Quality of access is all, which was clear in his preparatory work for *The House*: 'There were small negotiations early on to agree access, but having got that what's then needed is not to allow them to control what we're doing even though nominally everybody is saying that it'll be all right.'

When the first episode of *The House* was broadcast in 1996, critics were amazed that Covent Garden had allowed the camera crews in. But Waldman contended that the Royal Opera House supremo, Jeremy Isaacs, was shrewd for doing so. 'Isaacs said, "Perhaps we were naive." But Jeremy doesn't feel we abused his trust. He was slightly taken aback by what it all consisted of. The making of it was all-consuming. It was an endless game of political footwork.' Not to mention duplicity? 'There was a kind of duplicity about it. I couldn't say to the box office manager, "I understand you're about to be sacked, could I film it?" I couldn't say to X that I gather, on meeting A, you're likely to be sacked. Rather I would go to X and chat about the subject and reveal that they were having meetings and see how X reacted. One was juggling in one's head – it is intellectually very taxing. I was duplicitous in the general sense of not being able to reveal my knowledge.'

To be this duplicitous, Waldman had to ingratiate himself with everybody who worked in the opera house. 'I made it my business to form relationships with everybody from the handyman to the general manager.' And this paid off. He recalled filming a diva who was sick and yet still sang *Carmen*. 'I was doing an interview outside her dressing room door, listening to the music and knowing she would have to emerge at a certain point. At that point I hadn't gone into the dressing room because that would have been an interruption which would not only have been undesirable but intrusive. But the diva emerges and she faces the camera crew. She could have said get the camera out of here, but I took a deep breath and hoped she wouldn't. And she didn't: she thought it was nice Michael rather than the media. We had become part of the furniture.'

Is there more to his work than just intrusive entertainment? 'Heavens yes. It isn't just about a British opera house. It's about art in its widest sense. It asks the questions: what is beauty? What is splendour? It shows all the work leading to the pure beauty on the stage. It's also about Britain in the nineties – job insecurity, the class system.'

This is no doubt true, but perhaps the main reason *The House* and similar documentaries have been so appealing is that they disclose real life embarrassments at the heart of a British institution. The Covent Garden management was disturbed – but too late – that they had allowed their institution to become a soap opera house rather than an opera house. And, as the nineties went on, the Royal Opera House lost all credibility, both as a well-managed institution at the heart of British cultural life and, thanks to its closure, as a place where pure beauty or splendour could be seen or heard. This was hardly Michael Waldman's fault, and yet there is a great danger that the exposure of institutions in this way undermines their credibility rather than providing a helpful critique.

Waldman may console himself with the thought that his work on *The House* was chiefly about raising aesthetic questions or showing Britain's employment problems, but he was moreover supplying something much less easily defensible to an insatiable British viewing public. Thanks to his films, we became cruel voyeurs, enjoying watching others' mistakes. Better yet, these mistakes were being broadcast to millions around the country, thus intensifying the delight we could take in this public humiliation.

THE DARK AND BRUTAL SIDE OF TELEVISION

Just before Christmas 1996, the *Daily Mail* launched a campaign to 'curb the dark and brutal side of TV'. There was too much violence on television, it claimed, and the following day the then National Heritage Secretary, Virginia Bottomley, took up the theme. Or at least that's how it appeared: the Tory-friendly *Mail*, in fact, was preparing the way for a piece of politicking which, for anybody who reflected on what she actually said, seemed thoroughly cynical.

The *Mail* claimed that Bottomley's package would protect 'children from squalid and seamy programmes'. But what were those programmes that the *Mail* wanted to censor? It cited a scene in *Brookside* in which Beth and Margaret engaged in a lesbian kiss, arguing that this courted controversy. This was very puzzling: was the perfunctory kiss on the doorstep supposed to be an example of 'dark and brutal' television? No? Then perhaps it was 'squalid and seamy'? If so, that was puzzling, too. Who deserved to be protected from the fact that some women like to engage in same-sex, up-against-the-door snogs? Perhaps, the *Mail* sought to protect men in Tunbridge Wells who were hitherto like Queen Victoria, blissfully ignorant that such sexual activity took place. But, if they were ignorant, an additional argument needed to be given to explain why television should collude in keeping them so: didn't the old Reithian notion of broadcasting recommend that it should inform and educate as well as entertain? In what sense was a lesbian kiss controversial? What would be really shocking, surely, would be the revelation that lesbians don't kiss.

But this didn't seem to have much to do with television's dark and brutal side. Nor did *The Girlie Show*, which the *Mail* also singled out. The Channel 4 show had featured topless bungee-jumping over the Thames and a report on naked fat men. One presenter had a pierced belly button and fantasised about having sex in the rain. *The Girlie Show*, cancelled by Channel 4 after its second series, was always worthless, but the attention the *Mail* gave it was the sort of publicity that couldn't be bought. Let it be said, firmly, though, that when topless bungee-jumping, broadcast after the nine o'clock watershed, causes offence, it only does so to those who affect to be offended, by those who can reassure themselves about their moral purity even while they become voyeurs; the pretence of offence, after all, is what keeps the *Mail*, that bastion of British ethical duplicity, in white-hot moral rage year in year out.

But again, this seemed to have nothing to do with darkness and brutality. Instead, the *Mail* had brought in the Trojan Horse of TV violence and then released from it all the things it loathed on television: a heroin-related murder on *Brookside*; an incestuous relationship between a teenage boy and his half-sister born to a prostitute in *The Bill*; a gay kiss between Tony and Simon in *EastEnders* (which had been, in any event, cut short by the BBC shortly before transmission). But the *Mail*'s condemnation of *Cracker* did, at least, have something to do with its headline condemnation of TV violence. It cited Jimmy McGovern's drama about a multi-addicted criminal psychologist and his investigations of violent killers, as particularly dark and brutal. *Cracker* had already been censured by the Broadcasting Standards Council for an episode in 1995 which included two repulsive scenes. In one, blood was seen dripping through the ceiling from a murder victim on to another woman. In another, the victim's dead body was shown to be heavily bloodstained. The BSC upheld complaints that these scenes were unnecessarily graphic and went beyond the bounds of respectability. Over the years, the BSC has only upheld a few complaints against programmes that have transcended the bounds of respectability: *Cracker*, *The Governor*, Yorkshire TV's drama about prison life, and *Silent Witness*, the BBC's series about a pathologist.

What was striking about all of these programmes was that they included scenes that were deliberately shocking. Arguably, given their subject matters, they would have failed if they had not shocked: if audiences can watch programmes concerned with serial killers, the grimness of life in prison, and people who have suffered violent death, without seeing something dark and brutal, then something has gone terribly wrong. Perhaps the failing of, say, *Cracker*, was that the scene of blood dripping through the ceiling was dramatically contrived and thus appeared not to be taking its repulsive matter with proper seriousness. Better that, though, than the movies of the true glamorisers of violence, the Hollywood moguls, who saturate their films in violence without consequences; or, if their violence has consequences, then they are ones drawn on a cartoonish moral canvas.

Bottomley even conceded that there had been 'a fall in the number of incidents [of television violence], but that it is the nature of those incidents that we are concerned about'. But in her condemnation it was difficult to work out what she was objecting to. This was telling, since Bottomley's failure to be specific, like the *Mail*'s appropriation of lesbianism and topless bungee-jumping to assist a crusade against TV violence, was surely intentional: it set a nebulous political context in which anything anyone didn't like about the content of TV programmes could be deemed part of Bottomley's clean-up campaign. Bottomley said she was worried about 'very haunting, very powerful pictures' of violence on screen. This was as specific as she got. But that wasn't good enough, since haunting images of violence on television are often perfectly defensible. It's hard to think of more powerful images on screen than the crucifixion in Pasolini's *The Gospel According to St Matthew*, or the repeated slow-motion sequence of the second bullet ratcheting President Kennedy's head back in Oliver Stone's film *JFK*, or the news reports that showed bodies lying on the Sheffield Wednesday pitch after the Hillsborough disaster. Each one of these scenes has a defence for being dark and brutal; more than that, each one has a moral force absent from Bottomley's cunning politicking. The first two examples also have some aesthetic quality, a quality which is only enhanced by the unflinching way in which the violence is depicted. In *JFK*, for instance, the use of the slow-motion newsreel footage of Kennedy's assassination again and again during the film, would seem to be the worst kind of exploitative horror when taken out of context. In context, however, it expresses the grief that many felt not just at the president's death, but at the haunting horror of the way in which he died – an image that several generations, quite properly, cannot shake from their consciousness. Haunting? Powerful? There would be something wrong with someone who was not disturbed by watching this scene.

Virginia Bottomley also talked about children. Surely they should be protected from horrifying images of violence? This was connected, albeit nebulously, with a feeling that children were exposed to too much violence when they watched television. According to *White Dot*, a monthly anti-television magazine published in the United States, the average American child will have witnessed 8,000 television murders before he or she finishes elementary school. But what are we to infer from this? That it is better for children to see no violence on screen? That television destroys innocence? That television turns children, the suggestible and the unsuggestible alike, into violent youths? No, what we were meant to infer from this rhetorical deployment of murder, is that television is a demonic force out of control.

And yet these fanciful fears are allowed to thrive when newspapers like the *Mail* and politicians like Virginia Bottomley conduct moral campaigns that fail to address the difficult issues. In the histrionic climate to which they contribute, distinctions are steamrollered along with the difficult ethical issues about the proper role of the parent in protecting children from violent images, or which horrifying images they should be allowed, perhaps even encouraged, to see.

But the debates about the alleged ill-effects of television rarely get into the difficult areas. Take the researchers at the Johns Hopkins Bayview Medical Center. The *Daily Telegraph* reported in April 1998 that that these researchers had 'found a direct correlation between juvenile obesity and the hours spent viewing television. Children who watched four or more hours of television a day were significantly fatter than those watching fewer than two hours – having been robbed of exercise time and encouraged to consume high-calorie snacks and fizzy drinks'. If this was a fair report of the researchers' findings, then they deserved to be taken from Johns Hopkins and placed in a darkened room with only television re-runs of *National Lottery Live!* for company and force-fed supplies of pop and crisps until they recanted their belief that their evidence led to the conclusion. Clearly, these fat, square-eyed kids were fatter because of the pop and crisps and because, after four hours in front of the box, they or their parents or guardians didn't think it appropriate for them to go into the street to chase hubcaps or kill cats or whatever it is that passes for healthy exercise these days. Television no more 'robs' children of exercise than reading Tolstoy does. And yet the myth that television is necessarily harmful to the physical and mental development of children is allowed to persist.

THE CRUSH AT THE BOTTOM OF THE LEPPINGS LANE STAND

In 1989, ninety-six people lost their lives at the bottom of the Leppings Lane stand at the Hillsborough football ground in Sheffield during the FA Cup semi-final between Liverpool and Nottingham Forest. They were trapped by high security fences from escaping the overcrowded stand. Many of them were crushed to death. Five years later, Jimmy McGovern wrote a drama about these events and their aftermath.

His film started in a flurry of happiness. We flitted from one Liverpool-supporting family to another. Brother and brother, father and son, father and daughters, were all playing the same joyous game: teasing each other about whether they had tickets for the match. The precious tickets repeatedly appeared, held brightly aloft, and yet we the viewers understood they were one-way passages out of this world. It was a powerful opening which gave us an immediate emotional link with the victims: they were blissfully oblivious of their fate, while we knew that their happiness was dreadfully misplaced.

This was one of the most upsetting two hours of television I have ever seen. In one key scene, repressed and rational Trevor Hicks (Christopher Eccleston), who had just identified one dead daughter, was refused access to the makeshift morgue where he feared he would find his other daughter. The bodies were now the property of the coroner and he has no right to see, let alone claim the body, said the policeman barring his way. For once Hicks lost his temper, and I was surely with him, the righteously angry man treated with contempt by those ill-equipped to wield authority. Here, as in other little scenes throughout, I felt something of what it was to be on the receiving end of such institutionalised inhumanity.

Pain and anger were very much part of the proceedings, as they always are in McGovern's charged dramas. Indeed, as the victims' families struggled for justice in the disaster's aftermath they were shown at first behaving placidly, deferring to barristers and court officials. When their anger finally exploded after the inquest jury gave its verdict of accidental death on the Hillsborough victims, the representation of their rage was scorching, all the politesse of their earlier behaviour cast aside. If their exasperated anger was something we could not share, we could at least feel it thanks to the caustic power, particularly, of Ricky Tomlinson's performance as bereaved father John Glover, bawling at the shocked jurors after they had given their verdict.

It still remains for me one of the most powerful moments in television drama, not so much for its eloquence, but for its cunning manipulation of dramatic tension, for its daring as a piece of realistic drama. Few television writers – and who could blame them? – would have the confidence to risk unleashing the anger of the bereaved and then let it trample the feelings of all those in its way. Indeed, when I watched this scene, I felt some sympathy for the inquest jury: it wasn't them who were responsible for the deaths at Hillsborough, and surely they didn't deserve to be on the receiving end of John Glover's wrath.

'That was the one scene where I gave myself a wee bit of flexibility, because it wasn't actually like that at the inquest,' said

McGovern. 'The families internalised all that anger, but I gave it to Ricky to say.'

It was a typical McGovern scene, the writing of a man who is, if not quite a conspiracy theorist, then one who revels in spinning moral webs that entangle the unwary and the complacent. 'I remember saying to a parent who lost her child at Hillsborough that if we'd lost the Falklands War, her child would still be alive.' What bottle for saying that, or perhaps, what tactlessness. What did he mean? 'In 1982, Mrs Thatcher was the most unpopular prime minister in history. Then she sent young men to die in the Falklands. 1983, landslide in the election. 1984, smashed the working class [during the miners' strike], gave the coppers huge pay rises. By 1989 there was a police force that served only one master – the Tory government. Then Hillsborough.'

Everybody is to blame – even us sitting in our armchairs watching Ricky Tomlinson march up and down in front of the inquest jury, allowing his long-bottled-up frustrations to spill out. True, this didn't happen. True, we had entered a fantasy invented by the writer. True, it was the most upsetting, conflict-inducing scene in the whole drama. But then reality isn't the most significant thing to which we can be exposed when we watch television. For being merely presented with reality doesn't help us understand it; we can learn from drama because of its creative engagement with reality. If *Hillsborough* had merely reflected reality, after all, the families' anger would still have been hidden in their breasts. McGovern, through fiction, made it clear, messy and real.

CHAPTER 7

1987: The World As It Appears

BRYAN MAGEE'S CALVES

Sometimes, when two talking men sit in swivel chairs on television, my eyes trail down their bodies, down, down, until I reach those two inches of flesh just above the sock line. Those inches of leg tell me middle-aged men are talking too seriously to worry about how they look. As they talk, the trouser legs rise – two inches, three inches, four, five, more. There have been times when I've sat watching a man – Tony Benn, for instance, God bless him and his cotton socks – so carried away with what he was saying that I have thought that, any minute now, I was going to see something very special – a man's bare knee on television.

Sometimes I think those two inches of male calf are a rebuke by certain men to women. There they are, as matter of fact as you like – inches of shin, skin and bone, men's abject counter-revolution to women's sexual revolution, men's insistence on the insignificance of appearance, their denial of the sensual world. Men's unalluring nakedness on television tells viewers that bare flesh has no power, no aura, that it isn't a secret worth concealing. That was one way in which I saw these programmes, but I also thought for years that these inches of skin were a sign that the discussion would be worth listening to.

When the BBC broadcast *The Great Philosophers* in 1987, there were no swivel chairs, only a big, sagging sofa in which even the greatest philosopher would get as lost as if they were in the recesses of a particularly tricky part of the *Critique of Pure Reason.* They wriggled and writhed there week after week, and my eyes occasionally wandered to those inches of flesh appearing on screen.

I was intrigued to see if *The Great Philosophers* would work as a television programme, not least because I had studied philosophy at Oxford only three years before. I had swivelled, too, and I had sunk deep into the corduroy of a G-Plan sofa while I read out my essays and my tutor fiddled with coffee filter papers. When I finished reading, the earnest work of discussion would begin, and, as if to underwrite its loftiness, my tutor would sink deep into his chair and cross his legs. One calf would be exposed – that symbol of philosophical activity ever since Socrates stood unashamedly for hours in a town square thousands of years ago possessed by some puzzle and with nakedness measuring itself up from the top of his sandals.

The Great Philosophers consisted of fifteen weekly 45-minute programmes during which the host, Bryan Magee, discussed a philosopher or group of philosophers with an eminent specialist. From Plato to Wittgenstein, we followed a history of western philosophy of the kind that has been attempted many times in books but never before on television.

Of all academic disciplines, philosophy lends itself least to television. There are no meerkats in philosophy, and little opportunity for nice graphics. Incidental music doesn't help. *The Great Philosophers* consisted, as it had to, of pure discussion. But instead of a seminar with several guests, Magee chose to have dialogues, like my Oxford tutorials but with less coffee and fewer diversions into discussing films. Shockingly, there was only one woman in the whole series, Martha Nussbaum, who spoke about Aristotle, but for the rest of the series – in terms of gender at least – this could have been the Garrick Club, all self-assured, calf-exposing men sunk deep into the upholstery.

In his memoir, *Confessions of a Philosopher* (not as raunchy as it sounds), Magee wrote that he was criticised for not making proper use of television; he had not, apparently, appreciated that it was chiefly a visual medium. There is something in this criticism, but not much. True, television is overwhelmingly visual. And, true, now and again during the series, my glance would wander down to A. J. Ayer's legs as he spoke, nearly as well as he wrote, to check on his bona fides. But that very wandering was part of a deficiency in me caused by years of watching television and expecting to have my eyes gratified at every moment.

In fact, in the context of the rest of TV's output, *The Great Philosophers* was refreshing – even visually, since there was so little in the series to divert the eye. There were swivelling men elsewhere on television, but they were generally fractious couples. Most television discussion programmes, as well as relatively intellectual news programmes such as *Newsnight* or *Channel 4 News*, are combative affairs, with interviewees writhing in the upholstery as they wrangle with each other. Television discussion between talking heads has become as adversarial and thus as unsatisfying as the two-party political system. Indeed, there is a symbiotic relationship between television and politics: TV reduces politics to soundbites or facile dispute; the British political system offers television the lively but ultimately shallow adversarial debate that has evolved from the very confrontational structure of the House of Commons.

On *The Great Philosophers*, by contrast, men spoke with a grace that the medium has not often tolerated. Television hasn't just killed the art of conversation in living rooms; it has done so in the studio, too, reducing it to fractiousness or fatuity. In this context, *The Great Philosophers* was refreshing, even otherworldly. For example, in one programme, Magee discussed Immanuel Kant's philosophy with Geoffrey Warnock:

'First of all Kant tried to deal with what he called the Form of Sensibility or rather the two Forms, Space and Time. He argued that these were imposed upon our experience, upon the world as object of experience, but the nature of our sensibility –'

'I'm sorry, I want to interrupt you there because I think this is an extraordinarily difficult idea for many people to grasp. Kant was arguing that space and time do not characterise things as they are in themselves . . .'

'Yes indeed . . .'

'. . . but are inescapable modes of experience for us.'

'That's right.'

'So although it is only in those two dimensions that we can experience the world, they cannot be said to exist independently of us and of our experience.'

'That's certainly right. If you raise the question: "What about creation as it is in itself, what kind of spatial and temporal order does it display?" Kant would say "Not a discussable topic." All we can talk about, he insists, is that world which is an object of experience to us, the world as it appears.'

This dialogue brings into focus two things about the rest of television's output. First, that rarely do we see an interviewer insist on pausing in order to clarify or reiterate a point for the viewer. Secondly, that only very, very rarely does television stretch most people's intelligence.

In his memoirs, Magee conceded his TV television programme was very different from his philosophy seminars. In the latter, he could pause to allow students to mull over what they had just been told or discussed, but this was not tolerable on television. The best he could do to simulate this pause for reflection, was to use repetition at certain points. In seminars, too, he could allow questions, but television – then, at least – was not able to allow viewers to put questions about what they had heard to the participants.

When I read this, I thought wouldn't it be lovely if there was a television programme that paused for a moment and, instead of filling the screen with images, left it blank for five or ten minutes so that viewers could reflect on what they had seen? Wouldn't a pause not only be helpful, but pleasant, so that we could reflect on the discussion we had just witnessed? But, again, so little of television's output is substantial enough to warrant such a pause. Nor is it demanding enough for the presenter to say: 'Hang on a minute. What we're talking about is so difficult that we ought to express that fact so viewers don't feel left behind. And perhaps we could take this opportunity to reiterate what we've been talking about so far.'

Television doesn't dare to do this. Instead, it fills the screen with more and more information, and less thought. On the Bloomberg business channel, for instance, there is often an index of share prices rolling like moving subtitles at the bottom of the screen and also on the right a panel of currency values. All this information is thrown at the viewer while the newsreader talks or interviews. Football news programmes on Sky and some music video channels use the same techniques. Sport and business have become ideal forms of a certain kind of television: they thrive on information – statistics, scores, prices – rather than thinking. And because such information can be graphically shown on the screen, they seem to be lively affairs that exploit the medium to the full.

In this era of information overload, what seems intolerable is a series in which people sit and talk about something which might stretch viewers' intelligences. I can't imagine a series such as *The Great Philosophers* being commissioned at the end of the millennium. This is sad: there clearly is a great popular desire to read and reflect on philosophy – the sales of Jostein Gaarder's book, *Sophie's World*, alone surely shows this. Commissioning editors don't trust their audiences to watch programmes in which participants do nothing more visually enticing than swivel, carried away with their thoughts.

Perhaps intelligent television can only be made when there is a marriage of argument to image – as there is in the best natural history programmes – or when visual storytelling is especially entertaining and informative. Perhaps commissioning editors are right to think that this sort of swivelling discussion programme only works on talk shows like *Vanessa* or *Oprah*, where nobody's intelligence gets stretched at all, or news magazines like *Newsnight* where the emphasis is often, too often, on confrontation.

Having been brought up during the era of public service television, when there was some hope that a mass national audience would be educated by means of watching television, I hoped for more. Television, since the war, has been a medium of unprecedented cultural power that could have educated a nation of viewers about many things. It could have stretched our intelligences and given us a national identity based on shared experiences of something more than the Queen's annual speech or Cup Finals. But, because television has been so often surrendered to mere visual stimulation, our shared experiences have been impoverished. True, the Open University has educated millions, but it is hardly prime-time programming. We know next to nothing about philosophy thanks to television, but lots about the nocturnal habits of cute animals.

DAVID ATTENBOROUGH WHISPERING IN THE BUSHES

Life on Earth began with David Attenborough emerging from the bushes in his short-sleeved shirt and matching flares. 'The South American rainforest – the richest and most varied assembly of life in the world,' he began. When he crouched to point at something, there was not a hint of flesh above sock which, to my mind, was an unforgivable lapse, for Attenborough was and always will be a member of that threatened species, the intelligent broadcaster, carried away with a subject that was difficult to understand but very important.

A flurry of images followed as Attenborough warmed to his theme: 'The orchid needs the bee to pollinate it. The anteater couldn't have existed before the ants. So unless the whole complex was brought into existence by one flash of instant creation, different organisms must have appeared at different times. Which came first and why should there be such an immense variety? Such questions occupied a twenty-four-year-old Englishman who came to these forests in 1832. His name was Charles Darwin.'

Later, we cut to a graphic depiction of the double helixes of DNA. It was so difficult to understand I could have done with one of those pauses for reflection which Bryan Magee wanted. Better yet, I could have done with a video of the series, so that I could pause, rewind, replay, reflect. But this series was broadcast before I owned a VCR. The series was as dense as a book, but its graphics were of the kind that could only be shown then on television. Thanks to his narration and the unfolding helixes, I felt I understood the intricacies of DNA better than any science primer I have read. Better than that, I had the singular experience that others around the country were finding out something difficult too; they were having their intelligences stretched thanks to the use of a mass medium for something enchanting and worthwhile.

Most of the time when we watch nature documentaries, though, we kick back on leopardskin sofas, flick off our loafers made from gophers, grip our remotes with opposable thumbs and enjoy the parade of furry cuties doomed to extinction thanks to their evolutionary inability to adapt quickly enough to a world that we are busy adapting into oblivion. We don't learn very much at all.

The natural world doesn't exist for us to learn about it; rather, it's there so we can change it to make our lives more pleasant. For example, there are lemurs who live in the wilds of Madagascar whose existence is under threat. They live mostly on the forest canopy and have white fur crash helmets with black faces and black ears peeping out. John Cleese once made a documentary about them. They are as cute as buttons. They look like living Oldenburg sculptures, but that won't do them much good when they are in a high-speed collision with the forest floor, that's for sure.

If one of these lemurs did fall from the top of its tree, it would become too ugly to appear on television. This must not be allowed to happen. We must send very small, very hard crash helmets to Madagascar now to avert the extinction of this species. Send postal orders to Headgear for Lemurs as soon as you can. No donation is too small.

Imagine what a lovely film that would make: lots of furry cuties swinging from tree to tree in protective headgear supplied thanks to your generosity. True, a few of them might get strangled with the crash helmet straps or inadvertently suffocate, but wouldn't it all be worthwhile just to see how giving you were and how cute they are?

Only rarely are nature documentaries not complicit in exploiting the natural world for our delectation. Only rarely do we learn something about the natural world that's worth learning. When this happens, we are usually watching David Attenborough. Often, he tells us something much more interesting about the natural world than we could have expected. For example, carrion crows that lived in Sendai City in Japan found walnuts hanging from trees, but their beaks were not strong enough to crack the nuts, nor did they break if they dropped them from a telegraph pole or a lamp post. Instead, some of the birds would wait above traffic lights and drop the nuts in front of stationary cars. When the lights turned green, often the cars would roll over the nuts. Then the crows would swoop down and pick up the pieces.

On *The Life of Birds*, the BBC's 1998 series, we saw this in action. A crow, unnoticed by pedestrians, walked among them and picked up bits of nuts, carefully striving not to be run over. This was a magical combination of intelligence and visual sense. We could not help but focus on the ingenuity of the crows and so learn about their evolution in a man's world.

Attenborough's *The Life of Birds* was one of those series that only the BBC makes. It consisted of ten weekly episodes. It took three years to make, involved forty-eight cameramen and women in forty-two countries, 200 miles of film and demanded that Attenborough flew 256,000 miles – appropriate for a series about birds. This is the sort of series that David Attenborough has liked to make and that we have loved to watch for more than two decades. They have earned the BBC lots of money through sales abroad and video receipts.

And yet, when Attenborough came to make the first of these series, *Life on Earth*, in 1979, there were those who thought it was a bad idea. He recalled how he was told by one of his bosses: 'Thirteen hours? What do you start with? Green slime? A fifty-minute programme about green slime to launch a series that is going to take thirteen hours? You must be nuts!'

The problem with television is that increasingly there are too few people working in it who are nuts, too many dreary suits who want to crush nuts under the wheels of their boring Series 7 BMWs. There are too many people who commission programmes that risk nothing, there are too many very sane people who are passionate about nothing very much, but rather believe themselves to be cunning about giving people what they want.

Television at its best, though, gives people what they don't yet know they want. The best entertainment, the best educative and informative programmes are all like that. Before they existed, we didn't know that they would be entertaining. Before *Life on*

Earth existed and we were enchanted by David Attenborough whispering in the bushes as a group of gorillas sat menacingly nearby, we didn't know that natural history programming would captivate us so. The most truly creative programmes on television have been ones that have changed us in this way. They have created new forms of entertainment rather than providing variations on old themes that inevitably have diminishing returns over time. Instead of being enchanted, we inevitably become disenchanted with programming which only offers a choice between formulaic sitcoms or worthless docusoaps.

Among those truly creative programmes, the special ones that make television exciting, the best have been those that do not insult viewers' intelligences or assume that they haven't got the attention spans to watch thirteen-hour series or three-hour dramatisations. If the programmes are good enough, viewers will watch them. This was the sort of principle that inspired David Attenborough when he became controller of the fledgling BBC2 in the mid-sixties. Sound reproduction was improving then, and colour TV was being introduced, so he commissioned *Civilisation*, a series about beautiful things with beautiful music. Kenneth Clark's series wasn't the only ground-breaking successful programme Attenborough commissioned: he was responsible for *The Ascent of Man*, *The Philpott File*, *Cameron Country*, *One Pair of Eyes* – some revolutionary, some failures, but all risky.

Television has risked so little in recent years because too few people working in it believe in the Reithian ideals of public service broadcasting. This is understandable, for we can hardly return to Reith's world in which patronising broadcasters told people what they ought to listen to or see. And yet, surely, we can retain the best of the Reithian philosophy. There must be more creative risk and more scope for failure. Often the characteristic experience for me is to watch television and find it hard to choose between programmes that are all eminently missable and yet mildly entertaining. The growth of thematically organised cable and satellite stations prevents me stumbling across something that might move or enchant me and instead makes me by turns bored and anxious. Television needn't be like that.

David Attenborough survived by learning how to evolve. He found himself in a hostile world and yet adapted by means of a specialism that nobody else thought worthwhile. While other programme makers and commissioning editors prepare themselves for extinction because their programmes are so similar to others, Attenborough will endure if only on the video shelves and on repeats. As yet, he has no offspring on TV to carry his genes.

CHAPTER 8

1988: A twentysomething-thirtysomething

YOU'RE NO CLARK GABLE, HONEY

When I'm unhappy, I sometimes pretend to be an American. I put on a red poncho and matching woollen hat, perhaps an old pair of clogs, and go out with a spring in my step and a smile on my lips. 'Isn't it just great to be alive?' I shout to the pitbull convention in the park. Then I stand at a major crossroads with my hands on my hips and an expression that says: 'Hot diggety! I love this crazy old town!' Then, for sheer joy, I try to throw my hat into the air. Often, a passing cyclist will yell: 'You're impersonating Mary Tyler Moore, right?' 'No, Rhoda Morgenstern, you yutz!' I reply. One day, just one day, I am going to get that hat airborne.

For me, the point of American television is to cheer up tight-assed Britons, to make us forget the rain, to cure us of the Seasonal Affective Disorder that affects us each and every season. We are transported to a land where people have good teeth, more foundation cream than Brazil has coffee, hardwood floors and well-behaved, doe-eyed children. We are taken to a place where characters have nice little problems and impressive muscle tone.

It's good to watch American TV shows because they end happily. Each week at the conclusion of *Scooby Doo*, the evil, ugly, old guy will be unmasked and, just before the cops take him away, will blame those 'darned kids' for trapping him. In the epilogue of *The Streets of San Francisco*, Karl Malden will often make a lame joke and then will nudge Michael Douglas sharply in the ribs: 'Am I right, Steve? Ha? Ha-ha-ha-ha!' 'Yeah, chief,' Douglas will reply respectfully. 'Ha-ha-ha!' And then the credits roll. Nothing can go too badly wrong, and when it's time for bed, everyone will be safely home and tucked up. *The Waltons* regularly ends with the family shouting goodnight to each other from bedroom to bedroom of their vast house on Walton's Mountain. 'Goodnight, Jim Bob!' 'Goodnight, John Boy!' ''night, ma!' 'night, pa!' 'Jesus, grandpa, don't you ever think to cut your toenails? Why don't you go back to your own bed!' 'Hey, you guys, can it! We gotta go a-cow tipping tomorrow!'

But *The Waltons* is only a special case of the archetypal American TV show ending. It's very reassuring and goes a little like this: 'I love you, mom.' 'I love you, too, son.' 'I love you, dad.' 'I love you, too, son.' 'What about you guys?' 'Oh, sure, we love each other.' 'I didn't hear you say it. Will you say it now, please?' 'OK, son. I love you, Clint.' 'And I love you, too, Tippi-Anne.' 'That's not my name.' 'Don't spoil the ending, baby. I love you.'

And before the endings, there are dramas, but only ones that are appealingly trivial. In *Beverly Hills 90210*, for instance, nobody has anything much to worry about, but they have to worry just a little, otherwise the show wouldn't last more than five minutes. As a result, everyone is regularly conflicted about something or other. Brandon is conflicted about his lovers, Valerie about her mother, Ryan about his hair gel, Tom about his singlets. That kind of thing. The parade of bland beauties is so intense that I often wish I was Deryck Guyler, that grouchy old Limey stiff who appeared regularly in *Sykes* and *Please Sir!* and who was a virtuoso on the washboard. I would like to put Brandon or Valerie on my lap and strum their perfect stomachs until they didn't worry any more. 'Gee, that's real nice, Stoowart,' Val would say, 'but have you ever thought about seeing a dentist? I mean, yellow isn't this season's white, if you know what I'm saying. And the bad breath – I mean some guys could get away with it, but you're no Clark Gable, honey.'

I loved *Dallas*, too, because everybody had too much teased hair to be truly troubled, but they all affected to be vairy, vairy angraiy. I knew that the names were too daft and the stories too cock-a-maimie for me to take them seriously. For instance, after Jock Ewing died in that helicopter accident in South America, Miss Ellie married Clayton Farlow, a man with two surnames. These were reassuring handles for a grieving oil widow. 'Clayton' she cooed across the pillows, but if she forgot that name, 'Farlow' would have done just as well.

In *Dallas* there was a Leland Vaughn, a Casey Denault and a Carter McKay. Or maybe they were all the other way round. Lone Star State men were men, after all, and proper first names were for fags or Limeys or Limey fags. There was a character in the series merely called Sly, but not for long.

Women's names were a different kind of puzzle in *Dallas*, especially because they were pronounced so strangely. Swellin' was JR's alcoholic wife. Looseat was the pint-sized firebrand in red quilted jacket with matching gingham blouse. Pamair was either Bobby's wife or a Texan charter service. Sometimes, true, Bobby became Bobair and, to my mind, the resulting rivalry between these two aviation firms explained the couple's marital problems. Pamair was flown by Victoria Principal, which is an extraordinarily presumptuous surname, pronounce it however you will.

But women were always baffling in *Dallas*, especially to JR, a man who had a permanent crease in every pair of trousers he wore. In the very first episode of this, the most successful soap in TV history, for instance, Swellin' had been shopping for something to turn her man's head and had come up with some lacy lingerie: the sexual politics of *Dallas* bore not an instant's investigation. She showed her husband her underwear proposal and he showed her his best sarcastic glare. 'Hmm. Mmm. Well!' he said. There was and never would be any Swellin' in his permanent crease.

JR didn't have much more comprehension of Julie either, all teased hair and lip gloss, the woman who could have been his wife but had been terribly disfigured in the Fort Worth blow-drying accident of 1984. (You remember, the one that the Second Warren Commission tried to cover up. Who now remembers the second Clairol blowing from the picket fence? Who? No one – that's who.) 'Why?' he asked her. 'Why?' Julie, who had been spurned by JR one night and had immediately seduced Cliff Barnes, had betrayed JR. 'Why?' he asked again. He would never find out and I would never care.

It was all too wonderfully absurd. The names, the sexual politics, the dead budgerigars that seemed to decorate the hatband of JR's stetson, the rather nice office that JR occupied all conspired to make me forget about the whys and wherefores. In American television, the whys are hardly ever worth the attention.

DECOROUS NEUROSES

Sometimes, though it was different and I was supposed to take the problems of American TV characters seriously. This was very hard work indeed.

Once in *thirtysomething*, Michael came home from work and found Hope in the kitchen banging the wall with his racketball shoe. It was a lovely evening, the sun streaming through the windows, little baby Janey – all seventeen inches of her – sitting in her chair bathed in a heavenly glow. Michael looked good in his braces, and Hope looked good too, her hair tied back and her bone structure on display. They had made some good choices with the kitchen decor, and the hardwood flooring was to die for. But there was trouble in this domestic paradise. There were bugs in the house, and they menaced the perfect family.

'I'll call the exterminators tomorrow,' said Michael. 'They'll spray the place.' 'They'll come back in different strains,' said Hope. 'So we'll re-spray again,' said Michael. 'Janey will grow up stunted,' said Hope. 'So we'll move,' said Michael. 'We can't afford to move,' said Hope. 'We can't afford to live here so what's the difference?' asked Michael. 'I hate everything except Janey because she's perfect,' said Hope. 'What's not perfect?' asked Michael.

It was a dialogue from a self-help manual, the kind of conversation deconstructed in books like *Men Are From Mars, Women Are From Just Outside West Bromwich*: the woman complaining and the man wanting to make things right quickly so that he doesn't have to listen to her moan.

But Michael had a good point. What wasn't perfect? To me, twenty-five and back from work, slumped on a foam-filled sofa bed, stressed and sweaty, this sunny corner of Philadelphia looked offensively perfect. I lived with Kay in a huge house in London that had been meanly converted into ten flats. Our flat was a little box that would have probably accommodated Michael's sports shoes at a pinch. The living room was so small that I didn't need a remote to change channels without leaving my seat. I was wearing a suit I'd bought from Camden Market for £14 that pinched under the arms and flapped below the groin. If I had worn braces they would have probably pinged into my face. I had a bone structure, but not one you'd want to write poems about.

Outside, the Talbot Horizon was cooling its smug self after bunny-hopping me through the north London gridlock. The car was, I knew, preparing a whole new range of motoring miseries for tomorrow. Often, the Talbot Horizon made me think of the torture scene in *Elizabeth R*, BBC1's historical drama starring Glenda Jackson, in which some bloke was dissected while still alive and presented with his heart for his screaming inspection. It was that kind of car. Nothing was perfect.

In *thirtysomething*, everything was perfect. Even the bugs had probably just come out of a grooming salon. If you looked through a microscope you could see that they had cheekbones every bit as good as Hope Steadman's. Some of them spoke Latin with very authentic accents and spent their summers at their Tuscan villa, one reading Nietzsche aloud and the others nodding sagely. Then they would come back to Philadelphia to play racketball with Hope in the kitchen. It wasn't a bad life by any means, and I would have swapped mine for theirs.

The only problem for the bugs and for Michael was Hope. She was a Canute, trying to stop the waves of real life from washing over everything she held dear. She would never be happy until she learned not to mind those waves of reality lapping over her ankles.

When I first watched *thirtysomething*, I thought that it showed a world of feelings from which a chilly, emotionally repressed Limey could learn. I thought this televised corner of Philadelphia could give me a sentimental education. From it I could learn how to behave with my partner. But it wasn't like that at all. Instead, it was a place where I would do better to keep my eyes on the interior decor and ignore the reactionary social message. At first, though, I was impressed by how seriously the show took itself, and I thought I ought to take it seriously too.

Back in her kitchen the following day, Hope said: 'Can we never fight, please?' 'We never do,' said Michael. 'We don't need to fight because we have a great thing here.' 'Do we have a happy marriage?' asked Hope. 'I think you're like not supposed to say it out loud,' said Michael, smiling sentimentally. Their happy marriage, their seeming perfection, was porcelain: they daren't raise their voices for fear of shattering it.

Something was still wrong. The cockroach episode of *thirtysomething* included a scene that the programme makers also used on the opening credit sequence each week. Michael and Hope lay on the floor of the nursery with warm sun streaming in over their lovely bodies. He was bare-chested, she was wearing a grey singlet and grey panties. She was lying on top of him. They looked fantastic, all appealing muscle tone and clean, well-conditioned hair. Then baby Janey crawled into shot. In the credits, this was a nice comic moment, underpinning a scene of domestic bliss. In the context of this episode's drama, though, this was the moment the sex scene started to go wrong. Hope said she'd put baby Janey to bed so that they could make love. Michael started to leave the nursery. 'Grab that laundry, please?' Hope asked. 'Ha?' asked Michael soulfully or stupidly, it was hard to tell. 'That laundry you walked by without seeing it as usual.' That was what Hope thought was really wrong. Not the bugs, though they were a problem. It was Michael. He just didn't pull his weight domestically. Or maybe it was Hope. When they preparing for love making, she tried to get Michael to think about the laundry.

The series set up a social hierarchy that made its ideological message clear. At the top was Hope, the wife with sensible earrings and the pointy nose that made her other features seem equally severe. She was the mother in an idealised marriage. Michael was Jewish, warm and easy-going, while Hope was as taut as her tied-back hair. The daughter of a Calvinist, perhaps.

'Do you guys yell?' Elliot asked Michael in the office one day. 'She never yells,' replied Michael. 'I want to yell sometimes but I don't. Probably I should sometimes but I don't.' 'I yell,' says Elliott, sadly. But Michael didn't shout because he dared not disturb Hope. He didn't shout at his wife because that would stop his marriage seeming to be perfect. 'You guys don't yell because you're perfect,' Melissa tells him. The Steadmans had a lot of stock in everything being perfect. The admiration of the Steadmans' friends and their own self-esteem depended on this seeming perfection.

But there was a cost to all this. What kind of a recipe was that for perfection? Michael should have yelled at Hope. And she should have yelled right back at him. Otherwise they had an anaesthetised marriage in which they bottled up resentments and lived precariously so that anything – the bugs on the wall, the kid on the floor – could destroy it. This is what made *thirtysomething*'s notion of marriage so implausible to me: Michael and Hope were supposed by their friends and, arguably, by the proselytising scriptwriters and the creators Marshall Herskowitz and Ed Zwick, to be perfect. But they were not and could not be so, since they did not shout at each other. Their perfection was a sham. But American television was often like that for me: it offered a perfection that was only superficially alluring but deeply shallow.

Elliott and Nancy were next on *thirtysomething*'s social ladder. Nancy below Michael and Hope because her marriage was much less stable than theirs. Nancy above Elliott because he was a childish soul. You could tell that simply by looking at his shirts, the breast pockets saturated with dark colours that clashed with the rest of the shirt and with his tie. You could tell that he was a child, too, because when he tried to be nice to Nancy, to reassure her, he always blew it. In this episode, Nancy asked him for some reassurance: she wanted to write a children's book after spending five years on her own at home bringing up children. 'I don't know if I can do it or not and just need a little encouragement.' 'I think you would write a wonderful children's book and fourteen publishers would want it and you'd make $100,000 and we could move out of this house and I wouldn't have to work any more.' It didn't take a rocket scientist to recognise he was being hostile. He was angry that he had to go to work while Nancy stayed at home.

In a bunch near the bottom of the ladder, away from the sun

rays that bathed Hope and her baby, were Ellyn, Melissa and Gary, the neurotic singles. Melissa was depicted regularly as a wreck of a human being, desperately trying to get into a steady sexual relationship so that she could have a child and therefore silence that noisy ticking of the biological clock that filled her nightmares. In one episode she even had a fantasy sequence in which she was in a boxing ring wearing gloves and fighting with herself. Her friends were her seconds or her spit-bucket guys. Fighting with themselves – that's what single thirtysomethings did in *thirtysomething*'s unforgiving world; they didn't even argue with their significant others as Nancy and Elliott did; still less were they as seemingly serene as Michael and Hope, though that was what they aspired to be; instead, they were self-absorbed. Self-destructive Melissa, that kooky chick who sometimes wore braces over a singlet to hold up her baggy pants. She was a photographer who lived in a voguish loft apartment with exposed brickwork; a woman who finally opened her heart and her duvet to that very, very young boy artist who never took off his fingerless gloves even when he was indoors. Melissa would never be as serene as Hope.

And Hope's friend Ellyn was even worse than Melissa. She was a career woman with a top job at City Hall. But she didn't have time for a date and wound up in hospital bleeding from the stomach ulcers caused by the stresses of her job. That's what you get for being a single career woman in *thirtysomething*, girl. As if it wasn't punishment enough trying to get some action on the singles scene. 'You don't know what it's like,' Ellyn told Hope. 'It's a complete desert out there. Most people's idea of a great first date is a complete physical.' Much better to be married, preferably with children. In the opening credits, Ellyn was depicted sitting on a chair sexually seething in a short skirt and tight top – a study in frustration.

In later episodes of *thirtysomething*, Hope returned to work. She was a magazine researcher but could not keep pace with the twin demands of raising a child and working in a competitive job. So she quit and went back home. The episode concluded with Hope dancing around her sunny room with her baby in her arms again to the tune of Van Morrison's 'Tupelo Honey':

She's as sweet as Tupelo Honey
She's an angel of the 10th degree.

That four-in-the-afternoon sun shone through again on that smug breeder's serenity and little Janey. That was the real lesson for Ellyn: she should go home and make babies.

And Gary, the guy who looked like Björn Borg's taller, goofier brother? He was single, and so had to suffer. He had to be punished for the crime of being over thirty and not yet married. Once he tried to pull a nubile young student in a hardware store. But when he went back to her place, where, like a Monty Python milkman he thought that he would get some action, she only allowed him to repair a leak in her sink. It was the sexual humiliation of a man who should have acted his age instead of chasing tail.

Eventually Gary got involved with a stereotypically humourless feminist called Susannah. It was tough for Susannah because she was at the very bottom of *thirtysomething*'s hierarchy. Hope even sneered at her behind her back. And it was clear to me why: she rejected Hope's values. She didn't want a baby. When she first became pregnant, she contemplated an abortion, but eventually gave birth. Early in 1991, Gary, her live-in lover, was killed in a car crash. The dual punishment was complete according to the principles of *thirtysomething*'s creators: the laid-back guy who didn't see fit to get married had to die painfully; the feminist had been turned into a mother, but she wouldn't have a happy family to rival Hope and Michael's. She would suffer as a single parent.

As a twentysomething, I could see these thirtysomethings

thought they had problems. And yet, I wanted to have their lives, or more precisely their homes, their bodies, their clothes, their racketball shoes, that little basketball and hoop set that Elliott and Michael played with in their office. Sometimes the sun came through the little windows of our flat, but not often. And if we had had a baby and I had danced around the living room with it, I would have banged my child and myself against the bookshelves, the table, the sofa – maybe all three at once. One of us would have wound up in casualty and the other in care. And, if I'd played Van Morrison, dancing around the tiny coffee table with my baby held aloft, the neighbours would have banged the plasterboard walls until I stopped. When we shouted, I suspected that tenants throughout the house gathered in a bed in one of the rooms and cowered from the noise. Either that, or they laughed at the absurdity of our anger. When I wasn't banging into the walls, I was out in the street, putting plastic padding into the rusting wheel arches of our Talbot Horizon, respraying it or working to get the money to have the car's hopeless gearbox fixed. I don't remember Michael or Elliott doing anything like that. Life for them was too beautiful, even when it was miserable.

Not that I was complaining, but when I watched *thirtysomething* my overwhelming impression was of beautiful people in beautiful homes with decorous neuroses. Their neuroses were supposed to be the main focuses of the story, as were the moral and social lessons about love and marriage touted by *thirtysomething*'s scriptwriters, but I saw these as backdrops to more pressing issues on the show. At work we wondered about the show's lighting: was it really that sunny in Philadelphia or was that a simulated heavenly glow created in Studio 7? For pasty-faced, repressed Limeys who lived in a rain-soaked dime of a country, this wasn't a small question. I wondered, too, about Venetian blinds – would they look as good in my home as they did in Hope and Michael Steadman's? I was too absorbed in questions of these kinds to take seriously its undoubtedly reactionary message. In *Backlash: The Undeclared War Against Women*, Susan Faludi argued that *thirtysomething* proposed men should go to work and women should stay at home and have babies; anything else was punishable by car-crash death or disastrous spinsterhood. For me at the time, though, unmarried and living with Kay, both of us working hard and unable to afford children even if we had wanted them, this message seemed as distant as the sun that bathed *thirtysomething*'s world. This was a fantasy land that could not set the agenda for my life; instead I separated its material delights from its social agenda. I wanted the Venetian blinds and hardwood floors, I wanted a house as big as the one in which we lived but not divided up into ten flats; down the line maybe I wanted babies, too, but I did not want my partner to become as smug and yet brittle as Hope. And there was no way, no way that I was going to become like Michael. If I had to choose which one of the *thirtysomething* cast I would want to be, it would clearly have been Melissa, barren, screwed-up Melissa, poor Melissa achingly envious of Hope and Michael; daft, vulnerable Melissa who was proof to my twentysomething self that thirtysomethings needn't be repressed and neurotically obsessed with shoring up themselves against imperfection.

If I had taken *thirtysomething*'s social agenda seriously, I would have been a fool, since it advocated a way of life contrary to the one that I wanted to live with Kay. I wanted a happy, materially secure, sunny life, yes, but one that didn't become smug and defensive, one that didn't become boring or insistent on perfection.

This was the moral I took away from American drama: nice apartment, shame about the political message. But that spoiled my pleasure, since my own sub-texts proved much more engaging than whatever values the dramatists were trying to instil in me, or whatever the story was about. Even in the life and death of the *ER* room, for instance, when the human viscera are exposed on the operating tables, I cannot help but be distracted from the surface drama. Hasn't Julia Margolyes got fantastic eyebrows? Does Anthony Edwards' goatee really work on a man with such otherwise ill-defined features? Isn't George Clooney just too ludicrously good-looking to be working in what passes for a public health service in the United States?

A THIRTYSOMETHING-TWENTYSOMETHING

In 1988 I was a twentysomething watching thirtysomethings; in 1998 a thirtysomething watching a twentysomething who, like Hope Steadman, seemed to be a role model, though of a very different kind. When *thirtysomething* was first broadcast, there was a great deal of debate over what it said about American society, American mores, the backlash against feminism. The same happened when *Ally McBeal* was shown. Was she a feminist crusader in a short skirt or a post-feminist reactionary who was using her looks to advance her own selfish ends? For a little while I tried to watch the show with this question in mind, but ultimately abandoned making a decision.

As always seems to be the case for me with American dramas, it was the backgrounds and the sub-texts that proved engaging and enjoyable. In *Twin Peaks* I was much more engaged by Agent Cooper's trips to the diner for coffee and cherry pie than by the shaggy dog murder story. The distressed walls of the office in which Ally worked were very appealing. It would be so nice to work there rather than in my overcrowded office which had gaps on the floor where the carpet tiles should be. And her apartment, too, was very pleasant; not quite as desirable as Frasier's with its fine view over the Seattle skyline, true, but lovely in its own way. But more lovely than either of these were the customarily beautiful actors who thronged every episode. Perhaps this is why so many American programmes are about law firms – not because they encourage constant engagement with moral issues, but rather because lawyers have to wear smart, expensive clothes and work in smart, expensive offices and so, to make the equation complete, they must be staffed by people whose faces and bodies don't clash too much with the decor or the wardrobes.

This time, though, I felt angry about being manipulated into taking this character as a serious representative of anything. When I was a twentysomething, I was somewhat engaged by the stories of *thirtysomething*; now I was too old and sceptical to be suckered into accepting, not only Ally McBeal's persona, but the framing of questions about her significance. The intense debate about Ally McBeal's role in the battle for women's liberation seemed to be a manipulative device on the part of the show's makers and a supine media that missed the real point: Ally McBeal was too self-absorbed to be representative of anything but herself.

In 'Compromising Positions', for instance, the second episode of the first series, Ally, having been recruited into a law firm where her old boyfriend works, was worried that she had been taken on chiefly so that her looks could be used to lure clients and win cases. And there was doubtless something in this: during her first case she defended a co-worker who had been caught *in flagrante* with a prostitute, but the judge was prepared to dismiss the case with one proviso. He demanded only that Ally bare her teeth to him before he made a decision. 'Excuse me?' she asked. Bare the teeth, he repeated. She did so, and he dismissed the case. Outside court she learned that the judge also had a history of consorting with prostitutes and so did not really want to convict a fellow lawyer of crimes that he had also committed. The thing about the teeth? That was just the judge's whim.

Ally was angry, as angry as any feminist would be in such a situation. She had been manipulated into helping uphold a male conspiracy. She had been treated as something less than a well-qualified lawyer. She was trapped with a sexist employer who exploited a sexist legal system. Her body rather than her brain had been the focus of attention, even in court.

In the context of the script this was all true, but, really, anyone who worried about such issues was making a mistake. The real purpose of the courtroom scene was so that Ally McBeal could walk back through the windy streets to her office looking decorously lugubrious. There was a slight parting to her pouting, too-full lips, the wind swept her hair over her lovely eyes, her long, thin legs exposed, her hands pushed deep into her jacket pockets or crossed crossly under her breasts. She spent a lot of time walking through the streets in this and later episodes, looking beautifully grumpy as her voice-over meditated on whatever cruel fate had befallen her – so much time in fact that to me her beautiful, sulky appearance was the text and whatever it was she was complaining about only a pretext for her to walk down streets that will beautify her grumpiness and expose her appearance to the camera for as long as possible.

And when, later in the episode, she had a goodnight kiss with her firm's prospective client (as her sexist boss had hoped – the creep!), she didn't kiss him full on the mouth but turned slightly away from his so that her pleasingly demure face was tilted towards the camera, so that we in the audience could be part of her narcissism. We could enjoy looking at Ally who enjoyed being looked at and who – more than anything else in the world – took pleasure in her appearance. We became a surrogate mirror reflecting back our approval. We became complicit in her self-regard.

Now and again the script legitimised Ally's narcissism. Her flatmate was written as nothing but a cipher whose life revolves around Ally's intsy-wintsy-teeny-weeny life problems. Better yet, Ally's flatmate was black, which was effective for the construction of Ally McBeal's liberal self-image, but rather less so for a black character who was forced, as so many black American TV and movie characters have been, into a servile dependency relationship with a white character, while the white character was depicted as no longer racist because of their association with a black character.

In 'Compromising Positions', too, Ally intruded on other people's intimate conversations so that she became the key player in every drama. She told her boss that she had seen his girlfriend kissing another man and agonised about whether she should have done so – so much in fact that her moral agony became more intense than the misery of her boss. And later, when she learned that her former boyfriend was poised to admit to his wife that he had been unfaithful, she broke up their conversation in order that he couldn't reveal the truth, a truth, which, she decided, would destroy his wife.

Why was she so intrusive? asked her ex-boyfriend. 'I have this desire to butt into everybody else's business. I think I need to believe that it works – love, couplehood, partnerships. The idea that when people come together, they stay together. I have to take that with me when I go to bed at night even if I'm going to bed alone. That's a McBealism,' she concluded, as though she had said something profound.

It was a McBealism, too, one that revealed the paradox of her solipsism. For her other people only exist to help her reflect back well on herself. As a result, she could never have a partnership that worked, never have love that was based on mutual respect rather than one that was based on serving her need for approval. Couplehood? The only long-term, intimate relationships that Ally McBeal could have are with the mirror or the camera. She is an ideal TV character since for her to be is to be looked at.

There was an episode in which she fantasised about having a baby and, like *thirtysomething*'s Melissa, worried about the ticking of her biological clock. But for her the phantom baby that came to life dancing in her fantasy was a baffling problem. What was this perplexing, freaky thing before her? Would she have to love it? Would she have to look after it? No! She, for good or ill, could never repeat that scene in *thirtysomething* when Hope danced with her baby in her arms. When Ally danced as she did often, she did so mostly with herself – flanked by friends, to be sure – but with herself and badly, in order to relax or to steel herself for the tough world out there that she confronted each day. It was a world that existed to blow her hair appealingly across her eyes as though her life was a fashion photo-shoot.

FRIENDS FROM HELL

They killed him. They jumped on the man's ceiling, all six of those gorgeous narcissists, until he was wheeled out of the building to his final resting place. But that's what the characters in *Friends* did: they stomped on strangers, literally or metaphorically, until they changed countries or died.

Heckles had to be killed. He was a stock irritant, an ugly man in a shabby dressing gown over a stained T-shirt. It was symptomatic, though, of American sitcoms' unwillingness to deal with the truly seedy that his hair was always nicely conditioned and blow-dried. He was also obligingly bonkers. Heckles complained about the noise from their apartment: 'You're doing it again.' 'We're doing *what* again?' 'You're stomping. It's disturbing my birds.' 'You don't have birds.' 'I *could* have birds.'

Having heckled, Heckles went back to his apartment: 'I'm going to rejoin my dinner party.' As if. Nobody outside the charmed world of this sextet had dinner parties, or even lives worth talking about. Everybody else was sad, lonely, uninteresting, vulgar, but, above all, burdens on the beautiful sixsome.

Then he banged on the ceiling with his broom. And they stomped back. Didn't they realise, these self-regarding high-rise dwellers, that those of us cursed with ground-floor flats can hear every move they make, every breath they take, and every beat of their crummy Sting albums? But back to the plot: they stomped;

he banged; they stomped harder; he had a heart attack; they stomped; he died. To me, the scene symbolised the fact that beneath *Friends*' glossy comic surface was a drama of fear and hatred. It was very lovely comic surface that made me laugh a great deal: it reminded me of what P. G. Wodehouse said about writing novels. There were two ways: 'One is mine, making a sort of musical comedy without music and ignoring real life altogether; the other is going right deep down into life and not caring a damn.' So long as I could hear *Friends* as a musical comedy without the music, everything was fine, but I could only do that for the length of time it took to tell a joke. After that, I could hear it fall deep and dark into life, into a hateful relationship with the real world. If only, like the fans of the show, I could have stayed on the surface.

In one episode, for instance, Chandler realised that he was too demanding of prospective girlfriends – they always had some minor flaw which turned him off. Nostrils so big that you could see your date's brain. A New York accent so strong that it made Jackie Mason sound like Prince Charles. That kind of thing.

But that was typical of the way the Friends interacted with the outside world. Each new boyfriend or girlfriend sent a frisson of anxiety through the group that grew into a wave of revulsion. Marco, for example, Rachel's sexually-charged beau, seemed to have it all – Italianate looks, charm, names for both her breasts. For the breast-naming thing alone, he earned the other guys' contempt; then, when he manoeuvred on the massage table so that Phoebe suddenly found herself massaging a new set of muscles, he clearly needed to be reported to immigration and sent back to Rome. And when Emily, Helen Baxendale's Limey chick, hauled Ross off to London to marry him, this was only so that Ross and Rachel could renew their nauseating romance. Phoebe's short-lived psychiatrist boyfriend pointed this out: in *Friends*, any interloper, by interloping, deserved to be punished.

As a result, the romantic dramas of *Friends* – Ross and Rachel,

Monica and Chandler – were tantalisingly paradoxical. When these couples had sex together, for me, it had the aura of incest; and yet, they *had* to have sex with each other. How could Friends have sex with anyone outside their charmed circle? The rest of the world was too drab; to express commitment to anybody outside the group would be an intolerable betrayal.

Friends were the counterpart to Ally McBeal. They could only have sex with each other, and yet even that would be a perilous business. Ultimately Ally McBeal could only enjoy sex with herself because she would be the only one worth that attention, and yet such sex would not be good enough since there would be no one around to reflect back their necessary approval to her. Perhaps she could have asked the camera crew along to film her.

A SHOW ABOUT NOTHING.

Perhaps I liked *Seinfeld* so much because it was overtly about nothing, while many American programmes broadcast on British TV are about too many putatively emotional issues to be wholly appealing. Instead of being concerned with self-image or perfection, instead of overtly attempting to instil values, *Seinfeld* confidently immersed itself in trivia.

'I think there's a huge market for nothing,' Jerry Seinfeld once said of the sitcom in which he appeared, as himself. 'Nothing is in very short supply.' And he was right. In the mid-to-late nineties, *Seinfeld* was the most popular sitcom in the United States. More importantly, it was so popular with American 18–34-year-olds, deemed by advertisers as the biggest spenders and the easiest to influence, that it cost more than $400,000 for a thirty-second commercial spot during the show. In 1997, three stars of the show threatened to quit unless their pay was increased from $150,000 per show to $600,000. They were angry that Jerry Seinfeld, star and writer, had been given a pay award that put him on $1 million per show. Seinfeld, in an admirable display of solidarity with oppressed millionaires, said he would quit too if his colleagues didn't receive what they were claiming. They received their award and went on to make the eighth series. Not bad for a show about nothing.

Seinfeld took the petty neuroses and obsessions of other American programmes but did not take them seriously. Instead, *Seinfeld* played them for laughs. There was a motto among the writers and actors on the show – 'no hugs, no learning' – since so many US dramas and sitcoms (*thirtysomething* is just the best example) ended with sentimental hugs and unconvincing learning.

Seinfeld was never like this. Instead, each episode would be about nothing important and at the end nobody would have learned anything at all. One episode was about hiring a tuxedo ('There's a thrill – wearing a suit that's already been worn by eighty high-school guys on the most exciting night their glands have ever known'); another about a dry cleaning mishap ('What the hell is dry cleaning fluid? It's not a fluid if it's dry').

The most appealingly petty scenes were set in the local restaurant where Jerry Seinfeld and his insecure friend George Costanza would sit talking about nothing important. 'Look at this woman feeding her baby greasy disgusting coffee-shop corned beef hash. Isn't that child abuse?' asked Seinfeld. 'I'd like to have a kid,' Costanza replied. 'Of course, I need to have a date first.'

Sometimes they would be joined by Elaine (Julia Louis-Dreyfus), a character as pettily obsessed as Seinfeld. 'Who do you think is the most unattractive world leader?' she asked. 'If it's all time, there's no contest: it begins and ends with Brezhnev,' Seinfeld replied. 'Did you ever get a good look at De Gaulle?' 'What about Lyndon Johnson?' 'I've got news for you: Golda Meir could make them all run up a tree.'

'I'm an idiot,' George Costanza told Jerry Seinfeld once. 'You may think you're an idiot,' replied Jerry, 'but with all due respect

I'm a bigger idiot than you.' 'Don't insult me, my friend,' Costanza replied. 'Remember who you're talking to. No one's a bigger idiot than me.' I loved these exchanges: I wanted my friends to talk this way, to live in a fairyland of trivia and no commitments, to hear only this music of comedy – the flipside of *thirtysomething*.

George and Jerry met one day shortly after Jerry had broken up with a woman. 'She eats her peas one at a time,' said Jerry of Melanie, the woman fated as a result to become his ex. 'It takes hours for her to finish her meal. Corn niblets she scoops, but with peas it's one at a time.' 'One at a time?' asked incredulous George. 'Yes. That was what was so vexing.' Here Jerry and George realised that they were boys, not men and that when they did anything – broke up with girlfriends, quit their jobs, they would learn nothing. When Jerry tried to date a woman, he asked her: 'So, do you date immature men?' 'Almost exclusively,' she replied.

This, I realised, was mostly what I wanted from American TV – decadent, immature lives performed on TV for my pleasure. Ally McBeal's agonising? The moral self-righteousness of *ER*'s Dr Green? Hope Steadman's self-defeating quest for perfection? You can keep them.

UNDERACHIEVERS, AND PROUD OF IT

The Simpsons may have been set in the United States, but I loved it because it seemed so British. Admittedly, it fitfully laughed at the British, but even that was funny. When the show's dentist wanted to scare kids into scrupulous dental care, he showed them pictures of the British Royal Family. Pictures of yellowing teeth in disease-ridden mouths. 'You wanna wind up like these guys?' he asked. 'Do you?' I had to admit he had a point.

I quickly came to love *The Simpsons* because it exploited the comedy of failure, and that sort of comedy was part of Britain's broadcasting heritage, embedded in the national TV culture in which I was steeped.

As a result, to me, Homer Simpson was an honorary Briton because like Del Boy Trotter, Basil Fawlty and Harold Steptoe he was a ground-down anti-hero who was designed to be laughed *at*, hardly ever *with*. 'OK, brain,' he said when required to re-take his High School exams. 'You don't like me and I don't like you. So let's get through this, and I can get back to killing you with beer.' Even his paternal advice to his son Bart was hopeless: 'Son, when participating in sports, it's not whether you win or lose, it's how drunk you get.' This was the key difference between *The Simpsons* and that other US blue-collar sitcom, *Roseanne*: in the latter, for the most part, I laughed with the Conners' doomed struggles against adversity; in the case of the Simpsons, I often laughed because Homer was wallowing in failure and now and again had a tiny window on that failure, a tiny perspective through which came his ironic commentary on the mess of his life.

Homer may have suffered from radiation poisoning from working at Springfield's nuclear power plant, may have had his most intimate relationship with the telly, may have been addicted to beer and doughnuts, may have been intellectually inferior to his dummy-sucking daughter Maggie, but he was happy.

As in *Roseanne*, there is a double-edged celebration of blue-collar US culture: Kwik-E-Marts, Monster Truck Rallies, and doughnut concessions jostle for attention, but in Springfield there is a total absence of early music festivals and not one decent German literature club. It was the flip side of the American Dream. For the most part the Simpsons' America has stopped dreaming and instead has found succour in alcohol-fuelled conformism or by celebrating its mediocrity in a way alien to Hancock, Fawlty or Del Boy. Their feelings of shame, embarrassment or doom came from a British culture ill at ease with itself; the Simpsons were rarely so insecure. 'Underachiever and proud of it', was Bart's T-shirt slogan, and the shirt sold more than a million a week to US schoolkids at the end of the eighties. State schools banned it, but the slogan expressed a culture of cool anomie.

In a sense the *The Simpsons* had to be a cartoon, for it was in this form that Americans have been able to contemplate the hilarity of failure: the rake that would smack Tom in the face whenever he rounded the corner in pursuit of Jerry; the 500-foot drop that would open up below Coyote as he pursued Roadrunner over the cliff. The lingering double-take to camera, the rapid descent into converging verticals. In the US, when real actors appear on screen, such failure was not permissible.

George Bush rounded on the show in his '92 election campaign. 'We're going to keep on trying to strengthen the American family,' Bush claimed. 'To make the American family more like the Waltons and less like the Simpsons.' A bizarre way of devising social policy, whichever family you chose as the role model. When the clip was shown during *The Simpsons* Bart retorted: 'Hey, we're just like the Waltons. We're praying for an end to the Depression, too.'

One of the main virtues of *The Simpsons* was its cheery subversiveness. Much American comedy, though verbally biting, is timid in what it will represent or criticise. The dysfunctional alcoholics of *Cheers* were never depicted as drunk; yet, Homer and the other habitués of Moe's Tavern are virtually always drunk and stupid. The contented smoker is also excluded from sanitised American programming; and yet barely an episode goes by without Marge Simpson's husky-voiced sisters sucking noisily on twin king-sizeds. You will rarely see a parent shaking his boy by the throat: in *The Simpsons* this image of bad parenting is so regularly deployed that it has become a T-shirt illustration. American television culture privileges the beautiful and the healthy, but *The Simpsons* strikes a blow for the ugly and the the burger-obsessed. The characters may be two-dimensional and yellow, but they are more rounded, more real than the characters of *Ally McBeal*, *thirtysomething* and *Friends*.

Even at the level of animation, where it has been unfavourably compared to the sophisticated graphic artistry of *Ren and Stimpy* or *Two Bad Dogs*, the show is deceptively rich. *The Simpsons* family may look like yellow freaks with four fingers (it was a particular delight when Marge counted to five and had to transfer to a second hand) and preposterous overbites, but they have a remarkable amount of cartoon heritage written into their features. Homer's brown five o'clock shadow echoes the depiction of lower-class types from *The Flintstones* to the Ant Hill Mob in *Wacky Races*. The drawing eschews the thin-lined figures of Hanna Barbera's proto-dysfunctional toon, *Wait Till Your Father Gets Home*, preferring more readily identifiable caricatures which are nonetheless sufficiently schematic not to have the poncy finish of, say, Disney's menagerie or *Roger Rabbit*.

Like the best American TV imports, it is almost profligate with its gags – visual jokes abound behind the action, as do film references, some of which I didn't get the first time around. There is a justified assumption among the makers that some viewers will tape the show, play it back and dally with the pause button. There is a spirit of generosity towards the viewer that is all but inconceivable among British programme makers.

I'M GONNA KICK HER FREAKIN' ASS!

The Jerry Springer Show is like a trailer-park *thirtysomething*. Emotional issues get aired, people share their feelings to therapeutic effect. The main difference is that Jerry Springer's guests have not taken Hope Steadman's strictures about yelling to heart. They yell, they say things that they really should, but probably won't, regret, they fight, they tug each other's hair – or at least they did until Springer's show was compelled by Studios USA in June

1998 to drop all physical violence from its broadcasts. To me, this was like a Football Association regulation forbidding the scoring of goals during matches. *The Jerry Springer Show* was, until then, as rule-bound as any other contact sport: it started with blank-eyed looks, moved, as night follows day, into vulgar exchanges, escalated into one brief sucker punch, and culminated in a mêlée in which the security boys, who all looked delighted to be engaged in this diverting line of work, restrained all-comers.

Without this progression from glowers to mass brawling, there is no show, since the dramatic climax, such as it is, is denied. This progression and the satisfying thought on the part of the viewer that they would not be deprived of fisticuffs was surely what made *Springer* bigger than *Oprah.* True, some of the fights are staged but, as with wrestling, this knowledge does not deter the enthusiasm of the studio or TV audiences. Sometimes, too, the fights were not staged, since the vengefulness that resides in the breasts of Springer's guests clearly sometimes leaps into spontaneous hate. You only have to look into their blankening faces to see that the train of violence is steaming down the tracks and due to arrive any moment.

And, just as *thirtysomething* was to me not so much about emotional issues as about nice decor, so *The Jerry Springer Show* isn't so much about healing purgation as an extended homage to the feather cut. Never since the Bay City Rollers' heyday have there been so many dodgy hairdos and sartorial mistakes in one room. It inspired me to develop a variant of phrenology, whereby those with the worst haircuts are likely to do the worst violence.

The hair issue is rather different when women fight. If I had a penny for every time a security guard on Jerry Springer had bawled, 'Let go of her hair!' or 'Act like a lady, not a bar-room thug!' (which always provokes the rejoinder: 'I *am* a lady. I'm gonna kick her freakin' ass' – except they don't say 'freakin'), I would have enough money for a nice rinse and set. A woman guest is introduced, marches on, and before you can say 'Blimey, look at the bird's nest on that!' another woman is holding on to her locks for grim death.

The Jerry Springer Show has a limited sense of the permutations of human fallibility. I'm a Teen Call Girl! I'm Sleeping With Your Man! It's Your Bachelor Party . . . Or Me! My Sister Slept With All Three of My Husbands! These are just some of the chapters in the decline of the human spirit Springer has chronicled. There is never anything about the more difficult strife that humans endure. My Mother is a Hydrofoil! I'll Never Understand Predicate Calculus! I'm Too Stupid to Live! These are the shows that Springer would never dare to make.

Hannah Arendt coined the phrase 'banality of evil' when writing about the Nazis, and this phrase recurred in my mind while I watched Jerry Springer. Not that Springer is evil, though he is certainly banal. Rather he is morally contemptible, maintaining a physical distance from the grubby stage drama both in order to avoid getting hurt and to confer on himself ethical credibility.

Worse than all that, though, is his Final Thought, the dime-store philosophising that is supposed to justify the foregoing brawls. 'How boring life would be if there were no outrageousness,' he said once. True. But hold on. 'Television doesn't and mustn't create values,' he added. 'It's merely a picture of all that's out there – the good, the bad, the ugly. A world upon which we apply our own values, learned and nurtured through family, church and experience.' A noble vision! Or it would be if he really believed it. In fact, though, like the makers of *thirtysomething*, Springer always inserts his values into his television – unlike *thirtysomething*'s values, these are ones that he learned in the gutter and nurtures in the TV studio. These values are really the most outrageous things anyone hears on *The Jerry Springer Show*.

CHAPTER 9

1991: The Absence of War

BOOM BANG-A-BANG

When the firing began in the Gulf War, the BBC withdrew *'Allo 'Allo* from its schedules. Series seven of the Jeremy Lloyd and David Croft sitcom had begun on January 5 but was deemed unsuitable to be shown when the Allied artillery started shelling Iraqi positions on January 15. That was the deadline the UN had set for Iraqi forces to withdraw from Kuwait or face Allied attacks. At first, I wondered why *'Allo 'Allo* had been taken off air. After all, this was only a sitcom. True, it had always struck me as bordering on bad taste since a sitcom about the travails of a café owner in occupied France during World War Two risked trivialising Nazism and hiding the horror of war. But surely, too, it was merely funny and couldn't offend even those people who had relatives fighting in the Gulf. Could it?

'Allo 'Allo seemed to me to continue the repulsive stereotyping of so many British sitcoms of the seventies, especially *Are You Being Served?*. I'd hoped that this era was over. During the eighties, though, *'Allo 'Allo* kept the flame of this kind of comedy burning. In this sitcom, Germans were inefficient and sexually

ludicrous. The Gestapo's Herr Flick, in his pervert's leather trenchcoat, futilely sought gratification with his assistant Helga, the blonde ice queen. The British were to a man hopeless: they were typified by Crabtree, who survived in the occupied town of Nouvion as a gendarme who mangled French with every breath of his body. He could not speak French in a British sitcom since too few of the target audience would understand what he was on about, so instead he spoke something much more ingenious. To communicate how badly he spoke French to English-speaking viewers, he spoke in an ill-accented English: 'Good moaning . . .', for instance, was his customary greeting. And the French? The French were libidos on legs whose Resistance couldn't organise a successful ruse to save their lives. They spoke with accents that were hardly as comically ingenious as Crabtree's Anglo-French, but instead an English notion of the ludicrousness of French ('Leesen vairy carefully, I veell say zis arnly wernce . . .'). There could be no resistance to this comedy: look, it said, we are satirising the British too so we can't be racist. Every nation is funny here! No matter that this allowed French and German stereotyping to appear with all the crude vigour of a Benny Hill sketch. No matter at all.

Like *Dad's Army*, *'Allo 'Allo* was set during wartime but at a remove from the conflict. There were deprivations, perhaps, but no death camps; resistance but no violence, only comically inept subterfuge. There was no killing. The closest the sitcom got to a killing was when René feigned his own death at the hands of a Nazi firing squad. Unbeknownst to his would-be executioners, this unwilling ally of the French Resistance had arranged for blanks to be put in their rifles. René, the café owner played by Gorden Kaye, writhed on the ground in mock pain and then affected to die. We, the audience, knew that he had not been shot and that he would, when the firing squad had gone, get up and walk away.

Perhaps *'Allo 'Allo* was withdrawn because it made the German occupation of France seem mildly irksome, rather than deeply oppressive. Maybe if *'Allo 'Allo* had been shown during wartime, it might suggest to viewers that Iraq's occupation of Kuwait was similar to this representation of Nazi occupation. Instead of raping and murdering Kuwaitis, instead of taking babies out of incubators and leaving them to die (as Saddam's troops were falsely accused of doing), perhaps instead Iraqi soldiers did nothing more oppressive than sit in the cafés of Kuwait City, joining their host in complaining about the dreadful singing of the café owners' wives? That, perhaps, was the problem with *'Allo 'Allo*: it would give a message that military occupation need not be a bad thing at all, but instead, a fitting subject for comedy.

But, no, I believe that the real reason *'Allo 'Allo* was taken off air was that it depicted British airmen as nitwits, and, at a time of war, this could not be allowed. Flying Officer Fairfax and Flying Officer Carstairs only had small roles as two chaps whom the Resistance hoped to smuggle back to Blighty but, despite their impressively authentic moustaches, these were not the kind of fellows that the British public would want to imagine were linking up with the USAF to kick Saddam's butt.

'Allo 'Allo was restored to the schedules before the Gulf War ended. But there were many other programmes that were banned for the duration – not by the Government, but by TV controllers who were exercised, as they properly should have been, about questions of taste and sensitivity during wartime. Thus, *M*A*S*H**, the US sitcom about a military hospital during the Korean War, was taken off the air by BBC2. Viewers might have been disturbed to switch from reports of the war in the Gulf on the Nine O'Clock News on BBC1 to jokes about a field hospital on BBC2.

Elsewhere, the BBC pulled *Carry On Up the Khyber* and *Monty Python's Flying Circus*, as well as *Over My Dead Body*, even though this American series had nothing to do with war. Channel 4 postponed its series on the Vietnam war. The sight of the Vietcong's Tet Offensive would have proven too offensive: orientals beating Americans was not what we should be watching while the Republican Guard, or the elite Republican Guard as they seemed always to be referred to in news reports, retained their martial aura. LWT withdrew *A Perfect Hero*, a drama about a disfigured airline pilot. An episode of the nature series, *Survival*, which showed birds caught in the engines of an Israeli jet was not broadcast.

Before the Gulf War began, the BBC issued a list of records that were not to be played on its radio stations during the conflict. Abba's 'Waterloo' was on it, but not Olivia Newton-John's 'Long Live Love'. It's a fascinating list, which included: The Animals' 'We've Got to Get Out of This Place'; The Bangles' 'Walk Like an Egyptian' (perhaps because Egyptians were coalition allies and the song was perceived as derogatory); the Boomtown Rats' 'I Don't Like Mondays' (presumably because of the line *I wanna shooo-oooot the whole day down*); Roberta Flack's 'Killing Me Softly'; John Lennon's 'Give Peace a Chance'; Lulu's 'Boom Bang-a-Bang' (the silliness of Eurovision Song Contest lyrics suddenly took on a darker meaning, since Lulu was unwittingly evoking the sound of Multiple-Launcher Rocket Systems pounding out across the Arab desert); B. A. Robertson's 'Bang Bang' and Cher's 'Bang Bang' (My Baby Shot Me Down); Maria Muldaur's 'Midnight at the Oasis' (romanticising Arab culture, one suspects, was not deemed in good taste at this juncture); Rick Nelson's 'Fools Rush In'; Edwin Starr's 'War' (with its lyric *War – what is it good for? Absolutely nothin'*); Rod Stewart's 'Sailing'; Desmond Dekker's 'Israelites'; Blondie's 'Atomic'; Tears For Fears' 'Everybody Wants to Rule the World'; The Beatles' 'Back in the USSR'; Paper Lace's 'Billy Don't Be a Hero'; Donny Osmond's 'Soldiers of War'; Frankie Goes to Hollywood's 'Two Tribes'; The Temptations' 'Ball of Confusion'; 10cc's 'Rubber Bullets'; Stevie Wonder's 'Heaven Help Us All'.

On TV, advertisers withdrew commercials that might upset potential customers. Cadbury removed its chocolate commercial featuring a cartoon army of singing soldier ants. The commercial for Carling Black Label lager, which consisted of a pastiche of *The Dambusters*, was also not broadcast during the Gulf War. This was the advertisement in which our chaps flew on a night-time sortie to destroy German dams with marvellous British bouncing bombs. But the Nazi who was guarding the target that night was well matched to the task of protecting the dam from those ingenious proto-Smart bombs. Taking off his coat and propping up his rifle, he struck a goalkeeper's pose and prepared to deal with the bombs as they bounced across the lake towards their goal. He palmed one over the bar, caught and threw another dismissively away. In the Lancaster cockpit, one of the crew remarked 'I bet he drinks Carling Black Label', before wheeling frustratedly back to Blighty.

This wasn't the sort of stuff that would help lager sales or public morale during wartime. Advertisers, broadcasters, DJs and even the Victoria and Albert Museum (which cancelled an exhibition entitled The March of Death), were being very careful not to hurt the public's feelings. No TV station was going to repeat *Tumbledown* (the drama of a Falklands veteran) or the documentary about Simon Weston who was burned on the *Sir Galahad* during the Falklands War. Liz Forgan, Director of Programmes at Channel 4, asked: 'What does a nation feel when it is at war? The instinctive feeling is that we must be very careful not to upset people any more than they are upset already,' she told the *Guardian* on 2 February 1991. But does a nation ever feel one thing? And, if not, whose feelings were being considered?

I'd only been aware of one war in the past on television, though even then distantly. My chief television memory of the Falklands conflict is of the day that South Georgia was captured. It was 25 April 1982 and a reporter asked Mrs Thatcher a question as she marched into 10 Downing Street. 'Rejoice,' she shouted back.

'Just rejoice!' Of course, we must rejoice: we were in the middle of a war and that is what we did when our side had won a significant victory. But the main image that hums around my brain every time I think of the Falklands War is not one that I saw on television but one recreated in my imagination. I once heard a British soldier talking about how he killed an Argentinian soldier as the British forces fought their way towards Port Stanley. The Briton had his bayonet out and was stabbing the man in the face and all the while the Argentinian was babbling incomprehensibly in Spanish, words that the British soldier, reflecting later on his killing, felt sure must have meant something like: 'Hurry up and kill me. Kill me, kill me! Put me out of my pain!' But that is my private war, the one that I will never see on television: an Argentinian man stabbed repeatedly in the face until he can speak no more. Rejoice! Just rejoice!

In the Gulf War we were being prepared for something very similar. We would move seamlessly from impressive military build-up to war to rejoicing, and that little bit in the middle between the build-up and the rejoicing would pass by as though it never happened. Only later, years later, would we be told in documentary series what happened.

At the time, it seemed that broadcasters were almost exclusively concerned for the feelings of families who had soldiers at war, but little for those revolted by or opposed to the looming conflict. Why weren't the broadcasters alert to another and widespread sensitivity: the feeling of revulsion at seeing, hour after hour, the terrible weapons of war presented as sophisticated toys? The BBC, after all, had banned John Lennon's 'Imagine' and Nicole's 'A Little Peace' but the corporation, along with other broadcasting institutions, was happy to screen documentaries and news reports about the weaponry that was being amassed on the border of Iraq and occupied Kuwait.

The lull between Iraq's invasion of Kuwait on 2 August 1990 and the Allied military operation which started only in the middle of January the following year meant that there was little else to fill news reports. This bloodless interregnum and the military propaganda put out by the leaders of the Coalition to the effect that the looming war would be clean, with minimal casualties to the Allied side, made me feel as though the war, when it came, would only hurt the Iraqis. For five months there had been a massive build-up of Allied troops in Saudi Arabia and news reports were filled with details about the forces. More and more kept arriving, each group with its own story to tell. Hurrah! The Desert Rats were on their way, those men who had fought so gallantly against Rommel. Not the same men, obviously, but their equals, no doubt, in pluck and determination. Hurrah! Here was Prince Charles visiting the 'Death or glory boys', the 17th/21st Lancers, famed for their courage during the Charge of the Light Brigade. This time, I hoped, they wouldn't be using lances and this time, I suspected, they wouldn't be cut to ribbons. Before war began, there were 650,000 troops, 1,400 tanks, 120 armoured vehicles and self-propelled artillery, more than 500 fighter planes, 300 helicopters and more than 100 warships, including five battle cruisers. There were huge engineering, medical, command and control staffs prepared for a desert conflict or battle at sea.

Against overwhelming odds, I surrendered myself and watched a glut of documentaries about the military hardware. The centrepiece of the Allied naval force, for instance, was three US battleships twenty miles from Iraqi shores. The *Iowa*, the *Missouri* and the *Wisconsin* were World War Two ships that had been mothballed in the fifties and subsequently modernised. Each had nine 16-inch guns capable of firing a shell weighing one ton into the heart of Iraq. Each ship displaced nearly 45,000 tons and carried a crew of 1,900 officers and men.

I remember a documentary which said that missiles could do little damage to these ships because they were protected by armour plate up to twenty inches thick. Better than that, four turrets had been removed from each ship to make way for quadruple launchers for BGM 109 Tomahawk cruise missiles. These could carry nuclear or conventional high explosives or a variety of runway-cratering sub-munitions. The Tomahawk had a range of 500 nautical miles. It could also be carried aboard the Los Angeles-class of US submarine. Whether these submarines were stationed in the Mediterranean or the Red Sea, they could still hit Iraqi targets. Cruise missiles could be launched from their forward torpedo housings. When they broke the surface of the water, solid fuel rocket motors would kick in and then a turbo jet would power the missile all the way to its target. An on-board computer would constantly monitor approaching obstacles. The TV footage of cruise missiles was impressive and disturbing. There was an overhead shot of a Tomahawk missile rising out of one of its launchers on board one of these vast American battleships. To my eyes, which had seen so few weapons with which to compare this sight, the rising missile looked like nothing so much as Thunderbird 1. Thunderbird 1 was stored in a silo beneath the Tracys' swimming pool, but when International Rescue received the call telling them that the evil, unpredictable Hood – that Oriental fiend whose eyes would glow red when he was being particularly beastly to blameless Westerners – had committed some outrage, hydraulic motors would slide the swimming pool away and Thunderbird 1 would rise from the ground, before setting off on a mission to restore order in some far-flung part of the world.

The take-off of the BGM 109 Tomahawk cruise missile was similar. It rose from a snug housing in the ship, and seemed to me huge and hugely threatening, as it gleamed in the sun, trailing smoke fumes behind it. Though this footage did not seem to be of the missile being launched during wartime, the fearful image still remained: I wouldn't want to be an Iraqi with that kind of thing flying around my airspace. I wouldn't want to be evil Saddam Hussein, sitting in my presidential palace with my eyes glowing red and Kuwait prone under my oppressive dictator's heel, now that another international rescue mission was being mounted.

But more than that, I felt that this weaponry could win the war without Iraq's enemies setting foot in the desert or on the pavements of Baghdad. These weapons were so big, so impressive that our boys could destroy Iraq and everything in it by pushing a few buttons. It would be so easy that they wouldn't even break sweat or soil their white dress gloves. Or so it seemed.

During the months before the UN deadline for Iraqi withdrawal ran out, there was little war coverage apart from this kind of stuff. Yes, we did see reports of the Iraqi foreign minister, Tariq Aziz, and the US Secretary of State, James Baker, emerging from hotel lobbies after last-ditch negotiations, but by then war seemed so inevitable to me that the main impression of these meetings was surprise that Tariq Aziz had ventured out of his country. Surely now national sentiment demanded that he return to Baghdad and await big bombs dispatched by white-gloved Westerners.

The most purportedly human story relating to the Gulf that was reported before fighting began was Saddam Hussein's decision to arrest 400 Britons and 2,500 Americans and hold them, it was claimed, to provide a 'human shield' against attack. Saddam claimed, on the contrary, that these captors were his 'guests'. Among them was a British boy called Stuart Lockwood, who was presented to the world's TV cameras. He stood on Saddam's left, looking bewildered and a little bit cross. Saddam himself was seated, which may have seemed a good idea to his spin doctors since it prevented him towering menacingly over a small boy on millions of TV screens around the world, but it did have the unfortunate consequence that Stuart looked like a supplicant at a child molester's court. Saddam smiled at Stuart, put his arm around the boy's shoulders and stroked his hair.

'Are you getting your milk, Stuart?' said one of Saddam's aides from the president's right. Bent low, unctuously not blocking the cameras' view of his leader and yet still attempting to show that he was speaking to Stuart at his own level, perhaps even stooping to conquer the boy's confidence. Stuart mumbled something which may have been assent. He was thoroughly ill at ease, as were his captors, though he did not, as Saddam and his aide did, try to conceal it. Consequently, he looked natural and they looked false. The aide leaned further forward yet still did not cross our sight line to Saddam. 'And with Cornflakes, too!' he said. The aide seemed to have forgotten that he was trying to induce Stuart to speak of his pleasure at being held captive in Baghdad where he could eat cereals just as he could at home. Instead, the aide was speaking at though he was amplifying something Stuart had mumbled into his chest.

The aim had been to show that Western hostages were being treated well by their Iraqi captors. But this was terrible propaganda, not least because Iraq had made hostages such as Stuart the only humans on display. For the rest, we saw only tyrants, technology and men in suits. Aziz and Baker didn't count: they were dehumanised bit-players who stood in front of lecterns. Saddam, Thatcher and Bush, too, were leaders who made speeches, not humans who suffered. And the soldiers, all 650,000 of them, were only interesting in so far as they operated the Stealth bombers, Jaguars, Buccaneers, Falcons, Eagles, Phantoms, Scimitars, Patriots, and Multiple-Launcher Rocket Systems. The hostages had been elevated above the warriors. In the battle for human empathy that preceded the real conflict, they were the most valuable commodity.

When the hostages were released by Saddam Hussein, the gesture indicated that they had become worthless to him. Like a slave trader or an exploitative capitalist employer, this man had sought to trade in live humans but he had proved himself an incompetent dealer on the hostage market: he had not been able to gain anything from their release, not even a victory in the propaganda war. Women and children were released first, the cameras focusing on the mothers with children wrapped in blankets as they descended the steps from the aeroplanes. Later came the men, like early Christmas presents to the West. Once they were safe at home, our white-gloved technicians could bomb Iraq into submission without harming Westerners.

Saddam's attempt to manipulate TV viewers had backfired hopelessly. Instead of making him and his country seem humane, it made them seem mad, dangerous and ultimately weak. He may have even made attacks on his own country and his occupying forces in Kuwait more acceptable in the West as a result. To me this suggested that Iraq was not a worthy foe: it couldn't even do good TV propaganda. I was proud – in some unexamined, cobwebby part of my mind – to be British, to be Western, to come from a country where the propaganda was either non-existent or so subtle that it seemed to be non-existent. I felt a pride that I came from a country where we were so media-savvy that we wouldn't be conned by such a crude stunt. It would take much more subtlety to dupe an Englishman. What I didn't know then was that I had already been seduced into believing that there would soon be a war without Western casualties fought against a man who was the personification of evil.

In early January 1991 an article by the philosopher Jean Baudrillard appeared in the French newspaper *Libération* called 'The Gulf War Will Not Take Place'. During the conflict it was followed by an essay called 'The Gulf War: Is It Really Taking Place?', and after the conflict by one entitled 'The Gulf War Did Not Take Place'. I didn't read these until years afterwards, but they now make a kind of Swiftian sense to me. Like Swift's *A Modest Proposal*, 'The Gulf War Will Not Take Place' can be taken as a satire. Confronted by the build-up of weapons and the military's protestations that Western casualties would be minimal, the author took the argument a step further – there would be no war. At the time, this must have seemed a crazy suggestion; even in retrospect, it is hard to conceive that the author was anything other than utterly wrong – there was fighting, there were deaths and there there was a victory in the Gulf. Weren't there?

This was not the first time that images of war had appeared on TV screens, but it was the first time that they were to be relayed 'live' from the battlefront. It was not the first occasion during which the military censored what could be reported, nor one in which broadcasters withdrew programmes for fear of offending viewers, but it did involve a new level of military control of reporting and images. This was going to be no Vietnam in which footage of US disasters at the hands of the Vietcong and reports from the frontline contributed massively to public protests against continued American involvement in the area. Instead, the Gulf War would be more like the Falklands War in which the military exercised great control over what TV cameras and reporters were allowed to see of the conflict.

Before the fighting began, television proved itself unreliable as a source of information. The reports of US marines along the Saudi border with Kuwait being poised to make an amphibious landing were part of a successful strategy to deceive Iraqi commanders about the likely direction of the assault. In fact, the Allied attack was land-based and Allied ships stayed offshore. The Iraqis had been duped because they relied on television for their information.

Baudrillard, I think insightfully, saw this as symptomatic of a world that had become a hall of mirrors and in which truth, if it was anywhere, was not on CNN. He wrote: 'The fact that decoys have become an important branch of the war industry, just as the production of placebos has become an important part of the medical industry and forgery a flourishing branch of the art industry – not to mention that information has become a privileged branch of industry as such – all this is a sign that we have entered a deceptive world in which entire industry labours entirely at its counterfeit.' There was a lot of truth in this. At its worst moments, I felt the television industry was indeed labouring at showing me a counterfeit war, but they were hardly master forgers, since broadcasters as much as viewers were unwitting dupes. Journalists as much as the Iraqis were outmanoeuvred by the Allied forces.

Just before the fighting (if that's what it was) began, Baudrillard went further: 'We are all hostages of media intoxication, induced to believe in the war just as we were once led to believe in the revolution in Romania, and confined to the simulacrum of war as though confined to quarters.'

Stuck in my quarters thousands of miles away from the battlefields, with only a television to show me what was happening, prepared to see nothing that would upset me and poised to rejoice at any moment, I had become a hostage. I was hardly Stuart Lockwood, but this Stuart was held open-mouthed and wide-eyed by the magnetic rays of the television set. Like millions of others I was immobilised and unable to even frame my objections to the war. For me, even before it began, the war was over.

KILLING ME SOFTLY

David Lloyd George, who was prime minister during much of World War One, once said that if people knew what war was like they would not support it. Ever since 1856 when the British government invented military censorship in order to silence criticism of the way in which it was running the Crimean War, wartime news management has had two purposes: to deny information and comfort to the enemy and to create and maintain public support. In this sense, despite the massive build-up of journalistic technology alongside the military hardware during the Gulf War, little had changed since the Crimean War: we could not be told or shown the truth before or during the conflict. It was several weeks after the bombing started before any bodies were shown on television and even then the most horrific scenes were cut, not because of official censorship but voluntarily by TV companies in order not to offend.

Instead, what we mostly saw for the first few weeks were video games that bore little relation to what was really happening. For example, we were shown footage of Scud missiles fired from Iraq being intercepted by Patriot missiles before they could hit their targets over Saudi Arabia and Israel. After the war, the Israeli defence minister Moshe Arens admitted that not a single Patriot had brought down a single Scud, but that truth was not allowed to spoil our TV spectacle at the time, or to undermine public faith in the transcendent power of Western weaponry.

Military spokesmen, and occasionally TV reporters, spoke in a sanitised language. There was great emphasis on the 'surgical' nature of air strikes on military targets. The cancer could be cut out while leaving the living tissue – the civilians – unaffected, perhaps even stronger. As a result, ordinary Iraqis would be healthier and so more able to rise up against Saddam – so, at least, ran the rhetoric. 'Smart' bombs would take out military installations or command centres with 'pinpoint accuracy'; there would be little or no 'collateral damage', which meant dead or injured civilians. People weren't people any more but 'soft targets'.

Bombing military targets in the heart of Baghdad was 'denying the military an infrastructure' and saturation bombing was 'laying down a carpet'. The Allies were virtuosos at this newspeak; Saddam was an amateur by comparison, using that euphemism, 'guests' – a term so ludicrously distant from the truth of men, women and children held against their will that it could only be properly used sardonically.

As one of the civilians back home, I was reliant on television mediation for my visual picture of the fighting, was a consumer of war. I had no thought that the conflict in the Gulf could deprive me or other viewers of our right to sit and watch in peace. As a result, perhaps, it was no coincidence that the language of war had come to echo the language of shopping. Shopping is supposed to be pleasurable, or at least not disturbing and so the language that advertisers used to encourage us to buy is pleasingly seductive and banal. Increasingly, leaders and some journalists would talk about the war as they would talk about shopping. Sometimes there was misplaced insouciance (the *Sun* once had as its 'thought for the day' on its front page: 'Cruise at Ten'). The war was a comedy, the names of missiles were fit subject for wordplay. Sometimes the language was candy-coated: 'friendly fire' meant the deaths of British servicemen at the hands of Americans. But blood, bombs, death – such words, such *real* words, rarely got heard.

Eight years later another term was added to this colourless language – 'degrade'. As cruise missiles flew into Baghdad once more, just before Christmas 1998, Bill Clinton and Tony Blair seemed to be reading from the same script. 'I have ordered a strong, sustained series of air strikes against Iraq,' said the President from the White House. 'They are designed to degrade Saddam's capacity to develop and deliver weapons of mass destruction, and degrade his ability to threaten his neighbours.' 'If he will not, through reason and diplomacy, abandon his weapons of mass destruction,' said the Prime Minister, standing in front of his Christmas tree outside Number 10 Downing Street, 'they must be degraded and diminished by military force.'

What was most striking was not so much the transatlantic unanimity of expression, and the attendant, disturbing possibility that the Prime Minister was merely echoing His Master's Voice, but rather that an old verb had been unleashed in a new context. 'To degrade' sounds like something that would happen in another desert – a Foreign Legion officer degrading a disgraced officer by stripping off his epaulettes, breaking his sword and trampling his cap in the sand. Perhaps this is what Clinton and Blair intended to convey: they were going to overthrow and humiliate Saddam. Perhaps even throw his military beret symbolically into the Tigris.

But no, the word degrade was being used by Clinton and Blair in a much less specific sense. Although the most common meaning of the verb, according to the *Shorter Oxford English Dictionary*, is to 'reduce to a lower rank, depose from a position of honour', there are other senses. The dictionary also defines degrade as 'reduce in strength, amount or some other measurable property'. This Clinton-Blair sense of the verb, according to the dictionary, is usually reserved to refer to 'reductions in colour'. But that was appropriate. The colourless lexicon of modern warfare euphemisms – fatalities, neutralisations, and the rest – had a new addition. Like the others, it repulsively distanced me (but surely not just me) from the reality of war. What's more, its use permitted Clinton and Blair to be vague about their objectives. 'Degrade' did not suggest that Saddam's weapons of mass destruction would be obliterated; it did not entail that Saddam would be deposed by force; it did not say anything very much.

The only apparent constant down the long years of wartime rhetoric is patriotic sentiment. Blair spoke of British servicemen 'risking their lives', and thus ushered us into an unquestioning sentimental affiliation with a cause about which we might otherwise have been sceptical. Clinton's patriotic flourish invoked a complex national myth of the United States as a lion, slow to rise from its peaceable slumbers but decisive when it did, and yet paradoxically the global ombudsman of peace.

But patriotism has its proper place in wartime leaders' rhetoric. Once, the ancestors of TV viewers weren't just consumers of war but were directly embroiled in it. Churchill could not have afforded to use the rhetoric of shopping when he sought to steel civilians against Nazi invasion with his 'we will fight them on the beaches' speech.

But Bush, Thatcher and Major during the Gulf War, Clinton and Blair during Operation Desert Fox, were concerned with military action far away from their homelands and so could afford to speak of it without enjoining their civilian population to prepare themselves for struggle and sacrifice. Saddam never had that relative luxury.

Wars haven't taken place on American or western European soil for so long that we could experience them as akin to entertainment. Until Tony Benn spoke up on *Newsnight* in December 1998, telling the presenter Gordon Brewer that his pictures from Baghdad were contrived to entertain viewers, and concealed rather than revealed the reality of death and injury, no one saw fit to talk in such affecting truthful language on TV, and I felt shamed by his words. The Anglo-American Desert Fox, like Operation Desert Storm before it, had thrown sand in our eyes from the beginning, preventing us from seeing what was going on or talking about it properly. We were degraded from the start, in a third sense of the verb, which the dictionary defines as 'to lower in quality or character, debase'.

But wasn't the Gulf War one in which we saw what was happening in real-time thanks to the unprecedented numbers of journalists and cameras in the Gulf? It was not. We were spared close-up shots of dead or wounded bodies from the land war. We were not allowed to see the results of the 'turkey shoot' on the Basra Road, or the American bulldozers covering Iraqi conscripts with sand in their trenches. We did see some footage of Iraqi deaths at the Almeira camp in Baghdad, but when the BBC broadcast a report on this, it was accused of betraying the nation's cause during wartime. For much of the rest of the conflict, TV showed us an absence where the war should have been.

Only later did I read the stories about what had happened in the Gulf in 1991. The most memorable, for me, was the account of Sergeant Joe Queen, then a nineteen-year-old who was one of the first American troops to cross the Kuwait-Saudi Arabian border during Desert Storm. It was his job to roll across the Iraqi trenches in an armoured bulldozer, bury Iraqi soldiers alive then cover them smoothly so that the rest of his brigade could follow. 'The sand was so soft that once the blade hits the sand it just caves right in on the sides . . . So you are travelling at five, six, seven miles an hour just moving along the trench . . . I don't think any of them had any idea because the look on their faces as we came over the berm was just a look of shock.' Between 1,000 and 2,000 Iraqis were buried alive this way during the war. These are, again, unseen images that replay themselves in my imagination. A retreating Iraqi soldier recalled seeing tanks with bulldozer blades: 'Some of the soldiers were walking towards the troops, holding their arms up to surrender and the tanks moved in and killed them. They dug a hole in the ground and then they buried the soldiers and levelled it . . . It was horrible to witness. I stood there for about ten minutes. I saw one soldier and his body was just torn apart by a bulldozer. The upper part was on one side and the lower on the other side.'

Like the image of the Argentinian soldier stabbed in the face again and again, this Iraqi soldier's death is replayed again and again in my head. There, at least, no broadcaster could protect me and no spin doctor spare me from seeing a fantasy – a fantasy which was closer to what really happened in the Gulf than anything I saw on TV in January and February 1991.

THIS IS WHAT WEAPONS DO

In 1963, Peter Watkins made a film about the Battle of Culloden. It bears comparison with the way in which the Gulf War was shown on television. Admittedly, this was a dramatisation rather than a news report. Admittedly, it was the re-enactment by actors of a battle that took place during one hour and eight minutes on a Scottish moor in 1746. Admittedly, it was fought with nothing more sophisticated than bayonets and muskets rather than cruise missiles and B52s. But it was a moral film that depicted clearly not only the weapons used but the consequences of using those weapons, that constantly strove to highlight the political context and which was immune to government or military manipulation. That did, in short, everything that television news did not do during Operation Desert Storm.

As the drums beat out their dismal tattoo, and the rain soaked tartan and King's uniform alike, Watkins highlighted the differences between the two opposed armies by focusing on two men. First, the camera studied the face and uniform of one of the King's soldiers: 'Alexander Lang carries a .753 musket firing effective distances of sixty paces. He carries sufficient ball and paper and black powder for twenty-four cartridges. He carries at his hip a brass-hilted sword and a bayonet with eighteen inches of fluted steel.' Then we cut to a man introduced by the narrator as Alastair McQuarrie, in the opposing side: 'Alastair McQuarrie carries in his right hand an outdated dragoon pistol for which he has no further ammunition.' It was a woeful mismatch, rather like Iraq versus the Coalition.

What was poor, miserable-looking McQuarrie doing on the battlefield? The narrator said earlier that he was part of the system of human rent that was the clan system in the Highlands, and Watkins went on to explain this elegantly. First we saw James MacDonald, a taxman, whose position was set out. Then we moved on to McQuarrie, a sub-tenant of the taxman, who owned 'one-eighth of an acre of soggy ground and two cows'. Then we saw Alan Macoll, a sub-tenant of the sub-tenant, who owned a half-share of a tiny potato patch. Next to him was Alastair Macdonald, a servant of the sub-tenant. All of these men were on the battlefield because Alexander Macdonald, the chief of the Macdonald clan, had demanded their presence. If McQuarrie had declined to fight, said the narrator, he had been told that his cattle would be taken and his roof burned.

But there were not just unwilling, ill-armed men on the rebel side. There were 150 exiled Catholic Irishmen, come to fight against the Protestant King George II's army in order that they could practise their religion unmolested at home. On the other side, there were not just Englishmen, but Lowland Scots. There were men from Highland clans fighting on the King's side, too, often fighting for revenge against outrages perpetrated by rival clans. There were more Scotsmen than Englishmen fighting against Prince Charles Stuart's army. These complexities were patiently set out. The politics and complexities of this battle were laid bare, as they were not in the case of the Gulf War. During the Gulf War, by contrast, the Allies never made it clear that this was a conflict about oil. By invading Kuwait, Iraq put itself in control of a fifth of the world's oil and, if Saddam's tanks had rolled into Saudi Arabia, he would have controlled twice that amount. Only when the BBC made its Gulf War documentary in 1996 and during it interviewed one of the Coalition's commanding officers, General Brent Scowcroft, was that motivation made clear.

Watkins' narrator interviewed the chiefs of the Highland army, an initially bizarre device, since be-wigged lords have never hitherto had to justify themselves before battle to TV cameras. Prince Charles Edward Stuart was interviewed as he sat on his horse. Why, asked the interviewer, had he been drawn into a battle on flat, treeless ground that so favoured British artillery and cannon, contrary to the advice given by Lord George Murray, the Lieutenant-General of the clan army who had been responsible for the rebels' remarkable advance as far south as Derby? 'God is on my side and my duty lies in fighting today,' said Bonnie Prince Charlie airily, his Polish accent sounding uncannily to my ears like Michael Howard's – which was ideal since this reply was like that of an evasive government minister on *Newsnight*.

Once battle began, Watkins showed the effect of the weapons. We saw a cannon ball being loaded as the narrator spoke: 'A cast iron ball. 3lbs. This is round shot. This is what it does.' The cannon fired. The camera cut to a man writhing on the ground. 'Alastair McInnes, 20. Right leg severed below the knee joint.' We cut again. 'Malcolm Angus Chisholm, 24, disembowelled.' We cut to a boy, screaming wildly as another soldier tried to restrain him: 'Ian Macdonald, 13, shot.' This is what we so rarely saw in the coverage of the Gulf War on television: the impact of the weapons whose destructive power had been so salivatingly recorded before they were used and so elliptically depicted by means of military videos.

'Charles Stuart, in one hour eight minutes,' said the narrator as the rout unfolded, 'reduced the flower of the Highland clans to twitching, limbless corpses.' Of the 9,000 King's men who had marched from Nairn on the morning of the battle, 50 had died. For every one corpse in the royal army, there were twenty-four in the clan army. 1,200 men lay dead or dying on Culloden moor.

But that was not all. After the battle, the King's soldiers were seen sticking bayonets into prone bodies. 'Our British soldiers looked less like Christian men and more like butchers,' said one witness whose remark Watkins quoted in the film. I saw the scene and thought of bulldozers pouring sand over Iraqi heads, of Iraqi soldiers trying to surrender. Of two photographs: the scene of carnage on the Basra Road and the photograph of the Iraqi soldier in his tank that had been on that same road, the remains of his teeth bared, his head burnt black. Images that I never saw on television until years afterwards.

But neither was that all. After the Battle of Culloden was over and the rebels killed or put to flight, the King's third son, William Augustus, Duke of Cumberland, the royal army's commanding officer, allowed his troops to ride to Inverness, killing soldiers as they went. But the British soldiers, some of whom had been drinking after the battle, killed the women and children they encountered too. In one scene, a boy stood in a lane and a soldier on horseback rode past him. The boy fell to the ground, slashed by a blade. Nearly 100 people were butchered or maimed thus on the road to Inverness. I thought of the killing of thousands of retreating Iraqi troops and civilians on the Basra Road that I had never seen on the TV news during the Gulf War. As the Basra Road turkey shoot unfolded, US General Colin Powell had reportedly told other members of the war cabinet at its final meeting: 'We should stop now. Our pilots are just killing for the sake of it.'

20,000 BRITONS WOULD COMMIT SUICIDE

Two years after *Culloden* was broadcast to great acclaim, the BBC banned Peter Watkins' film *The War Game*. This was a fifty-minute drama-documentary which depicted the preparations for a nuclear attack in Kent, and the horrific, chaotic aftermath.

During the fifties, broadcasters at the BBC had considered making a radio documentary about the effects of the hydrogen bomb, but the programme was never made after ministers expressed alarm at the project. *The War Game* was made, however, and the chairman of the BBC board of governors, Lord Normanbrook, gave the film a private screening for Home Office officials (who were in charge of civil defence), the chiefs of staff of the armed forces and some senior BBC executives. Although some reservations were expressed as a result, the BBC was left to censor the film itself: the Director-General Sir Hugh Greene banned the film, even though it later received public cinematic screenings, because of its power to disturb. But is this any reason not to have shown it? If these sensitive people have the right to vote, drive and own televisions, couldn't they also be expected to have the intelligence to realise that something would or wouldn't be too disturbing for them to watch? And what if they were disturbed by the programme? Surely they have the right to be disturbed; indeed, anybody who saw *The War Game* and wasn't disturbed would be a very peculiar human being. But, just as children are regularly invoked by those who seek to prohibit the depiction of violence, the supposed special vulnerability of certain sections of the viewing population was deployed rhetorically and patronisingly to protect all of us. Or maybe there was another political agenda, similar to the one expressed by the Ministry of Defence just before a decision was taken in the fifties not to make the H-bomb radio documentary. Then, the man from the ministry said that while they did not 'desire to keep the public in complete ignorance; on the other hand they did not want to stimulate the feeling so easily accepted by the British people because it agreed with their natural laziness in these matters, that because of the terrible nature of the hydrogen bomb there was no need for them to take part in home defence measures . . .' What a wonderful argument! The British public should not be encouraged by a documentary to reflect on the possibility that civil defence could perhaps be pointless, and so not bother to take such measures as might, perhaps, be useful in some eventuality. Hardly the remarks of an official who thought the British public sufficiently mature to make for themselves a reflective decision about their own welfare.

Many people complained about the banning of *The War Game*. As a result, the BBC sent out a letter which revealed something of their, and perhaps subsequent broadcasters', thinking about what we should see of war or the representation of war on television. Part of the letter said: 'When the film was completed and screened for senior programme staff, most of those who saw it were very deeply affected, and believed that it had the power to produce unpredictable emotions and moral difficulties whose resolution called for balance and judgment of the highest order. The horror of the film was, in their view, of an entirely different quality to that which is contained in the recognisably fictional presentations of some television films. It was also different in its impact from the objective presentations of past horrors – such as scenes which might be shown in documentaries on Culloden, the Hiroshima bombings or the extermination of the Warsaw Ghetto. Such scenes, because of their fictional nature, or because of their historic setting, do not have the personal application that would come from the broadcast showing of *The War Game* which conveys the sense that what it is showing could happen to the people who might be watching it. The BBC has, therefore, decided that because of its nature, this film cannot be broadcast. No matter how late at night it was screened, and whatever warnings might be given before the showing we could not be certain that the audience would not include some for whom its horrors would have reached the point of danger.'

Peter Watkins wrote in a newspaper article in 1985 that he had been told privately by the BBC that it had expected 20,000 people to commit suicide in Britain if *The War Game* was broadcast.

In 1985, as part of the commemorations of the 40th anniversary of the Hiroshima and Nagasaki bombings, the BBC finally showed *The War Game*. For Watkins, this was despicable. At the time, he wrote: 'The BBC is only now screening *The War Game* because it believes it is finally safe to do so. It believes that the consciousness of the public has been sufficiently diverted – that the concern over the issue of nuclear arms has been sufficiently subverted – to allow *The War Game* to be finally aired, to be swallowed up in the mish-mash of TV, and forgotten with all the other spurious images.'

★

ANGELA RIPPON'S LEGS

When television news began in Britain, there were no presenters on screen. Instead, disembodied voices read the bulletins from scripts. It was only in 1948 with BBC Television Newsreel that news footage was broadcast, but still viewers did not see the announcers. Even in 1955, when Richard Baker became the first presenter of BBC Television News, he did not appear on screen for fear that his expressions would detract from the objectivity of the reports. When he was joined by Robert Dougall later in the year, the pair appeared on screen, but read from scripts with their heads down.

How things have changed. Now news programmes have become as choreographed as ballets, as filled with cunning camera angles as a sophisticated movie. The presenter is no longer a stuffed shirt with a script, but a celebrity master of body language – projecting their own reassuring, sometimes ironical, often sexy presences as much as the substance of the news. Think of Michael Buerk's wink, satirised into absurdity by Chris Morris on *The Day Today*. Think of Jeremy Paxman's sardonic farewell as he shuffles tomorrow's front pages into order. Think of Angela Rippon's legs. Now try to concentrate on a report on the latest GNP figures.

Today many of the most highly-regarded news programmes are presented by beautiful people who spend as much time in make-up as preparing stories. Thanks to the autocue they can look at the camera and, as it were, at the viewer and thus establish a bond, with a wink here, a reassuring smile there, that says 'I'm a regular guy, the kind of chap you can trust' or, more often, 'You fancy me, don't you?'

This is no longer just the era of the newsreader as celebrity, but of the newsreader as sex symbol. We have gone beyond the newsreader-viewer relationship recalled by Robert Dougall in his memoirs: 'Television breeds a closeness and intimacy unlike that of any other medium. You become as it were a privileged guest at innumerable firesides . . . [The newsreader] builds up over the years a kind of rapport with the public.' This is, rather, an era in which Anna Walker, who presents Sky News' prime-time bulletin, publicises her travel series *Walker's World* with a calendar depicting her in various stages of undress. This is an era in which only women of a certain type – bright, sensible, with rootless accents, somewhat submissive, generally sunny and blonde, and undeniably pretty in an antiseptic way – are deemed suitable to read the news.

TV news has become as formulaic and fetishised as costume dramas. The glamorous newsreader, whose looks are deployed more or less intentionally as news dallies with becoming entertainment, is an impediment to communicating information.

As TV viewers, we have surrendered to this change. During wartime, we were protected from seeing too much reality on television. We put up our hands and gave in to the Ministry of Defence, the Government and over-scrupulous broadcasting bosses. In peacetime, we have waved the white flag to broadcasters who want to make the news akin to entertainment. When *Network 7*, the news programme in Janet Street-Porter's *Def II* strand of teen shows on Channel 4, was shown, its makers explicitly contended that the programme was entertainment. Otherwise, they argued, who would watch it? At first, I thought this was an obscene argument: news, I thought, should be empowering to viewers; it should help citizens understand their political system; it should strengthen democracy rather than undermine it; it should expose us to reality rather than protect us from it. But when news programmes are obsessed with courting viewers by any means necessary and by choreographing their presentation, we are often exposed to a reassuring, fantasy view of the world. The world is an exciting spectacle brought to us up-to-the-minute.

It's all Angela Rippon's fault. The most important moment for British broadcast news happened, paradoxically, on the *Morecambe and Wise Christmas Show* in 1978, when she stepped from behind the desk and revealed what some viewers had suspected didn't exist. She not only had legs, but legs that would make Shirley Maclaine weep with envy. High kicking and singing 'Let's Face the Music and Dance', she invented the newsreader as celebrity glamour puss, a role inherited with relish by her successors.

In most news programmes, though, the exploitation of sex is rather more subtle. Men, often grizzled old foreign correspondents, play the elder roué. They are often shot at a slight angle with one shoulder casually forward, the glance not quite three-quarters, or leaning on the desks, while women are mostly shot full-face, sitting primly and tensely. Men occupy more space than women: they used to do it on buses and now they do it when they read the news.

The men may not be themselves handsome, but they still fulfill the sexual stereotypes. The man commands, the woman follows. Male newsreaders make their women partners laugh like drains at the lamest continuity gags. In one Sky News bulletin, for instance, there was a report about a man who had bought carloads of bananas to expose a loophole in Tesco's loyalty bonus scheme. Then we cut back to the studio. 'A latter-day saint. We love him,' said Frank Partridge. Off camera Anna Walker laughed heartily, if unconvincingly, as she was obliged to do. For, no matter how bad the joke, at least one person, the presenter's sidekick, must laugh to keep the reassuring, conspiratorial mood alive. At the end of the show Partridge wound up to camera, and swivelled to look at his sidekick Walker, his body language saying 'Your place or mine?'

This is not to lampoon Sky in particular, because what is striking about most mainstream TV news programmes is how similarly structured they are. There are two main presenters, usually a man and a woman, sometimes two women, but never two men. On one side of a long desk both on Sky News and BBC *Breakfast News* is the business editor, on the other the sports editor or the wit who assesses the day's papers.

Only the camera angles and editing are different. BBC1's *Breakfast News* has been the most cumbersomely choreographed: the eight o'clock bulletin starts with a fast montage of the globe, a shot of Parliament, people walking down a street, and newspapers, before cutting to an angled shot across the long desk with Justin Webb in the foreground, and Juliet Morris smiling in the background. Disastrously (I thought), as Webb read the first item, Morris regularly remained in shot, with nothing to do but carry on smiling. Unless of course the news was grim, when she adopted a suitably forlorn expression. Robert Dougall wrote in 1973: 'A newsreader is not playing a role, not appearing as another character, or in costume, but as himself.' This description has become increasingly less applicable to modern presenters.

Rather, what we see are role-playing newsreaders, people whose job it once was to command authority, to reassure but hardly ever to entertain. The latter has now become more important. It's significant to say the least that Anna Walker said: 'The key part of our job is to get the best out of our guests.' She's no doubt right, but it's revealing that she talked of guests rather than interviewees – there is a thin line between Anna Walker and Des O'Connor, between hard news and soft chat. No wonder that Kirsty Young, who presented Channel 5 News when it first started also had a chat show.

The mixed double act also helped to blur the distinction between news and entertainment. Editors of TV news try to cultivate presenters as husband and wife, or girlfriend and boyfriend – wittingly using sexual relationships to help structure the news. And when the partnership doesn't work, there has to be a divorce – as in 1995 when Connie Chung was dropped as co-anchor with Dan Rather on the CBS evening news in the US after their on-screen chemistry was judged to be too volatile and threatening to ratings – a problem which is almost inconceivable among the cosy marriages of Britain's prime-time newsreading couples.

It's all far removed from the world of Baker and Dougall, or indeed from the prototype of all newsreading double acts, Chet Huntley and David Brinkley, the popular pair who presented NBC's news together in the fifties – even though one was in New York, the other in Washington.

Once, Reginald Bosanquet and Sandy Gall presented ITV's *News at Ten* together, but nowadays it looks odd if both presenters are men, although two women are tolerable. But why do we need two presenters? During a long bulletin they are deemed important, partly to allow one to rest, and partly to break the monotony of one newsreading voice.

When Channel 5 News began, it tried something different. It made do with one presenter but had her wandering around the studio and chatting to correspondents at their desks. In March 1997 the then new network argued that the under-forty-fives didn't watch news. So to try to capture that advertiser-friendly under-forty-five demographic, Channel 5 ditched the boring middle-aged suits sitting behind a desk and replaced them with Kirsty Young, a young suit who read the news while standing in front of a kidney-shaped desk.

As someone very much under forty-five at the time, the presentational structure did not float my boat. When Young roamed the studio on Channel 5's first night on air, chatting to political editor Mark Easton about the looming election, I could have done without the incidental disco music, or the party political rosettes that fringed Easton's desk and indicated to even the most stupid viewer that his journalistic specialism was politics. The sports editor had a football on his desk, just to simplify matters.

To me, it would have been better if Kirsty Young had *run* through a battlefield with shells exploding left and right, and correspondents rushing up with notes, shouting things like: 'Liverpool 3, Man Utd 2! Sah!' or 'Nikkei up three points! Sah!' That's the sort of stuff that will get the under-forty-fives watching TV news again, especially if the ammunition is live.

Those news programmes where the accent is so much on user-friendly presentation rather than breaking stories, in-depth analysis or challenging one's intelligence lend themselves readily to satire. Chris Morris's *Brass Eye* and its predecessor *The Day Today* mocked the way that bad TV news has surrendered itself to choreography. And the media-cynical under-forty-fives, especially, who form the biggest audiences for such satire are the ones most sensitive to farcical presentation overwhelming content.

With the growth of rolling news networks the role of the news presenter is likely to change. There will be a greater accent on live coverage, unmediated by anchor men and women back at the studio. This may be welcome, since it will, one hopes, reduce the use of re-shot questions, library footage which is not labelled as such, and virtual reality newsrooms. There is, nonetheless, the danger that the quality of 'liveness' that TV news editors prize, can be just as easily choreographed as today's news programmes.

Presenters, especially the glamorous ones, cannot be so easily dis-invented. They are likely to require a growing share of broadcast news funding, though the old gag from the *New Yorker* cartoon may go too far: 'Owing to cutbacks in our news department, here is Rod Ingram to guess at what happened at a number of places around the globe.'

The result could be that those with few professional skills but looks aplenty provide our windows on the world. It was an age predicted in the 1987 film, *Broadcast News*, where a bimbo newsreader (William Hurt) proves more attractive to network executives than those who have learned their journalistic trades. 'Don't forget,' says his cynical, skilled journalist colleague, Albert Brooks, sarcastically, 'We *are* the news.' We may not yet be at that degraded level, but the pressures are undoubtedly there to make it happen.

I often feel that Live TV, the cheap and cheerful cable channel which during the nineties offered that self-conscious nadir of broadcast journalism, News Bunny, missed a trick. Surely, if Live TV really wanted to make a mockery of broadcast news, they should have ditched the rabbit and made all those models who played topless darts, and all those men who bounced as they played lunchbox volleyball, present news bulletins. 'And now an in-depth report from Terry Torso in Bosnia . . .' 'And now the vital statistics from our topless business editor' . . . It can only be a matter of time.

The niggling doubts I have had for some years about TV news weren't just invoked by presentation – though they were symptomatic of a divorce between news as a tool of democracy and news as entertainment. No, for years I couldn't quite put my finger on it, but I knew something was wrong. The obsessions of my journalistic colleagues with news made me wonder: is there something wrong with me for not sharing their concerns?

Then, in 1998, the French sociologist Pierre Bourdieu published a book called *On Television*. In France it became a bestseller. In Britain it aroused only a glimmer of interest. But for me, it helped bring into focus some of the scepticism I felt about TV news. For him, news was a self-reflexive addiction, a parade of spectacle. I'd been a journalist all my working life, so this wasn't exactly what I wanted to hear, and initially I was indeed rather threatened by his contempt for the media and his diagnosis of its ills, but all around me journalists seemed obsessed by news for no other reason than that it was the news. Not because it mattered, told us something about society, or because it was instrumental for a healthy society.

Bourdieu wrote: 'I think that television poses a serious danger for all the areas of cultural production – for art, for literature, for philosophy and for law . . . I think that television poses no less of a threat to political life and to democracy itself.' Why? Because television is run by the mediocre, a mediaocracy, people who know little, and yet have a 'monopoly over what goes into the heads of a significant part of the population'.

TV news 'suits everybody because it confirms what they already know, and above all, leaves the mental structures intact.' What did he mean by mental structures? Consider, he suggested, the painter Manet. His work upset the teaching of painting in the nineteenth century. Like the greatest poets, scholars and artists, he effected a symbolic revolution that changed the way we see and think. But TV news doesn't do this because it needs to be popular. He compared TV news to the way people talk about the weather: 'People talk so much about the weather in day-to-day life because it's a subject that cannot cause trouble.'

Instead of real debates on TV, too, Bourdieu detected a masquerade of controversy, an ultimately meaningless controversy since conflict was fomented in order to prevent viewers being bored. What is important is to have a conflict that prevents the viewer flipping channels.

Bourdieu argued that the makers of TV news see the world 'as a series of apparently absurd stories that end up looking the same – endless parades of poverty-stricken countries that, having appeared with no explanation, will disappear with no solution – Zaire today, Bosnia yesterday, Congo tomorrow. Stripped of political necessity, this string of events can at best arouse some kind of vague humanitarian interest.'

What gets left out in most TV news, then, are the things that are difficult to report. Flaubert wrote that it took a lot of hard work to portray mediocrity, and journalists on TV aren't prepared to put in that work, especially when they get higher ratings for the sensational, and when audiences are conditioned to watch spectacle rather than something that might challenge their view of the world.

Instead, Bourdieu argued, news is premised on the sensational or the exception. Again, this initially made me feel defensive, since I had been trained in the belief that news was more substantial than that, and I had assumed that the exception or the sensational was illuminating rather than an end in itself. But, once I reflected on what I saw on television, I stopped believing this. Is a story at the top of the agenda of the Nine o'Clock News because it is the most important item? And what does most important mean? Important in holding the viewers' interest and keeping ratings up? Important in that it fits into everybody's mental structures that will not risk challenging news presenter or the audience? Or because it is the key political issue of the day? A profound moral debate? When a sports story tops the news, as increasingly happens, or when a weather story is given as much prominence as genocide, as sometimes happens, and when TV news prefers cheerful images to dark and brutal ones, we are not watching news but an unchallenging entertainment.

Should television protect us from powerful, haunting images of violence, or from too much misery? Sometimes it seems that newscasters have decided that it should. Why else did *News at Ten* routinely end with an 'And finally . . .' item about something reassuring, even though its earlier news reports may have been about wars, famines, murders, rapes? It's hard to resist the conclusion that the ultimate purpose of *News at Ten* was to reassure rather than to inform; still less is its purpose to upset – even though the proper reactions to, say, a famine in Ethiopia or ethnic cleansing in Bosnia, should involve just that.

Humankind, perhaps, cannot tolerate too much reality. Either that, or television producers dare not give us too much of it, for fear of losing ratings and advertisers, upsetting politicians or depressing viewers. But what if every evening, after watching the TV news, we felt the weight of the world's problems on our shoulders? How could we tolerate that? How could we live? We would be like Father Zossima's brother in Dostoevsky's *The*

Brothers Karamazov. The brother tells his mother: 'My dearest heart, you must realise that everyone is responsible for everyone and everything.' But how can he live with that burden – how can he do the right thing at all? Similarly, if television news showed us horror after fresh horror every day we would not be able to cope, and we would not know what to do.

Perhaps. Or perhaps we would become more sensitive to the sufferings of others that we saw on the news, rather than allowing ourselves to be distanced from reality by the structure of some news bulletins.

I come from a generation that is more sceptical about what it sees on screen than ever before. No wonder people of my age are responsible for, and revel in, such media comedies as *The Day Today*, *Knowing Me, Knowing You With Alan Partridge*, *The Mrs Merton Show*, and *The Larry Sanders Show*. We don't believe what we see, we don't trust TV presenters, and we console ourselves with irony and biting attacks on the mediaocracy who we don't trust any more. These are programmes that are popular in a time of cynicism and disappointment: the media doesn't give us what we want, and the best we can do is laugh at it.

But if you want a war, television can give you one. Heads down everybody, there's a hot one coming your way right now!

THE LAST SCINTILLA OF DOUBT JUST RODE OUT OF TOWN

'Tonight's stories. Euro MPs' new headsets play the sound of screaming women. Bryan Ferry's bathmat poisonous, says lab. And bouncing elephantiasis woman destroys central Portsmouth. Those are the headlines,' said Chris Morris, sounding as virile as any man who has ever read a sentence with the phrase 'central Portsmouth' in it. Then he modulated his tone to mimic Michael Buerk's sentimental voice: 'Happy now?'

Next, Morris had footage of a senior politician with some children. He set it in its proper context: 'A warm handshake from Michael Heseltine for the boys and girls he's about to take into the woods and shoot.'

'The Day Today,' said the disembodied voice with even more virility than Chris Morris could manage, 'because fact into doubt won't go.'

More news. The Bank of England was in chaos following revelations that the pound had been stolen. Some men made off with it in a Montego. The Bank of England, said Morris, 'refused to confirm rumours that the pound was vulnerable because they had removed it to play with at lunchtime and forgot to put it back.' The pound had been replaced by an emergency currency based on the Queen's ova – several thousand had been removed for just such an eventuality in 1953.

More City news from Collaterlie Sisters. 'Thanks, Chris. "You do it. Get it now! No! You do it! It's over there!" Arguments like that broke out on the international markets today when Spain withdrew from the world and began trading with itself. The peseta burst open at 4.'

There was just time to look at the international finance arse. Two rotating globes appeared on the screen. One was the United States cheek and the other the Japanese cheek. 'The day started with a gap of 2.4, but by lunchtime that had narrowed. In summary then: Oh, no. Chris.'

More news. The homeless are to be clamped if they're found on the streets after 9 p.m. 'The reaction has been strong,' said Morris. 'So far we have spoken to Kim Wilde.' 'I didn't know about that,' said Kim, daughter of Marty and a singer in her own right, to her interviewer. 'That's awful.'

'The Day Today,' boomed the disembodied voice with utter conviction. 'The last scintilla of doubt just rode out of town.'

But Morris had some good news. After years of sanctions and

sanctions busting, Australia and Hong Kong had signed a trade agreement. Gavin Hawtrey, the Australian foreign secretary was on the line from Canberra. And Martin Craste, a British Foreign Office minister with special responsibility for the Commonwealth, was in the studio. Morris asked Craste what he would do if Australia exceeded the agreement. 'This is a good day. If the limits were exceeded, we would be back with a firm line, but I don't think that's going to happen.'

Morris, detecting the scent of discord that could lead to the trip wires of full-on military conflict, said: 'Mr Hawtrey, he's knocking a firm line in your direction. What are you going to do about that?'

Hawtrey: 'Well, in that case we would re-impose sanctions as we did last . . .'

'Sanctions! Hang on a second,' said Morris, swivelling to face Martin Craste. 'They've only just swallowed sanctions and now they're burping them back in your face!'

Craste: 'That's rather premature. If there were sanctions, we'd have to respond with appropriate measures.'

Morris: 'I think appropriate measures is a euphemism, Mr Hawtrey. You know what it means. What are you going to do about that?'

Hawtrey: 'Well, I'd have to go back to the cabinet . . .'

Morris: 'And ask them about what?'

Hawtrey: 'Well, I don't know. Maybe it's a matter for the military.'

Craste: 'I think military measures are totally inappropriate and way over the top.'

Morris: 'It sounds like you're being totally inappropriate. Are you?'

Hawtrey: 'Of course I'm not being inappropriate. Martin Craste knows that full well.'

Craste: 'This is just the sort of misunderstanding that I thought we'd laid to rest.'

Morris: 'Misunderstanding it certainly is. It certainly isn't a treaty, is it? You're both at each other's throats. You're backing yourselves up with arms. What are you going to do about it? Mr Hawtrey – let me give you a hint: bang!'

Hawtrey: 'What are you asking me to say?'

Morris: 'You know damned well what I'm asking you to say. You're putting yourself in a situation of armed conflict. What are you plunging yourself into?'

Hawtrey: 'You'd like me to say it?'

Morris: 'I want you to say it, yes.'

Hawtrey: 'The word?'

Morris: 'The word, yes.'

Hawtrey: 'I will not flinch –'

Morris: 'You will not flinch from –'

Hawtrey: '– war!'

'Gentlemen, let me put you on hold,' said Morris, swivelling away from Craste and Hawtrey who had served their journalistic purpose for the time being. 'If fighting did break out it would be in Eastmantown in the Upper Cataracts of the Australio-Hong Kong border. Our reporter there is Donald Bethl'hem. Donald,' said Morris, turning to the monitor which showed a man in a flak jacket crouching before the camera, 'What's the atmosphere there like?'

'Tension is very high, Chris,' said the wild-eyed reporter. 'The stretched twig of peace is at melting point. People here are literally bursting with war. This is very much a country that's going to blow up in its face.'

Morris swivelled back to face his guests. 'Well, gentlemen, it seems you have little option but to declare war immediately.'

Craste: 'That's completely impossible. I couldn't possibly take such a decision without referring to my superior Chris Patten and he's in Hong Kong.'

Morris: 'Good. Because he's on the line now by satellite. Mr Patten, what do you think of war now?'

On the TV monitor, Patten nodded. It was old footage of a dreary moment from a Tory party conference. Patten looked half asleep as he consented to something, probably Peter Lilley threatening another crackdown on social security scroungers. But that wasn't important now. It looked as though he was nodding at Morris's question.

Craste: 'Very well. It's war.'

Hawtrey: 'War it is.'

On the monitor, Donald Beth'lem chipped in: 'That's it, Chris. War has broken out. That's it – a war.'

Chris: 'That's it. It's war.'

The word WAR appeared in big red neon at the back of the studio. Suddenly lights appeared from overhead – the same sort of lights that used to illuminate Churchill's war cabinet, no doubt. Morris was marching across the studio, straightening his suit, a media warrior barking at his audience over the exploding incidental music: 'From now on *The Day Today* will be providing the most immediate coverage of any war ever fought.' Douglas Hurd was on a monitor, ready to supply his opinion. It was never sought. But it was good to know he was there. Another studio reporter was keeping up with up-to-the-minute developments from *The Day Today* news pipe. Whatever that meant. And Suzanna Gekkaloys was ready to rush off in her heels across the studio, to what Morris called 'the inside of the fight, like some crazy Trojan'.

But first, let's put the war on hold and hear about the weather with Sylvester. Sylvester's head peeped through a map of Britain somewhere around Walsall. He swivelled around in this map-cum-collar, and as his nose came into line with say, Bristol, he told us what the weather was going to be like in the South West. The things those chaps can do with graphics these days!

Back to the war. 'Donald, what's the latest?' 'As I swilled the last traces of toothpaste from my mouth this morning,' said

Donald portentously, 'a soldier's head flew past the window shouting the word victory.'

The Day Today had its own smart bomb with a nose camera called Stephen. A TV monitor showed how Stephen was homing in on his target. 'There it goes,' said the studio expert. 'It's trying to locate the soldier. It's found him. It goes in through the mouth, down the oesophagus, into the stomach and it explodes.'

'Absolute bang!' shouted Morris. 'That's *The Day Today* – bringing you another tear on the face of the world's mother.' He moderated his tone more than somewhat. 'Now sport with Alan Partridge.' Hang on, though. Wasn't that *The Day Today*'s smart bomb?

'Some late football results from Division Two,' said Partridge, with a face more serious than those of the war correspondents. Which is just as well because football is much, much, more important than anything. 'Hull Paragraph 5, Portsmouth Bubble-jet 1. Sheffield Hysterical 3, Chunky Norwich 1.' There was a match in Scotland that had been abandoned because the referee couldn't stop the teams playing.

By now *The Day Today*'s reporter was inside the fight. Whatever that meant. 'Suzanna Gekkaloys has broken through to the front line. This is her contribution to history.' Suzanna had changed her newsreader's suit for khaki, but the supercilious expression, stupid voice and the microphone in her face told you it was the same woman we'd seen in the studio minutes earlier. She jumped out of the jeep with shells exploding all around her, broke down the door to a house, shot a wounded man dead and set up her cameras in the home of a cowering family, knowing that the presence of a TV crew would make the place a prime target.

A very good, brave, cutting edge dispatch, but we didn't have any more time for war reports. Just a moment for Morris to show viewers tomorrow's front pages. The papers didn't seem to have anything about the war. *The Times'* top story, for instance, was:

'Crazed wolves in store a bad mistake admit Mothercare.'

The news was over. You could tell because as the credits rolled Chris Morris came in front of his desk and lay down on his face in the shape of a crucifix. How could they leave us like this? Who had won? Who had lost? Where was the documentary that would explain what had happened? Were there many casualties? How could we find out? This was how: 'Available now on commercial video, *The Day Today: This is Our War*, featuring the men and women who sacrificed themselves at the altar of fact.' It was only £10.99. But that wasn't all: there were 1,000 pop classics on the video too, all with appropriate footage. The enemy (whoever they were) surrendered to: 'Hands up, baby, hands up – give me your heart, baby.' Fires raged to: 'Burn, baby, burn – Disco Inferno.' These were songs that we couldn't hear during the real war. That is, if what we saw on screen was a real war.

RUBBER BULLETS

The Day Today was especially disturbing because its satire changed nothing. Michael Buerk and Jeremy Paxman still perform on their news programmes with substantially the same self-regard as before they were satirised by Chris Morris. Buerk still maintains his vast range of reassuring vocal and facial twitches, Paxman his delicious superciliousness. Local news bulletins still strive desperately to find something, anything, more absurd than sponsored bed pushes and delayed trains from Fenchurch Street. And City news is still as looney-tune, just as laughably incomprehensible to those who aren't among the cognoscenti, as that reported by Collaterlie Sisters. The parade of absurdity carries on.

Baudrillard would have loved *The Day Today* and its failure to have much real impact. *The Day Today* deprived TV news of any claims to be taken seriously, and yet it carried on regardless.

In fact, it got bigger, more bombastic and affected in the wake of *The Day Today*. Twenty-four-hour news networks mushroomed in the mid and late nineties, graphics became even more fanciful, the dimwit double acts of news presenters became more ludicrous, the exasperation of TV journalists with the unyieldingly dreary quality of their stories more apparent. A couple of scintillas of doubt rode back from their exile: Could it be that TV news was using *The Day Today* as a role model? Was the idea that TV news now meant to be funny?

I became very conscious of the useless virility of TV news when I was watching a live broadcast of the nail bomb that exploded in Brick Lane, east London, in the spring of 1999. I first saw the news in a bulletin on ITV and thought, now I'll find out what really happened. I flicked over to Sky News where there was already a camera at the end of Brick Lane pointing past a reporter who stood with a microphone in his hand. He was being interviewed by the anchor back at the Isleworth studio. But what could he know as he had been standing answering questions from the anchor for ages, rather than being permitted to go off-camera and find out what, if anything, was happening? There were no casualties to photograph and, as yet, few witnesses to interview. Over on BBC News 24, there was amateur video footage from an upstairs window of a flat on Brick Lane which showed smoke and the arrival of the fire brigade. This short film was repeated again and again. Nowadays, I have three twenty-four-hour news networks – Sky, BBC News 24 and CNN – all of which exist to give me and other subscribers the news as it happens. But, as in the case of the Brick Lane nail bomb reports, there is often nothing to say, but plenty of airtime in which to say it. Our hunger for news and for spectacle is often unsated by the sheer recalcitrant tedium of the reality on which TV news is frustratingly sometimes dependent.

The Day Today's satire would not have worked if it had merely consisted of showing tedium. It would have been as unwatchable as an Andy Warhol film, or as a video film of smoke pouring into a street in Brick Lane. Instead, it showed what TV must do if it is to satisfy our hunger for news. Admittedly, TV news has never fomented a war, but, it's hard not to think, if TV journalists were really following the logic of broadcasting to the extreme, they really should. War has everything that TV news wants: spectacle, human tragedy, the all-consuming journalistic need to appear more virile than their rivals, the opportunity for novelettish prose, bang after absolute bang. If war didn't exist, TV news would have to invent it. And then, once it had invented it, it would exploit it until it was usless and then, by the final headlines, forget it had ever happened.

It doesn't matter if CNN can tell us exactly what is happening, that it can have a camera in every foxhole, when our hunger is not for political analysis of a situation, for an understanding of what happened, but for its dramatic simulation. What *The Day Today* showed us satirically is that this dramatic simulation is the creation of dim but ruthless artists.

The war episode of *The Day Today* was broadcast in 1994, three years after the Gulf War ended, at a time when the speciousness of that war's coverage was still fresh in our minds and the boasts of news outfits like CNN had some novelty value. But its satire achieved something miraculous, and miraculously depressing: it blew up TV news and the fragments descended back into exactly the same places as before the explosion.

TV satire used to be different. The sixties show *That Was the Week That Was* upset the butts of the jokes in a way that is inconceivable now. Back in 1962, a Conservative MP urged that the BBC be impeached because the show ridiculed MPs. It was so offensive to the government that the Postmaster-General considered banning the programme; only Harold Macmillan's intervention ensured that it continued to be broadcast. Better to be mocked than ignored, he wisely reasoned; better take the stick than use it.

One critic attacked presenter David Frost and producer Ned Sherrin for being 'pedlars of filth and smut and destroyers of all that Britain holds dear'. Frost regularly attacked the probity of the then Home Secretary Henry Brooke, who was dubbed by the show 'probably the most hated man in Britain', though Frost usually ended by pretending to correct himself: 'Seriously, though, he's doing a grand job.' *TW3*, as it became known, was finally taken off the air because of fears that it would influence voters in the 1964 general election. Never since has a satirical TV programme been so feared or loathed.

In the late eighties and early nineties, *Spitting Image* strove for a similar effect but, arguably because British political culture had become less deferential in the intervening years, it proved incapable of causing equivalent upset. Admittedly, some Tory MPs were outraged by its attack on British public life, but by that time, though, most of the targets of the satire were too astute to complain. Michael Heseltine even tried to buy his latex puppet but changed his mind after he was asked to make the cheque payable to the Labour Party. And yet his attitude was symptomatic of a change in politicians' attitudes: now they would cosy up to the satirists.

As a result much TV satire has become a conservative force: it has turned politics into a spectacle which we can only laugh at cynically, having surrendered any hope of real change. Typical of this are John Bird and John Fortune, whose parodies of ministers or captains of industry work by confirming the audience's sense of futility at the political process.

Every time I saw an MP on *Have I Got News For You*, for instance, it was hard for me not to think – hasn't this lemon got some constituency work to do? The relationship between satirists and satirised has become too cosy. No matter how much of a whipping politicians received from Hislop and Deayton, their very presence on the show destroyed the impact.

Only a handful of TV satirists have seemed capable of doing

something more winningly offensive during the nineties. One was Michael Moore, whose *TV Nation* series was, he claimed, a new genre called 'docucomedy' which involved creating stunts in order to satirise big business or the political process. The other was Mark Thomas, whose stunts have been much more dangerous and upsetting to the establishment. In one, Thomas ambushed a nuclear train in Kent with two tanks and forty hooded 'terrorists'. In another, a multiple sclerosis sufferer confronted Jack Straw and asked if the Home Secretary, who is opposed to the legalisation of cannabis, would mind if he lit up a joint to ease his pain. Police cautioned him but later discovered there was only tobacco in his roll-up.

Thomas also tackled the arms industry. He and his colleagues invented a company that would supply much-needed PR to the arms industry and set up a stall at an industry fair in Athens. The coup was to get a leading member of the Indonesian armed forces, Major General Widjojo, to participate in a mock interview with the PR firm, aimed at helping him get his message across in the media. Torture was necessary. The massacre of 271 civilians in a church yard was necessary. That sort of thing. Widjojo answered questions in which, for the first time, an Indonesian official admitted that civilians were tortured by members of the country's armed forces.

I hope that Thomas gets danger money for his work because, when you're making monkeys out of torturers, their wrath is more fearsome than that of Tory MPs. Somehow I can't imagine Ian Hislop or Rory Bremner having the wit to pull this kind of stunt. In fact, I can't imagine many TV reporters going undercover in this way either to expose corruption or deceit. Thomas has walked into something of a vacuum in this respect: news series such as *World in Action*, which we used to rely on for investigative reporting, have been cancelled. Instead, we have to rely on stand-up comedians to do the work of highlighting political abuses. In this respect, it's appropriate that Mark

Thomas isn't especially funny; now it's news rather than satire that strives to be entertaining and as a result manages to be funny.

CHAPTER 10

1995: Wet, Cold and Dentally Challenged

ALIENS IN CHESTER

When *Hollyoaks* began in 1995, I couldn't quite believe what I was seeing. Here was a children's drama set in Britain in which for once everybody seemed reasonably well adjusted. The characters lived in nice new homes in suburban Chester and had blameless romances with partners who had sexy bodies and, often, their own means of transport. Some of *Hollyoaks*' leading protagonists were even tanned. Everybody in the show was groomed with the careful attention hitherto reserved in this country only for dogs in the final stages of Cruft's.

This wasn't so much Britain's first teen soap as a salute to our national dentistry. For years British soaps had answered the bronzed bodies and white teeth of *Beverly Hills 90210* and *Neighbours* with bronzed teeth and white bodies. No longer, said *Hollyoaks*. The days when the good-time hopes of programme makers would founder on the yellowing stumps of a cast of verité trolls were over. Over too were the days when Kenneth Clark would invite viewers to look over his shoulder at one of the great achievements of western civilisation – Chartres Cathedral, say –

while his audience would remain transfixed by one of the great failings of western civilisation, his teeth. Thanks to *Hollyoaks*, though, British television for once had a cast of handsome actors who could smile without shame throughout each half-hour episode. And they did – heaven knows *why*, but they did. Admittedly, Alvin Stardust did pull the pints in the local pub, but let's not spoil the story.

I remember Channel 4's advertisements for the show which were plastered on the sides of buses. Kurt, the serial's teen stud, was pictured along with the caption: 'Kurt's got the best seat on the bus.' Imagine! The advertisement was drawing attention to the pertness of an Englishman's bottom. There was a time when an Englishman's bottom was his own private domain, something to be kept in the darkened privacy of his trousers except in the direst emergency. If it did come out at all, it would do so in the form of a comical builder's cleavage, or to bob coitally in a scene of traumatising sexual disgust in Dennis Potter's *The Singing Detective*, or, most commonly, for windy outbursts of toilet humour. Never before in the field of mainstream British television was the male bottom considered the fit object of sexual attraction, or fit in any way at all. Its possible existence as a curvaceous peach of fun was never to be mentioned in public, still less was it to be broadcast in large type on the side of the Number 38.

For me in 1995, aged thirty-three, and with a lifetime of watching British television behind me, this was all very shocking. On this country's television, in its documentaries, political programmes, sitcoms, dramas, news bulletins, advertisements, games shows, even in its sports broadcasting, nobody was well adjusted. Very few had much fun, curvaceous or otherwise. And yet Phil Redmond, the former scriptwriter and creator of *Brookside*, who devised *Hollyoaks*, had quite explicitly sought to bring the feel-good production values of American and Australian soap operas to British television. We, too, could run through the surf flexing pristine pectorals and wearing brief briefs into the arms of pneumatic beach bums of whatever gender took our fancy. We didn't have to paddle at Blackpool with rolled-up trousers and knotted handkerchiefs on our heads any more.

British teenagers enjoyed Australian soaps and *Beverly Hills 90210* partly because they were wafted somewhere exotic and sunny but viewers of all ages demanded that home-grown television should give them something different. British viewers wanted to see British characters whose teeth were more brown than theirs, who were more aesthetically displeasing than them, who suffered more than them, who were not, and never would be, happy. And by watching these characters suffer on screen, we might feel slightly better about ourselves. Think of *EastEnders*, the ultimate feelgood British soap. The reason people watch *EastEnders* in such numbers, surely, is because it cheers them up. You feel good watching the endless round of Albert Square woe, because you can take pleasure in other people's misfortunes – at least you don't have Pat Butcher's lifestyle, Phil Mitchell's consonant-free diction or the cuckold's horns of Ian Beale. We study the misfortunes of other people who resemble us and that makes our lot easier. That, or so I thought until October 1995, was what television in this wet, cold, dentally-challenged country, was for.

Naturally, *Hollyoaks* didn't change the agenda of British television drama, but instead found itself a quiet little early-evening niche where its singularity could be contemplated by baffled media studies students and savoured by those rare Britons who have uncomplicatedly sunny dispositions. To the rest of us it was as strange and unpromising as a road movie set on the M50 – a fundamentally foreign genre which it seemed misguided to import.

Yes, American and Australian programmes are popular in Britain, and their characters have only trifling troubles that darken their lives like a wispy cloud in an otherwise blue sky. But we demand that the characters of British programmes suffer or make fools of themselves for our delectation, so their suffering or their shame makes ours more tolerable. Happy British fun seekers are all but incomprehensible to the collective sensibility of British viewers.

PLEASURE? THE VERY IDEA!

Three of the most important and, perversely, cherished, characters in British television history make this point clear – Ena Sharples, Albert Steptoe, and Basil Fawlty. Consider, first, Ena Sharples. British viewers loved this breathtaking tartar, this gossip of *Coronation Street*. Here was a troubled woman, as nosy as Mrs Honeyman in *Camberwick Green*, but with worse headgear. Ena Sharples thought nothing of wearing her hairnet jammed tight over her head when she went out in public, and, quite frankly, nor did anyone else, though they did not dare to tell her so. She could get away with this sartorial mistake not only because she was the *Street*'s all-powerful matriarch, but also because the hairnet represented her modest, British world view. Her hairnet announced incontrovertibly that she was living from day-to-day a second-best life. It told the world that she was going nowhere special and so would not release her thinning curls anytime soon upon the soft, damp breeze of north-west England. Her hairnet would only come off for ceremonial occasions, funerals perhaps, or other rituals associated with misfortunes, such as redundancy parties or hospital visits. As for those occasions that might cause Ena Sharples to whip off her hairnet and share in the sheer joy of life – but no, these were not likely, not likely at all. In this respect, like Miss Havisham's bridal dress, Ena Sharples' curls were kept in readiness for something that seemed less and less conceivable as time marched furiously on.

Ena Sharples' coat was buttoned up as far as it would go and her scarf was knotted tightly around her throat. The only bits of human flesh that one could behold on her formidable frame were that part of the head below the hairnet line and, at the ends of her raincoat sleeves, her hands. The left hand would more often than not rest on her lap or on the table as she sat in the snug of the Rovers, leaving the right hand to perform the vital functions of matriarchal office as she held court. Three fingers of this hand would be clutched around her glass of stout, that dark effervescence-free drink, as plain, flat and as serious as her life, and the index finger would be held in reserve to point at some soft article who had foolishly intruded into her domain. 'Now look here, young man,' she would start, her index finger at forty-five degrees to the horizontal and ready to fire pointed venom from its tip into the dizzy young thing's chest.

Her head was even more compelling. The big ears, adapted by natural selection for hearing everything that went on in Weatherfield, were held flat against her head by earrings which, I imagine, were little lead weights designed to make her lobes even longer and her ears even more effectively large. The ears rhymed with the pendulous bags under her eyes, and were brought on, no doubt, by years of sleepless nights reflecting on the inadequacy of the humanity all around her. Her eyebrows, long, sculpted affairs, rose and fell at first, but finally sloped and thickened as they converged on the dense pinch of flesh above her nose, which, in itself, bespoke anger and worry. Her eyes were blank and furious, like a shark's. The face, in sum, was a picture of the longtime moral outrage of a woman who thought herself unimpeachable and yet lived in a fallen world of flibbertigibbets and men who were, by definition, as impressive as used dishwater.

Violet Carson, who played Ena Sharples, was dead long before *Hollyoaks* appeared to Phil Redmond in a dream. But if she had been offered a guest role in the programme (perhaps Kurt could have been her long-lost secret great-grandson, or her Dickensian ward), she could have destroyed the smug milieu of *Hollyoaks* in minutes with a glower and a string of monosyllables. Ena's words bounced like bombs from her tongue into the fast-chilling air around her, when she had a caustic exchange with Pat Phoenix's Elsie Tanner or even with Doris Speed's Annie Walker. Yes, Ena even took on Annie Walker, even though Annie had the natural advantage of running the Rovers, which made her as near to royalty as *Coronation Street* could muster. But Ena wouldn't defer to that royalty, nor indeed would she have any truck with Annie Walker's scented hauteur or the moral corruption betrayed by Annie's received pronunciation. There was no deference from Ena to Annie, just hard stares. That's how hard Ena Sharples was. She would take on anybody. She was as hard as nails, and yet, as time wore on, as brittle as pressed flowers.

True, Violet Carson did play the piano on TV variety shows and on those occasions did smile, but this seemed obscenely out of character. For the rest, I cannot believe that Ena Sharples ever had fun, except – and even this would be as unlikely as Stan Ogden uttering some brilliant aperçus – at somebody else's downfall. I cannot, for the life of me, imagine Ena Sharples on a donkey at Blackpool Pleasure Beach, even sidesaddle. Pleasure? *Pleasure*? The very idea!

Albert Steptoe was a repulsive wreck of a man, who, even more than Ena Sharples, was dressed in such a way that he was not fit to be seen in public. He only washed his socks when he had a bath, and this did not necessarily mean that he took them off. Never, until Homer's dad's teeth in *The Simpsons* burst from his mouth and into our consciousness, have false teeth been so repulsively mobilised in a sitcom. Albert's were a blackened set, no doubt partly because he kept them overnight in a glass of his favourite drink, gin and tonic. His chosen dress, knackered old trousers with collarless shirt and a threadbare woollen waistcoat, was merely a prelude to considering the decrepit mess that was his head. Wilfrid Brambell's chin was long, nearly as long as Bruce Forsyth's and as tapered as Jimmy Hill's.

Albert Steptoe's face set into a rueful pose whenever he was caught out by his son Harold. For years, I would imitate this expression, hunching my shoulders and pushing my head into the chest. This preparatory work done, I would pull the sides of my mouth down and raising the upper lip towards my nose, squinting with my eyes and, the pièce de résistance, stuck my tongue between the front teeth of the bottom jaw and the lower lip, to emphasise the chin. Sometimes my schoolboy friends would join me in this. There we would stand in a corner of the playground, hunched, scowling, collectively whining in falsetto: ''arold! 'arold!'. And we wondered why no girls were interested in us.

In Egremont, a small town in Cumbria, they have a contest each year to determine who is the best gurner. A gurner is a man – and I think only a man, though there seems to be no logical reason for this restriction – who can pull his face into the most ugly shape. Only in Great Britain, surely, would such facial ugliness be so prized. This isn't because Britons have a global monopoly on ugliness (though the rudimentariness of our dental care and the pastiness of our complexions do help us to command the awe of many other countries less favoured by our shortcomings), but because only they could thwart ugliness's evil power by considering it a virtue and enshrining that virtue in the form of a competition. In any event, there is no evidence, not a shred of it, that Wilfrid Brambell, either in character as Albert Steptoe or as a budding gurner in his own right, ever competed in Egremont's prestigious contest. Were he to have done so, ugly men with advanced cases of facial mobility, flaccid-faced frighteners from John o'Groats to Lands End, might as well have packed up and gone home, aware that their pretensions to notoriety would have been trumped by the most hideous card in the deck. Albert, or indeed Wilfrid, could have been the reigning monarch of Uglyville if only had he so desired.

Despite this hypothetical claim to fame, Albert Steptoe's lot was not in fact a happy one. He lived in a rag-and-bone yard, a home as filled with junk as his son's head was filled with dreams of escape. He spent the autumn of his days in constant fear that Harold would leave home. The drama came from the fact that his perilous life was lived on a knife edge: if his ingenuity slipped, if he failed to realise some scheme to keep Harold's itchy feet under the kitchen table, he would be left devoid of human contact, unless you counted the skeleton that dangled in the living room, or unless you are the kind of person who is prepared to make remarkable claims to the effect that Hercules, chewer of hay and puller of tat, was really something more than a horse. Harold was nearly forty and so there was the possibility that he would still find a woman to share his world. There was more life out there, he realised, than there was in a tramp's, or indeed his father's, vest. And he wanted a little bit of it before he got old. For his part, Albert's chief purpose in life was to prevent Harold escaping, in order that the son would look after the father as decrepitude took an even firmer hold on his unspeakable self. It was an Oedipal struggle every week. Once, Harold brought home a woman to sleep with him, in an intentional affront to his father. (Why, Harold? Why did you bring her back home to this house that would make a battle-hardened member of the SAS run away like a little girl? What were you thinking of?). He lured her home to sleep on his groovy new water bed, but of course at the vital moment that punctured like his dreams of escape, dampening her ardour and yet warming the cockles of his dad's heart.

In *Steptoe and Son*, the Oedipal struggle was never resolved and was instead grafted onto a theme regularly played out in Russian literature, that of the child who is compelled to set aside their own life to care for an ageing parent. The frustration and resentment bred in this child as a result of being psychically suffocated in this way was just the thing for gloomy Russian dramas, and yet here it was played for laughs, poignant ones though, since anybody who clearly remembers their childhood or has ever been a parent could understand the dynamics of Ray Galton and Alan Simpson's sitcom. Even if Albert did not feel guilty for what he was doing to his son, we loathed him for it.

Albert Steptoe was more like Miss Havisham than Ena Sharples could ever be. He was surrounded by the weight of history, the mess of discarded human acquisition. Nothing would ever find its proper place, be used again for its proper purpose. His wife was dead and her memory was daily defiled because Albert used it to make Harold feel guilty and stay at home. But was Albert happy? Hardly. His only power was to ruin his son's life, and this he did. Like Ena Sharples, his chief role in life was not to add to the sum of human happiness, rather to subtract from it.

Later, the film director Terence Davies would use Wilfrid Brambell to play a dying cancer patient in the last part of his *Trilogy*. In the context of Brambell's TV persona, this made perfect sense, even though his slow death was almost unbearable to watch. And, even worse, to hear: that harrowing cough that echoed around the hospital as his racked body collapsed towards easeless death did have its comically overplayed grisliness, yes, but even so it was not to be compared with, say, Little Nell's expiration. This was the death that Harold would never witness in his many years of devotion to his father: in television sitcoms such as *Steptoe and Son* there can be no such resolution, since resolution takes away the fundamental premise of the drama.

Easeless death – that was Basil Fawlty's life. His life with Sybil at Torquay's least enchanting hotel was a long slow march to the grave with only the light relief of being able to hit his Spanish waiter on a regular basis for consolation. As trapped as Harold Steptoe in a suffocating milieu, thwarted in a marriage whose only principle was mutual hatred, and unable to leave a job as a hotel manager – a post which demanded skills of human warmth and service which he was temperamentally unable to supply –

Basil Fawlty did once escape. In a laundry basket. Things had got too much for him, the panic of the plot had reached a point where he could do nothing but leave, even if it was to be in a box of linen soiled by strangers. There has surely never been a more graphic depiction on British television of shame and humiliation, of panic and the overwhelming urge to take flight from a sea of troubles; no clearer expression of the need for immediate therapeutic intervention, and yet we loved to laugh at his misfortune, surely not only because the script was so well done or the drama so well handled, but because, when we watch television we want to see a theatre of cruelty. We want to sit in upholstered security and watch others suffer for our pleasure.

While other leading male characters in British television have driven cars that expressed their success and implied their masculinity was just what it should be (Simon Templar's Volvo, Morse's Jaguar, DI Regan's Ford Granada, Jason King's Interceptor, with its cream leather seats, wooden steering wheel and, quite probably, a cheroot holder and a little well to hold the optional ice bucket), Fawlty drove an Austin 1100 which bespoke a symbolic castration every bit as severe, though with fewer comic overtones, as Del Boy's choice of motor in *Only Fools and Horses*, the Reliant three-wheeler. Not only did Fawlty drive a bad car, but he compounded his error by treating it shamefully. The episode in which Fawlty has to transport in his car a posh French meal from Antoine's top-notch restaurant, culminated with him psycho-sexually thrashing his stalled car in the street. This is one of the funniest scenes in one of the best written and performed sitcoms in British history and yet its comedy is rooted in voyeuristic cruelty. When a man beats a car for its inability to perform, he is, in a symbolic and all-too-public sense, impugning his own masculinity.

These were the characters who impressed themselves on me as I grew up watching television. A tartar, a selfish martyr and a brilliantined stick insect. From them and their like on television,

I composed my notion of the British character and saw it confirmed in reality. The best things about my country, it seemed to me then as it seems to me now, were that it knew its hopelessness so well and it was brave enough to create TV characters who reflected this. For decades these characters would become Britain's chief means of entertainment and of attaining a national self-knowledge. A paradoxical self-knowledge, to be sure, since it was sublimated, buried under large rocks of irony and other distancing devices, but there, still there. There is not much *Hollyoaks* Kurt in most British people, not much sunniness of disposition; but in each Briton there are varying proportions of Ena, Albert and Basil – little concentrations that, I feel sure, we have only been able to recognise when we see them represented on television. It has been an incredible alchemical transformation – to take Britain's rain-soaked souls and make them into TV gold. These things, through thick and thin, have made me proud to be British, while those programmes overtly staged to stimulate such feelings – royal weddings, royal addresses, royal funerals – have not.

THE CROWNING MOMENT OF BRITISH TELEVISION

After the war, there were great hopes for television in Britain. It would hold this crumbling kingdom together since, more powerfully than other forms of mass media, television would supply moving images direct to the living room, straight into the otherwise impenetrable heart of British life. But few then contemplated that, as a result, our living rooms would be full of Enas, Alberts and Basils. Or that nationwide television would connect the individuals of this nation through soap operas, still less through sitcoms, through a shared cultural memory densely criss-crossed with threads of frivolity, vulgarity, catchphrases, sport, games shows, stuffed bears, cookery programmes, and finally, costume dramas, cop shows, or fly-on-the-wall documentaries.

No, after the war, broadcasters hoped television would be a much more straightforwardly unifying affair. In 1949, Norman Collins, then controller of BBC Television, wrote: 'With nation-wide television, when the King leaves Buckingham Palace the Mall will extend as far as the Royal Mile and the King will ride simultaneously through the four Kingdoms. A Royal Wedding will be a nation's wedding. On Remembrance Day the shadow of the Cenotaph will fall across the whole country and on great rejoicings the fireworks of Hyde Park will burst and sparkle at every fireside.'

Collins only had to wait four years for his notion of television as national unifier to come true. After the death of George VI in 1952, Elizabeth was crowned Queen in 1953 under the arc lights at Westminster Abbey and television was crowned as Britain's most important cultural institution. Elizabeth's coronation was the moment, after all, when television overtook radio as the chief national broadcasting medium: 11 million tuned into the wireless to hear the coronation, but 20 million, 56 per cent of the population, watched it on television and heard Richard Dimbleby's narration. Even though there were only two and a half million television sets in Britain at the time, Britons found screens that would allow them to see that then supremely important national transformation, the mutation of Elizabeth into Queen Elizabeth II. In the early fifties, television schedules were tucked away at the back of the *Radio Times*, rather as the radio schedules are now. Sales of TV sets (then £85 each) soared in that year, including the one bought by Kenneth Halliwell. If the film *Prick Up Your Ears* is anything to go by, he immortalised and, for some, immoralised the event by having sex with Joe Orton in a narrow bed while the Westminster Abbey coronation unfolded on his neglected screen. Thus was Britain's national television born.

Twenty million isn't all that many viewers – nowadays *Coronation Street* and *EastEnders* sometimes command those sorts of viewing figures and, as recently as 1996, the *Only Fools and Horses Christmas Special* was watched by more than 26 million festively-stupefied couch potatoes expressing national solidarity in the only way they could after turkey and pudding. And yet the coronation marked the point at which television became a national mass medium. In those days there was only one channel (ITV first started broadcasting in 1955) and, as a result, television's power to command a mass audience all watching the same thing was then unimpeded.

Since the coronation of Queen Elizabeth II, the most important national events have been primarily television events (the 1966 World Cup, Charles and Di's 1981 wedding, for instance). This was easier to achieve when there were fewer channels, when everybody watched *Hancock*. But even today, when British television consists of five terrestrial channels which, with some regional variations, broadcast nationwide, television is still the most powerful culturally unifying force in the country. And yet, the era in which TV was the chief cultural national unifier is doomed, that strange period during which each family's domestic space, its private world of fantasies and frustrations, became a place where that family united most significantly with the rest of the country.

In *The Enchanted Glass*, a book about Britain and its monarchy, Tom Nairn wrote: 'There is no power to see ourselves as others see us, and like anyone else the British look into a mirror to try and get a sense of themselves. In doing so they are luckier but ultimately less fortunate than other peoples: a gilded image is reflected back, made up of sonorous past achievement, enviable stability and the painted folklore of Parliament and Monarchy.' Television, too, is an enchanted glass, but one that has reflected back something more troubling than this lucky reflection Nairn speaks of, for in television's images we have not just seen the national identity as defined by the Crown (though we have been able to see that banal image, and more awfully clearly than Nairn imagined), but as expressed through Mrs Slocombe, Eric, Ernie, Basil, Ena, Albert. We have been able to glimpse ourselves ungilded and unappealing, and yet these enchanting reflections have entertained as well as reflected us.

Nairn reckoned that Lord Reith, the first director-general of the BBC, was like Fleet Street proprietors, a stage manager to the monarchy. He was, but British television since then has fallen from its Reithian grace. It, and British newspapers, have become stage managers *of* the monarchy rather than *to* it: the chains of deference have fallen away like water, and this has had a profound impact on the nature of television. Instead of royalty commanding the media stage, it has become a soap opera barely as compelling as *Coronation Street* or *EastEnders*. Now, The Windsors is a soap which has many of the characteristics of other TV soaps: it seems to be endless; it has its cycles of dreariness and melodrama; it can tell us something of the society we live in but not much, since it is mostly a blissfully unedifying entertainment; it has no secrets worth speaking of, since if it did, they would not remain secrets for long. Royalty, partly thanks to television, is no longer intrinsically special, no longer mysterious, no longer always interesting, and, above all, no longer awe inspiring. Lord Reith would have hated what television has done to our monarchy.

When I imagine Lord Reith surveying British television at the end of the millennium, I fancy that he looks like Ena Sharples, a weathered Cassandra who lived to see his prophecies come hatefully true. After the war, Lord Reith was often seething and outraged to see what had happened to the British Broadcasting Corporation that he had brought into being. This was the Presbyterian who would ask applicants to the BBC 'Do you accept the fundamental teachings of Jesus Christ?' and yet would live on until the time when profanities were uttered during *Till Death*

Us Do Part. He died on 16 June 1971 and so was never exposed to Mrs Slocombe's pussy.

Had he lived to witness this very British double entendre, Lord Reith would surely have retreated to the Rovers Return snug with Ena to contemplate the ruin of their values. There they would sit, he the very tall figure with the unimpeachably soft drink, she the one in the hairnet. For hours they would sit in silence trading nothing but the two hardest stares that have ever been stared in Britain. Occasionally they would speak – agreeing with each other about the nightmare the world in general and television in particular had become – but this would happen not often.

CHRISTMAS DAY, 3 P.M.

'A merry Christmas and a happy New Year. There is something wonderful in the way those old familiar warm-hearted words of the traditional Christmas message never seem to grow stale.'

I want to use my Playstation. Can we turn the telly off?

Sshh!

Listen to her. Not stale? What is she thinking of? Has she been drinking?

Not as much as you. Ssshh for five minutes.

'This year I am talking to you not from Buckingham Palace, but from Sandringham, where my family gathers every year for Christmas.'

Are we ever going to eat?

Ssshh!

'Like many families, we have lived through some difficult days this year. But Christmas is surely the right moment for us to try to put this behind us and find a moment to pray for those, wherever they are, who are doing their best.'

Isn't she grey? Was she this grey last year?

Try turning the colour up.

No, I mean her hair is greyer than it was last year.

'My husband and I –'

Oh God.

'– are greatly looking forward to revisiting New Zealand and Australia in the New Year. I have visited almost all of the thirty-two independent Commonwealth countries –'

Here we go. The Commonwealth. Here we go.

'In October, I was in Brisbane for the Commonwealth Games –'

She really has no dress sense at all, does she?

'– and then went by sea in *Britannia* –'

***Britannia*. Oh God. She's talking about *Britannia* again.**

'– to visit a number of those beautiful Commonwealth island countries in the Pacific.'

Do you think she's said 'Commonwealth' enough yet?

'I hope that your children are enjoying themselves as much as mine are –'

I'm not. Not any more.

'– on a day which is especially the children's festival –'

Doesn't that mean we should turn it off?

No. Sshh!

'– kept in honour for the Child born at Bethlehem nearly two thousand years ago.'

THE INSCRUTABLE PRIVACY OF THE BRITISH LIVING ROOM

What kind of society is the one created by British television? A paradoxical one, surely, in which we are more alone and yet more together than before. Like a row of joggers on treadmills at a gym, or a traffic jam of motorists in the rush hour, we are alone in our little bubbles and yet more aware of those around us because we are engaged in the same activity. And yet, television is different since we cannot see those with whom we are sharing an activity, apart from those in the same room, but a bond is established nonetheless. We are linked by a shared memory bank of TV experiences.

True, the experiences I have of watching, say, *Morecambe and Wise* may well be different from yours, but we can still share something of those experiences, even if it merely consists of being able to sing 'Bring Me Sunshine' together and imitate Eric and

Ernie's parting dance, the one where they put their right hands behind their heads and then flick their left legs out, then they put their left hands up and their right legs out. Left, right, left, right, dancing in parallel towards the back of the stage until they diverge and Eric exits stage left and Ernie stage right. You don't think so? Go next door now and ask what's her name to join you. She will, you know.

When Graham Swift won the Booker Prize in 1996, he referred in his speech to the strange intimacy of writing a novel that was fated to be read privately – in bed, in the private bubble of a Tube train, alone in a restaurant. Television's relationship with viewers is rather different: yes, you can watch television in bed, just as you can read a novel in bed, but in the age of nationally unifying television this has hardly been a straightforwardly private, intimate experience.

In this age, you may not know your neighbour, but you can often be sure about what they watched last night, not just because you can hear it through the walls of your semi, but because in Britain we spend between a third and a half of our leisure time in front of the box and, until recently, with only four terrestrial channels to choose from, it was not hard to guess what Mr and Mrs Jones at Number 33 were tuning into during the evening.

This change in society infuriates anti-TV groups such as the White Dot campaign, which urges us to turn off our televisions and go and do something less boring instead – perhaps talk to the neighbours across the fence, or go down the pub for a singalong. This, after all, was the kind of face-to-face society that Richard Hoggart hymned in his book *The Uses of Literacy*: there he wrote, mournfully, about the slow death of the working-class culture he prized – the oral tradition, the importance of the neighbourhood, the sense of a community rooted in a place (rather than a virtual one rooted in the cyberspace of the Internet or the unifying and distancing space of terrestrial television). Instead, mass culture was seducing us from these healthy forms of interaction into a candy-floss world of spectacle, a rootless and shiftless society titillated by commercial popular songs, sex-and-violence novels and cheap popular papers.

Writing in the mid-fifties, Hoggart wasn't in a position to appreciate television's impact on this society, since it was then only starting to spread, mutating into a virulent virus that seemingly couldn't be cut out of our social fabric without destroying its host. This common culture that television produced in the years after the coronation arrived at the same time as the suburbanisation of Britain. The typical British viewer these days probably knows more about the Duckworths in *Coronation Street* than about the Joneses at Number 33 – most of us have been into the former's bedroom, but perhaps nobody but the Joneses themselves has been into theirs.

If this culture is coming to an end and this virus has lost its ingenious hold on our attention, then perhaps we shouldn't lament its passing. The common culture of television may have held us together, but at the same time it kept us apart, preventing us from knowing each other. It helped to make us rootless and anxious, while offering us the false hope of a community in an increasingly selfish, isolating world. Paradoxically, though, it kept that face-to-face culture alive: in its window night after night, television kept a flame burning for neighbourly communities that talked in the street and went to the pub for a singalong, just as television was undermining that way of relating to other human beings. When we watched *Coronation Street*, *EastEnders*, *Brookside*, we saw face-to-face communities that existed in our time, in the television age, but seemed very far removed from the ways in which we lived our lives. As a result, soaps, which are partly soothing, have also made us anxious: the rich interconnections between neighbourhood characters in soap operas could only contrast with socially impoverished suburban Britain. We should be more like Mrs Honeyman or Pat Butcher or even Hilda Ogden.

But there is no way back to that face-to-face culture. Instead, in the future, we will live in a non-society of people sitting in their living rooms watching different programmes from their neighbours, rather than a national community linked by a common culture of television. In the digital age, the virus of nationally unifying television will be killed. Television at last will become like other consumer durables, a lump of technology which is supposed to do no more than satisfy the desires of desiring machines. We will, or at least digital TV companies say we will, be able to choose what we want to see.

In the near future, television will converge with the Internet. We will sit in our living rooms with keyboards on our laps chatting electronically with physics professors at MIT and shanty town dwellers from Mexico City. These chats will take place on screens similar to the ones in front of which a nation used to sit transfixed from eight to eight-thirty on Thursday evenings, hanging on the every comically miserable syllable of Tony Hancock. In fact, we may sit watching *Hancock* on UK Gold while at the same time chatting happily with each other about the show's shortcomings and former cultural power on Internet Relay Chat.

The result may not appeal to the likes of Richard Hoggart, but on the Internet social groups will be much less passively constructed. You won't talk to somebody because they happen to be on the other side of your garden fence, but because there is something about them that interests you or because you want to explore the world beyond your postal district.

The British living room will become inscrutably private once more. Your neighbours will not know what you are up to in there, while, by contrast, businesses, Internet service providers and digital TV companies probably will. To fight against these incursions, we will retreat further into the darkness and become more apparently alone than ever before.

CHAPTER 11

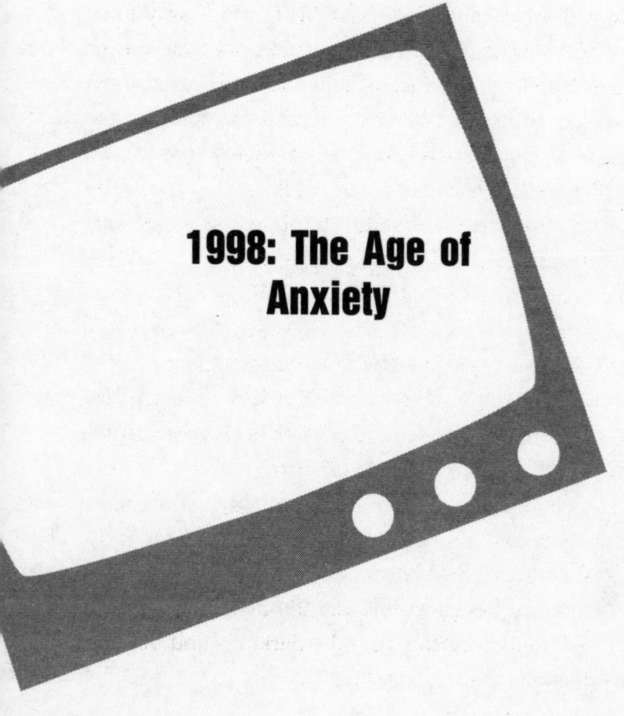

1998: The Age of Anxiety

THE SENSIBILITY OF A KING CHARLES SPANIEL

Something really needs to be done. For too long the thing's been allowed to offend our eyes. We must do something very radical indeed. Perhaps a bit of stencilling here and, I don't know, a little rag-rolling there, might make the thing look presentable. The big problem, though, is the hair. Hand me the staple gun. No that won't do it. Let me try the gas-powered nail gun. Blimey, that has a powerful recoil. It does look a treat now, though. Maybe just a quick dip in the acid bath? A few quick smacks with the claw hammer? There, that's perfect.

When I watched *Changing Rooms* in 1998, I felt it wasn't radical enough. It wasn't the rooms that needed overhauling, it was the celebrity decorators. Here's a money-saving tip. Never trust a man who looks like a King Charles spaniel. What's more, never trust a man who looks like a King Charles spaniel and wears leather trousers with a velvet coat and protruding cuffs. And never trust such a man to redecorate your coal house, let alone anything in the real house.

In one controversial episode of *Changing Rooms*, Laurence Llewelyn-Bowen was charged with the task of making a dining room lovely. Glamorous but traditional, cheap but expensive-looking, posh but homely, protestant yet catholic – you know the kind of thing. He proposed to redecorate in the Queen Anne style to achieve these ends, but with rather more Perspex and MDF than had been employed on such projects in the seventeenth century. He threw back his locks, mixed the loganberry emulsion with some Artex and started work. It was downhill from then on.

The overwhelming poverty of his aesthetic vision for the dining room of Russell and Susan Dukes, an appealing couple of chip shop owners from near Hull, became clear when Laurence returned from the National Portrait Gallery. There he had picked up two laser prints of portraits of Samuel Pepys and Nell Gwynne which he managed to graft on to pictures of Russell and Susan's heads. He placed the resulting montages in frames decorated with fruits of the forests (pine cones, twigs, but not, I hoped, tin cans and condoms) which had been sprayed with gold paint. 'Not only have you got a seventeenth-century family portrait,' said Laurence, 'but you've got a Baroque frame to match.' No they hadn't: they had tacky twig frames with repulsive laser prints which made worthless historical allusions.

But these were merely the finishing touches to Llewelyn-Bowen's project. He had painted the walls in loganberry and the floor in black and white squares to simulate the style of dining room floors of the Queen Anne period. He and *Changing Rooms*'s stereotypically grumpy handyman, Handy Andy, had constructed a mock fireplace which was stuck on to the back of a door. His pièces de résistance were the candlestick holders which were held with Blu-Tack to the walls. The possibility that the results were ugly, vulgar and contemptible, it seemed clear, had not occurred to him.

It had, however, more than occurred to Susan. When Laurence had finished spending £500 on tacky things to shove in her room, aided by two of Susan's neighbours Phil and Caroline Cockin, she was shown the decorating job by the show's host, smiling Carol Smillie. After an agonising pause, she uncovered her eyes: 'Oh, my God!' She loathed what Llewelyn-Bowen had done to the room, which, to my mind, confirmed that she was a woman of taste and discernment. As soon as the production team left she spent hours trying to restore the room to something like its previous state.

But there was time, amid all this aesthetic horror, for a touching human moment when Susan confronted the neighbours who had assisted Laurence. 'I hate it,' she told Caroline and Phil. 'We thought we would get a house we were proud of, not one I'm ashamed to show friends. I love you both, but . . .'

In saying these honest, kind words, Susan had deprived TV viewers of the denouement – the neighbourhood feud fomented by floppy-locked fops from the new Restoration era. If only we had been allowed our fractious ending, then our entertainment would have been complete. What we demanded – thanks to the manipulative conceit of the programme – was that the Dukes and the Cockins should wind up brawling in the background of the living room, as Carol Smillie, in the foreground, told the camera: 'Well, as you can see, not everybody who appears on this show is happy with the results. But that, as they say, is *Changing Rooms*. See you next week!' Otherwise, though, this episode had everything I could have expected: the drama of domestic anxiety, the potential for tears and injury with a high-velocity gas-powered nail gun, the contemptible delight I took in other people's shocking lapses of taste.

In *Changing Rooms* each week two pairs of neighbours agree to help redecorate a room in each other's house. Each couple is advised by an expert decorator (Laurence Llewelyn-Bowen, for instance). Each team is given £500 and two days to redecorate the room. This relatively small sum and the brief amount of time available gives the show its thriller structure: the clock is always counting down and the budget is so limited that corners have to be cut. Will the room be finished on time? Will it look as good as it was envisaged by the expert? What will the neighbours think?

At the end of the episode, Carol Smillie leads each couple back to their house to see what they think of the results. They stand with their hands over their eyes and then look at the room. The camera takes in their first non-verbal reactions which, I often suppose, are the true ones, only modified into politesse by their subsequent remarks.

Changing Rooms gives viewers what they hadn't known they wanted to see. It is public service broadcasting in the age of anxiety. DIY programmes hardly commanded large viewing figures before *Changing Rooms* existed. The show is ingenious because it exploits a widespread mood of anxiety about appearances, an uncertainty about good taste, and combines these with a voyeurism that television is well able to satisfy. Television once promised to bring the world to our living rooms; with *Changing Rooms*, it brings other people's living rooms to our living rooms so that we can study others' lapses in taste, other people's domestic dramas. As with soap operas, especially *EastEnders*, we like to see the sufferings of those who remind us – but not too much – of ourselves. This is hardly a new impulse in British television viewing, since we have watched the spectacle of other people's failure and suffering in soaps, sitcoms and docu-soaps for years. *Changing Rooms*, though, is more inward-looking, symptomatic of a neurotic, decadent viewing culture that has reduced spiritual aspiration to rag-rolling.

Changing Rooms has become not only one of the most popular television series of the late nineties, but also one of the most suggestive programmes about the nature of British society during that time. What's more, it's a programme that indicates how television has contributed to changing Britain. Since its inception, television has consolidated the suburbanisation of Britain, making us retreat from our streets and doorsteps into our living rooms where we were offered spectacles for our entertainment or where we became caught up in a community of people – a nation, a network of football fans, an interest group – whose members we need never have met. This domestic space has, thanks to television, become the focal point of many people's lives. When we watch it we are confronted with many different, too many different, ways of living the good life, and, yet, being exposed to these TV good lives makes us increasingly anxious: how can we get the good lives that we see for ourselves? Television contributes to making us uprooted and anxious. Many of us, at the end of the nineties, are just like Richard Hoggart's scholarship boys in the fifties: we are anxious, uncertain how to proceed since we are uprooted from the communities that shaped our ancestors' lives and gave them the principles by which they lived their lives, and even decorated their homes.

The first cookery and DIY programmes on British television may have merely been aimed at assisting people to acquire the necessary skills to improve their meals and their homes. But, by the time *Changing Rooms* came along, something much more complicated and not altogether noble was going on. Instead of acquiring skills, this programme encouraged viewers to watch people deploy their skills and often badly so that we could take pleasure in their ineptitude. But the pleasure we took in this was born of anxiety: confronted with endless possibilities of how to make our homes or ourselves beautiful, we enjoyed seeing others making bad choices and seeing tyrants of taste create monuments of tastelessness.

As Kay and I devoted ourselves to redecorating our home in 1998, I often felt we were travelling without a map. We had no Laurence Llewelyn-Bowen to help us, and instead were only guided in our choices by the presence of the insipid, cold colours with which the previous occupants had decorated the place. Hospital-corridor green, the drabbest of greys. The house we lived in was, as a result, very cold indeed. In rebellion against this, we transformed the house into a womb of warm colours. When we were tiling, sanding, painting, crying in frustration, bad-mouthing whoever had built the house we had bought, cursing the people we had bought it from, we became ultimately convinced that we were not just improving the place for ourselves materially but, by making the house an expression of what we wanted, making ourselves a home in which we could be ourselves. It seems inconceivable to me that *Changing Rooms* could have achieved the same effect, since what we wanted was too personal. When we painted the living room dark red, in order to transform the room's colour from chilly pale green, it may have looked as though we had thrown buckets of blood onto the walls; but for me the room provided uprooted and anxious me with a soothing place that no one other than Kay could disturb. A neighbour looked through the window and said: 'Severe, isn't it?' And, yes, it was, because we had happily pursued our own obsessions to the limit without the help of anyone else.

Part of the pleasurable pain of watching *Changing Rooms* is that it gives me the spectacle of seeing ordinary people admit strangers into the intimate rooms of their homes, and see them risk having their worlds torn apart by these tyrants of taste. I despise their desire for self-publicity, but at the same time admire their courage. But for me the appeal of the show doesn't end there: when the tyrants do ruin someone else's room, this helps me and surely others in the TV audience overcome our anxieties about issues of taste, since then we can see, often all too clearly, that these experts do not deserve the authority that they have been accorded. This is a very British coup: a revolt against experts on the part of those who were anxious about their own amateurishness; a revolt which restores to the amateur the self-assuredness and confidence to make a mess of their domestic space howsoever they wish. What is more, thanks to the conceit of the programme which allows only a small amount of money and time to be spent on the redecoration, even the experts, the decorators and their craftsman Handy Andy, have to cut corners – a Rawlplug and screw hammered into the wall rather than properly fitted by means of a drilled hole and a screwdriver; an ill-cut piece of MDF shoved somehow into place. This is very satisfying for DIY viewers such as me, since we may well bodge in the same way; but to have that bodging underwritten by the experts is very appealing.

If *Changing Rooms* performs a useful social function then, it is that the programme gives us back our confidence in an age of anxiety and of false judges who purport to know how things should look but do not, to our satisfaction, really know what they are talking about. And yet, most of the times the rooms have been converted to the satisfaction of the couples who have risked public humiliation on television. Then, we viewers become merely envious, since they now have what we want: a room tastefully converted and a relationship with the neighbours perhaps strengthened as a result. It's better, much better, when the room is made horrible and we realise happily that the BBC has a policy of not paying for or helping with alterations if participants are unhappy with the results. Then, instead of envy, we can feel voguish *schadenfreude*.

This was surely the purpose of *Signs of the Times*, a programme that pre-dated *Changing Rooms*, but paved the way for its exploitation of domestic neuroses and the attendant desire to take delight in the bad taste of others. For several weeks during the early 1990s, this series showed couples who allowed their domestic spaces to be photographed and demanded that they provide an on-screen justification for their often horrible decorative choices. The last shot of each profile was always the same: the person or couple standing in front of their home in a still image, defiantly if misguidedly defending the choices that had made us laugh, sneer or, very rarely, feel envious. This was a television of cruelty.

In the case of Susan Dukes, though, I didn't want to laugh or sneer. And I certainly did not feel envious. True, I felt a sense of voyeuristic titillation, since I did enjoy seeing her revolt against what had been done to her living room, but at the same time I empathised with her. Her living room had been ruined and her domestic sanctity not merely breached but roughly painted over and mangled on national television. Victim Support offers emotional help for those who have gone through the trauma of burglary; Susan had been through something very similar, but what emotional support could she have? What could she do but roll up her sleeves, join her husband and make her ruin of a room right?

At the time, many newspapers wrote articles about Susan's reaction. Even Carol Smillie – sensible, smiling Carol – was reportedly so taken aback by Susan's reaction that she started shaking. 'It was an awful moment,' said the show's executive producer Linda Clifford. 'Susan's eyes filled up with tears; she was really upset. No one had been so horrified on the programme before. We had to cut out the bits of her crying.'

Paradoxically, this brutal voyeurism was part of what made *Changing Rooms* so ingenious: it echoed, manipulated and exacerbated the cruel and yet guilt-ridden temper of our times. It combined shopping with the spectacle of other people's suffering – suffering about which we may not have felt entirely happy, but yet which we enjoyed watching at the same time as blaming somebody else (Laurence, Carol, the production team) for its existence.

Until the late nineties, DIY programmes were hardly prime-time entertainment. But, in the wake of *Changing Rooms*, came a glut of shows – *Home Front*, *Gardening Neighbours*, *Ground Force* among them – that strove to entertain with the drama of domestic makeovers. The theme was always the same – ordinary people, extraordinary improvements. Previously, such domestic programmes had marginal places on the schedules. Gardening programmes, for instance, offered two things: the spectacle of floral beauty and the patient explanation of the skills one needed to achieve such beauty in one's own garden. In the late nineties, instead, the most popular gardening shows added to depictions of floral beauty the drama of improvements by experts and the agony of material self-improvement.

Before the rise of gardening and DIY dramas, we had to rely on sitcoms to depict the neuroses of suburban living. John Esmonde and Bob Larbey, in their sitcoms *The Good Life* and *Ever Decreasing Circles*, showed us the perils of this retreat. In the former, Tom (played by Richard Briers) and Barbara Good (played by Felicity Kendal) lived in Surbiton, that Surrey commuter town that sounded as though it could be nothing but suburban. When he turned forty, Tom decided to quit his job designing plastic toy gifts for breakfast cereals, and turned his garden into a pig sty in order that the Goods could live self-sufficiently. Next door were Margo and Jerry Leadbetter, Surbitonian suburbanites both – especially Margo, who was upset that their friends next door had ruined The Avenue by turning their home into a farm with chickens, pigs, a cockerel called Lenin and a goat called Geraldine. At its most profound level, the sitcom asked what was the good life – did the Goods lead it, since they had opted out of the rat race to follow their own dream, or did the Leadbetters, who led lives of conformist material security? The show's answer was the Goods because they were relaxed and dirty and had chosen lives that were their own, while Margo, poor Margo, was a coiled spring, who could be set off at any moment and explode into her ear-piercing shriek: 'Jerry! JERRY!'. She was like *thirtysomething*'s Hope Steadman, a domestic Canute keeping the waves of grubby reality at bay, though never close to Hope's domestic serenity.

In *Ever Decreasing Circles*, Margo's neurotic seventies persona was darkened and pushed towards absurdity in the character of Martin Bryce (Richard Briers again, in arguably his best TV role), a neighbourhood do-gooder who spent his best moments in his box room, completing rotas for neighbourhood groups. He had to do all the work himself because he could not trust anyone else to do them properly. The ever decreasing circles of the title were those that Martin traced as he ran faster and faster trying to keep his part of suburbia orderly, neat and perfect. And yet, in the selfish eighties, Martin was not wholly to be condemned: he may have been a dying breed, flapping hopelessly in his box-room death throes, but he was a suburbanite who had not yet given up the battle and thus had not retreated into his living room for good. In a decade of selfish acquisition, he was a small, but intense light of communitarian spirit, tragi-comically fighting the inevitable – the collapse of neighbourhoods into discrete households connected chiefly by nothing stronger than the fact that they probably watched the same things on television the night before.

In the nineties, his role was taken up by Hyacinth Bucket (pronounced, at least by her, as Bouquet) in Roy Clarke's *Keeping Up Appearances*. She was less community-spirited but more, much more anxious than Martin Bryce. Her overwhelming anxiety over presenting a pristine, unimpeachable surface to the world consumed everything and everyone around her. If a cushion was not properly plumped or if her common brother-in-law Onslow appeared on her doorstep in his stained singlet and stubble, Hyacinth Bucket would be overtaken by a neurotic twitch in one eye that could not be easily removed. To prevent this eventuality, Hyacinth needed an army of supporters. The most striking difference between Martin Bryce and Hyacinth Bucket was that he was a lone ranger against neighbourhood collapse, while she was a highly strung, high-maintenance suburbanite, who needed the help of other people to realise her socially aspirant schemes and prevent her mental collapse. Her meek husband Richard, as a result, was merely a lifting device while she busied herself with the neurotic feminine tasks – ensuring that the coal was freshly scrubbed and that every object in the house (even Richard) rested on at least one doily. Her neighbours, especially Elizabeth and Elizabeth's divorced brother Emmet, existed to help her keep up the appearance of her home. For her, well-being was not something she achieved for herself, but something that could only be conferred by outsiders. In this sense, *Keeping Up Appearances* was the necessary television prelude to *Changing Rooms*. Hyacinth would have loved a complete makeover by Laurence Llewelyn-Bowen, but only if she could have made herself believe his Queen Anne-style redesign of her dining room would have helped improve her social standing.

FANNY CRADOCK'S EYEBROWS

Television has offered recalcitrant Britons the hope of domestic improvement for many decades. In the case of cookery, where Britain upholds a proud heritage of being laughed at by every other nation for its culinary ineptitude, such improvement has been deemed an achievable political goal by commissioning editors. Culinary tyrants of taste were unleashed like excitable dogs on the British viewing public many years ago in order to improve our cooking skills. But have they succeeded? Quite possibly not: sales of pot noodles have risen with the increase in the number of TV chefs; the phrase 'motorway service station cuisine' remains an oxymoron.

This great, unfinished revolution began with Fanny Cradock who, in the fifties and sixties, occupied a cultural position of pivotal importance. It was her job to educate British palates and lead a nation of powdered-egg enthusiasts into the fresh new world of gourmet cuisine. Her chosen medium was television, her chosen assistant was the comedy lush, Johnny. He stood at the back of the studio clutching a stiff drink and wearing a monocle in his eye. Sometimes he handed her a gin or a glass of champagne, but mostly he didn't so much assist as lend his presence, the historic role of certain kinds of men in certain kinds of kitchen and proof that a woman needs a man like a fish needs raspberry jus.

Fanny would be bent, in evening gown and pearls, over a whirring whisk or a blurring knife, her proselytising role in British culture weighing heavy on her slender shoulders. Either that or they were particularly heavy pearls. The nerve of the woman! There never was, and never would be, an apron for Fanny. Owing to her slightly crossed eyes as well as their wild, nervous disposition, and to the fact that she had plucked her eyebrows with the viciousness she should have reserved for cutting open lobsters, Fanny looked totally crackers. Perhaps her fraught demeanour had something to do with Johnny, a man who would drive any woman to stuff something rich and alcoholic in a blender.

For years they were a double act: who could forget Johnny's catchphrase in that soap powder commercial when she caught him with dirty shirt collars and cuffs and a guilty expression? 'City dirt, Fanny' – that was his catchphrase and his excuse. As with Captain Mainwaring, the phrase 'Stupid boy!' seemed forever poised to leap from Fanny's lips.

With hindsight, one can see that the politico-cultural purpose of Fanny and Johnny was to prepare an unsuspecting nation for another comedy double act, Maggie and Denis. Like Johnny, Denis Thatcher was the stiff with a drink who did something in the City, a symbolically castrated male who had taken succour in the 19th hole, while his omnicompetent wife did the things that women did – bought groceries, made tea, ran the country.

Fanny's TV mission to whip Britons into frothy peaks of culinary achievement began in 1955 when she and Johnny, who had been restaurant critics for the *Daily Telegraph*, were hired first by the BBC and later by the newly-created ITV. From the start there was a great deal of sadomasochism in her cookery. For instance in 1956, she and Johnny were filmed on stage at the Albert Hall. She demonstrated how to make a soufflé. As she beat the ingredients of a little bowl into shape, Fanny said in a French accent: 'And then you think about the woman next door that you have never really liked but you have never really told her and so you take it out on the sauce. And that is the perfect way to make a soufflé.' Anger and energy were folded into Fanny's cuisine. Nobody could stand in the way of her noble mission. Her post-war task was as serious and urgent as the creation of the welfare state: her role was to demonstrate that above the safety net of pork luncheon meat dangled the tantalising ladder of hollandaise sauce. We could climb that ladder into a better, tastier, more colourful world, but only if we didn't mind scampering up while Fanny whipped at our heels with an egg whisk.

But there was more to Fanny than pain. With the advent of colour television, Fanny was able to unleash her gaudy food decorations on an unsuspecting, drab Britain. British food, hitherto, had been in black and white, eaten by grey people in grey homes. Fanny aimed to change all that. But she went too far. On *Fanny Cradock Invites* and *Fanny Cradock Cooks for Christmas* she relied too heavily on food dye. Her brandy butter was pale green to tone with the little bits of glacé cherries, angelica and nuts that she decoratively appliquéd to the buttery mound. Her mashed potatoes were often green and sat, unbecomingly, around a piece of fish.

That said, Fanny Cradock was inspired by the best of motives. Colour had been criminally ignored by British cooks, as had the importance of food decoration to a pleasing table. Her melon basket, dotted with flowers, is still beautiful in my mind's eye, long after I forked her green mash into my mental waste bin.

But she came to a quick end as a TV chef. In 1976, she was invited to appear on *The Big Time*, a show hosted by Esther Rantzen in which ordinary viewers were given the chance to achieve lifelong ambitions. It was the show that was responsible for taking Sheena Easton from obscurity in clubs to international stardom. But it was also the show that served to destroy Fanny Cradock, that pushed her off the pale-green brandy butter mountain of culinary celebrity.

She was invited to appear with a woman called Gwen who had won a magazine competition that had awarded her the title Cook of the Realm because of a particularly splendid menu she had created with her own fair hands. She met Fanny at a restaurant to discuss her achievement and receive praise from this tyrant of taste. Gwen's menu started with seafood cocktail and then went straight into duck with blackberry sauce. Fanny rolled her wild eyes and raised what was left of her eyebrows. She puffed up her cheeks and exhaled noisily. She was not happy. Gwen said evenly that her menu had been good enough to win the Cook of the Realm award. Fanny glanced at her sharply and said: 'Yes, dear, but now you're among professionals.'

This seemed particularly cruel. After all, women such as Gwen had taken on culinary aspirations thanks to the likes of Fanny. They had set aside their tinned spaghetti and dreamed of higher things. But Gwen had aspired to excellence only to be crushed by her mentor. In one scene the great culinary proselytiser had been revealed as a megalomaniac chef who no longer deserved viewers' respect. Fanny Cradock never made a cookery programme again.

Hundreds of chefs rushed to TV kitchens to fill Fanny's void. Today, if you were asked to complete the proverb, 'Too many cooks . . .' the correct answer would be '. . . on TV.' But none of them has finished the revolution that Fanny began. Our mulish disregard for the culinary arts has even been expressed in the title of a popular programme: *Can't Cook, Won't Cook*. That title would have been inconceivable in Fanny's heyday. 'Can't Cook, Won't Cook, eh, dear?' Fanny would have told some unwilling lump who had intruded into her kitchen. 'Will Cook. Will Cook. You Damned Well Will Cook!'

Nowadays cookery programmes stray from the revolutionary

path outlined by Vladimir Ilyich Ulyanov Cradock in her text *What is to Be Done (About British Cookery)*? Instead of mere practical demonstrations of culinary excellence, served up rather impatiently, we have, in *Celebrity Ready Steady Cook*, minor characters from *Coronation Street* to help us cast off our shackles. Like *Changing Rooms*, it has a thriller structure to fill our hearts with proper fervour. The proselytising is still there: guests bring along silly ingredients for under a fiver, and from these, the celebrity chefs make something wonderful in only twenty minutes, using everything they can. Cardboard thermidor done to a turn. Plastic bag pâté. That kind of thing. There is some unfairness in this, since each chef has a well-appointed kitchen behind them, teeming with fresh herbs, eggs, pasta makers, flour, sugar. What's more, when someone brings along only a lobster (£4.99), it is mentioned in passing that the thing has been cooked. Which, to my mind, is cheating.

No matter that the celebrities were Z-list, or that the host had a line in banter that made Bruce Forsyth seem like Stephen Hawking – this was remedial cuisine from the Cradock School for Successful Soufflés. In one programme, chef Nick Nairn was presented with some cooking apples, potatoes, four prepared Yorkshire puddings, sausages, a tin of mushy peas and sweet onions by the woman who played Fiona in *Coronation Street*, Angela Griffin. 'I'm a Yorkshire lass and I like Yorkshire food,' Angela confided. Nick proposed to fill the puddings with caramelised apple, roasted sausages on a bed of mushy peas. There was also talk of onion marmalade on the side. Fern Britton, like a less world-weary Judy Finnigan but ultimately of the same, banal stamp, looked at Angela as the ex-*Coronation Street* star's mouth watered at the prospect.

'Happiness?' she inquired. 'Oooh yes, mega-happy.' 'She's happy,' Fern confirmed to a nervous studio audience. Is that Professor Hawking? Your TV presenting career is waiting for you. Whenever you're ready.

The ensuing twenty minutes used the typical tropes of a thriller, a clock counting down, disaster bubbling away on each hob, lots of time-wasting handwringing and mocking glances to the heavens. It was like the film *Speed*, edgy but ultimately doomed to a happy ending since only the expendable (burnt potatoes, Dennis Hopper) wouldn't make it through.

THE BLAIRITE NICENESS OF DELIA SMITH

Fanny's high heels were quickly filled by Delia Smith's sensible flat shoes. Delia is the ice to Fanny's fire, the mineral water to her gin, the twice-baked goat's cheese soufflé to Fanny's green mash. She's like Fanny only in that she has the aim of improving British cookery. But, unlike Fanny, she suffers fools – or at least British viewers – gladly. Delia is slower. More patient. Less patronising. We tried the austere Leninism of Fanny and found that it fell into a vile cult of personality. Temperamentally, we are better suited to the sensible Blairite niceness of Delia.

The main similarity between Fanny and Delia, is that they have no truck with aprons. During one instalment of Delia Smith's *Winter Collection*, for instance, she wore a neat green blouse and autumnal waistcoat. She made three soups, two-tomato chutney, wild mushroom risotto and spaghetti alla carbonara without an apron – like a self-assured high-wire act waving away the net. With a menu like that, I would have donned oilskins, goggles and maybe even a sou'wester. But Delia's seductive art is to suggest that this food of the gods is as easy to make as – heaven forfend – a cup of instant coffee.

While the hedonistic likes of Keith Floyd offer boozy spectacle, Delia serves up an unexcitable, patient half-hour, made on the premise that these recipes will be used and used again, analysed closely – just as Delia and her teams of helpers have done with each dish. It is all presented considerately, without a hint of being patronising: it is just what culinarily-challenged Britons require.

When she said 'The good news is that fresh tomatoes don't have to be skinned for chutney' sighs of relief went up in living rooms around the country. When she demonstrated a neat trick to eat spaghetti without spilling it down your front, viewers mouthed thank yous to the television screen.

There is something about Delia that always sets me off asking the great imponderables. Is she going to bequeath that fabulous garden over her shoulder to the National Trust? And just who does her washing up? There is a remarkable profligacy with utensils in television cookery that suggests some poor sucker is going to be up to their elbows in suds for months on end. Or perhaps, like used tennis balls at Wimbledon, the pots and pans get a well-earned retirement after short, selfless lives. If so, could I put my name down for that pan in which she made Roasted Pumpkin Soup with Melting Cheese?

Delia is often accompanied by tinkling ambient music, which may well have been lifted from a new age, positive vibes album, and feelgood slow-motion photography – the lingering close-up of black bean salsa poured over crème fraîche into a soup was surely as sensual a moment as cookery programmes can manage.

The only drawback was that Delia didn't seem to have all that much fun. She's the last TV chef in the world who was likely to shove the last drop of red down her neck as she waved goodbye, flush-faced, over the closing credits. She never indulged herself as she should have done. At the end of a patient explanation of the making of pasta putanesca, for instance, she ends by rolling up a forkful of spaghetti: 'Am I going to eat it? No, I'm not going to eat it. I'm just going to say goodbye.' Oh *Delia*! Let yourself go a bit – you've earned it.

★

THE TINGLE FACTOR

Advertising on television has mutated like a particularly ingenious virus. It now clothes itself in the form of drama, and plays peek-a-boo with viewers, concealing and revealing its identity and titillating viewers with cliffhanger endings. It resembles the way in which DIY and cookery programmes have changed: we cannot be sold things, just as we cannot be told how to improve ourselves, without distancing or distracting devices – irony, false romances, mock-thrillers, tea-drinking chimps, TV gardener Charlie Dimmock and the manipulative way she has with her breasts on *Ground Force*. For Lord Reith, commerical television was like the bubonic plague: it may not be quite that bad, but advertising on television has been able to reinvent itself and retain its power in a way that the plague would have envied.

Gibbs SR toothpaste was the first product advertised on British television in 1955. In one early commercial for the product, a stream was photographed cutting through snow to the accompaniment of cheery flute music. In the foreground was a large block of ice that held a toothbrush and a tube of paste. 'It's tingling fresh,' said the narrator. 'Gibbs SR toothpaste – tingling fresh toothpaste that does your gums good too,' he added. But then came the really interesting part. 'The tingle you get when you brush with Gibbs SR is more than a nice taste. It's a tingle of good health and it tells you something very important.' What could this important thing be? Who could say, but in any event we were now looking at a nice, blonde-haired young girl brushing her teeth. I felt sure her name was Tippi Tingly. What was it that was important, then? 'You're doing your gums good and defending them against infection and, as this chart shows, gum infection is the cause of more tooth losses than tooth decay.' The chart, which had replaced Tippi's vigorous brushing, did not really show anything. True, on the left was a bar with the words 'gum infection' and on the right one with the words 'tooth decay', and the former was bigger than the latter, but, as we were not told what was being plotted vertically or horizontally, no real information was being conveyed. Thus began TV advertising's long history of baffling the viewer with non-science.

Although there are some elements to this advertisement which you can see in today's TV commercials – the appliance of science, a healthy-looking girl – it all seems too ludicrously direct now. The repetition of key words seems to leap from a manual rather than the creative minds of copywriters. Today we are used to the name of the product being somewhat muted, to see entertaining rather than putatively informative advertisements. That said, there was once a commercial in which someone exclaimed: 'These Odour Eaters really are *odour eaters*!' The name of the product was seen as semantically distinct from its function and yet, paradoxically, the name was repeated so that you could remember what to ask for in the shop. A quite brilliant piece of copywriting.

The failure to name products in advertisements sufficiently clearly, by contrast, can cause confusion. When Cinzano was sold on television by means of a long-running little drama in which Leonard Rossiter would contrive to pour a glass of the stuff down Joan Collins's cleavage, this seemed to me to be the apex of advertising achievement. It was witty, it was well acted, it was stylish, it was directed by both Alan Parker and Hugh Hudson, noted film directors in their own right. But there was one problem: most of the viewers surveyed thought that Leonard and Joan were trying to sell them Martini. The name of the product was not lodged in viewers' collective unconscious by the ad. It needed a concluding line: 'Joan and Leonard have been trying to sell you Cinzano, understand? Cinzano. Now buy some.'

We have become bad faith viewers when we watch television advertising. We know that during commerical breaks people will try to sell us things, but we delude ourselves into believing that we are also and mostly being entertained. In December 1992,

30 million viewers – more than half Britain's population – watched the original Gold Blend couple finally declare their love for one another. To me, it seemed Britain had gone mad: the drama, such as it was, captured the nation's hearts – or at least the hearts of insane, hat-wearing, *Daily Mail*-reading Britons, and prompted a bestselling novel called *Love Over Gold* and a tie-in CD of love songs. In 1997, 15 million people watched the Gold Blend couple's final tryst, and I was one of them. Mark jumped on the train to diffidently plight his troth. 'I can't believe you took the coffee,' he told Louise. 'You know, if we're going to have any kind of relationship, you're going to have to learn to share.' The camera then pulled back and the train rolled on through the South American landscape, taking the pair, their boring romance and their filthy coffee off our screens for good. This was the end of Nescafé's decade-long advertising serial that boosted sales of the instant coffee by 70 per cent and made my life more miserable by at least 200 per cent. It was a woeful campaign, and encouraged a drift towards poorly written narrative, cliffhanging advertisements. Worse yet, they weren't even discreet about their product placements.

At the end of the commercial break which had seen the Gold Blend couple disappear into the South American landscape, up popped a cute little story for Cadbury's Roses. They had become sponsors of *Coronation Street*. A chocolate cat bounded across the terrace rooftops and leapt at a chocolate pigeon, which flew off (clever that) across Weatherfield. By the time *Coronation Street* began in earnest, though, I was too dramatically challenged, too purged, to take in self-righteous Sally's boring complaints about philandering Kevin Webster. This was the second revolution in narrative advertising: instead of a drama in the commercial break, we now had a drama that associated itself with the drama that was to follow, that basked in the glow of *Coronation Street*'s popularity. There was now one more Coronation Street than those I had seen at Granada Studios in Manchester, a chocolate one that in many respects was better than the real others.

This second revolution in narrative advertising was and is grisly to behold. These advertisements mar the programmes, insult the intelligence of viewers and undermine actors, writers and directors. They have a big future. Maybe Lord Reith was right: the bubonic plague of commercials is slowly killing off broadcasting. But this suits the anxious, decadent age: we are fitted for nothing more than watching people sell us things or other people decorate their homes. In the future, it's going to get worse.

YOU KNOW, I DON'T THINK I'VE SEEN A SQUARE FRYING PAN BEFORE, VANESSA

'Do you know the secret to perfect cooking? It's not the recipe. It's not even the ingredients. It's The Best Cookware In The World That Money Can Buy!'

For someone raised by television to take the strictures of Fanny and Delia with regard to perfect cooking seriously, this seemed simplistic advice. Surely the secret to perfect cooking Was A Mixture Of All Three? And What's More, Why Are We Talking In Capital Letters?

Why? I'll tell you why. I have seen the future of television, all hard sell and uninteresting interactivity and it is TV Shop Europe. Broadcasting here consists of long, sometimes, half-hour programmes, pitted with interviews and reports. There is a studio audience, too, paid (I hope) to bray their endorsements. The shows are hosted by nice people in kitchens or by gym bunnies in mufti. After a while, these people become plausible, particularly as they broadcast almost exclusively during the night and so I am vulnerable and insomniac as I watch. The man who devised the Ab Isolator says 'Gimmicks don't work,' which, to my mind, is true. 'The Look Cookware is what you've been waiting for,' says someone else, which is even truer.

But let me ask you this. 'Do you like omelettes, Brian?' 'Yes, but I have never been able to cook them, Vanessa.' 'Well, that's going to change, Brian.'

Brian and Vanessa, like Tweedledum and Tweedledee with sex organs, have an on-screen thing going on of the most vile kind. Their deployment of sexual chemistry is solely in aid of offloading lorryloads of pans on to bleary-eyed suckers, such as myself, who sit watching them through the early hours. 'I'm interested to know how the pan feels in my hands, Vanessa,' says Brian, smiling. 'It's sturdy without being heavy or bulky,' he adds. There must be, please God, some sexual subtext to all this. If there isn't then I'm afraid, Brian, the time has now come for you to feel the steel of my vast collection of cooking knives, available on a 30-day-satisfaction-guaranteed-or-your-money-back-but-you-get-to-keep-the-worthless-fridge-magnet deal at only £129.99, you sad, *sad* man. No human being wants to know how a pan feels in their hands.

This is the way that Brian and Vanessa lure dead-eyed viewers into the twinkling fairyland of Icelandic pots and pans. We cut to Ragnar Wessman, head chef of the Hotel Saga, Reykjavik, for what passes for professional endorsement. He fries some fish and announces: 'It's a very even flow of heat.' True, no doubt, but isn't it a bit feeble to have the International Chefs' Collection of pans endorsed by some bloke who works five minutes down the road from the pan factory?

Meanwhile, back in the kitchen, the romance has begun to cool like a neglected omelette pan. 'You know, I don't think I've ever seen a square frying pan before, Vanessa.' Vanessa's eyes narrow. 'Well, professional chefs have been using them for years, Brian.' To my mind, she couldn't have made her feelings about Brian's sexual inadequacies any plainer.

Later that same evening, the screen is well and truly filled by a man called Tony Little. He has a ponytail and buns of steel. He looks as though he can crack nuts with several parts of his anatomy and me with a mere glance. But he's more than just crackers. 'I'm considered to be the world's number one trainer, which I Thank the Lord for!' He does tend to shout, which at this time of the morning, cannot be good for Ab Isolator sales.

His Ab Isolator (a sort of strap with two things at the end, so far as I could judge) comes with Tony's explanatory video. 'I'll motivate your butt!' yells Tony, flexing his many muscles. I don't care for his tone one bit.

'Take control of your life!' shouts Tony just before the credits roll. 'Make the choice that matters most in your life!' Good advice. I have resolved never to watch this stuff again. I will never again let people I don't trust sell me things I don't need, or let TV experts advise me on how to lead the good life.

CHAPTER 12

Why Sideshow Bob Tried to Destroy Television

At the start of the summer holidays in the seventies, BBC1 would often broadcast a programme called *Why Don't You Just Turn Off Your Television Set and Go and Do Something Less Boring Instead?* As a title, it was risky – as off-putting as calling a programme *Hetty Wainthropp Investigates* or displaying Matthew Kelly's name prominently on the credits. On the show, there were lots of boys and girls in white T-shirts with Bristol accents who knew how to have fun without watching television. In those days, fun didn't involve chasing hubcaps, smoking crack cocaine or torturing cats, but building or collecting things. Every one of the well-scrubbed bunch who appeared on the show, I felt sure, would have been able to follow John Noakes's instructions on how to make a *Blue Peter* brush from two balls of wool and a wire coathanger. They were doers, not watchers. I imagined that all around Bristol there were happy mums and dads who were proud of their handy children, who kept them supplied with perfect pipe racks and crocheted doilies.

There were seven weeks of holiday looming and during this time, according to *Why Don't You*, viewers could build up an impressive stamp collection or make an exhaustive study of local pond life. You could study traffic flows in your town centre and display your data on an overhead projector in your darkened living room before impressed contemporaries over squash and crisps. You could form a bridge club and write to Omar Sharif asking for expert advice. *Why Don't You* had location pieces in which little boys (with daddy out of focus in the background, puffing on a pipe) showed off their huge train sets, or little girls tempted the camera crew with filo pastry parcels. They were the sort of kids who would get at least as far as the semi-finals on *Ask the Family*. Some of the boys wore floral ties and matching orange shirts.

Why Don't You made me anxious. I wanted to do nothing more than pull the curtains and watch television, or lie in a star formation on a playground looking into the sun, turning round and round, until I was sick and blind. *Why Don't You* urged me to aspire to higher things. But, as when any TV programme has tried to tell me how to live, I have ignored it, switched over or off and made my own choices, with only a twinge of anxiety to remind me that I should be doing something less boring instead.

This anxiety was always misplaced. Sometimes I would be stupefied, sick and blind, yes, but at other times I would be borrowing books from the library and reading Dostoevsky or Orwell. I didn't grow up into a Martin Tupper, with only television to frame my world, but with lots of things to entertain and inform me. I grew up, too, doing lots of pointless things that wouldn't qualify me to be a floral-tied boy on *Ask the Family*, but about which I didn't feel guilty or anxious.

But television has left its mark on me. When I feel lonely and the house seems too quiet, sometimes I turn on the television. I've done that for years as, I'm sure, have lots of other people. It helps me forget my loneliness and fills my living room with soothing noise. Instead, I could go out to the pub, pick up the phone and call someone. But instead I turn on that false friend, knowing that it won't quite give me what I want and that it silences real human contact. But it will always be there, always dependably filling the unbearable spaces. I wish I wasn't like that, but I am. I feel sure that children of later generations will not be like me in these respects, and I am glad for them. They will watch a new kind of television, and find that it doesn't enchant them very much. They won't have the poignant childhood television memories that I have and that are brought to life by tin foil cups, but they will have others. They won't live in a virtual community of national TV viewers, but they will have time to form other groups – perhaps better ones. The rise of Digital is going to do a great favour to these kids: it will make them less interested in television than I was. And it's doing me a favour too: it's curing me of the need to watch television.

On *The Simpsons* once, Sideshow Bob threatened to detonate a 10-megaton atomic bomb unless all Springfield's television stations ceased transmission for good. 'Wouldn't our lives be so much richer if television were done away with?' he asked as he appeared on TV to announce his threat. 'Why, we could revive the lost arts of conversation and scrimshaw. Thus, I submit to you that we abolish television permanently.' To me this sounded a great deal like the paternalist philosophy of *Why Don't You*? It proved too much for Homer Simpson. He stood up, shook his yellow fist at the screen and yelled: 'Go back to Massachusetts, pinko!'

Digital television makes me want to go to Massachusetts, to look moodily out to sea and never hear Andy Gray analyse a Wimbledon v Spurs match into oblivion again. To ponder life's bitter mystery rather than exercise my right to purchase things that are not worth buying from the shopping channels at my disposal. To sit on the sea shore and pick up the sea shells. Perhaps to take them home for a spot of scrimshaw. Or maybe for some conversation. Or maybe I should steal a nuclear device and really explain things to Rupert Murdoch.

It all began when the man arrived to install the satellite dish. I say man, but really I mean 'entertainment paramedic' if the advertisements are right. Which they are not. 'It's very stylish, don't you think?' he said as he scaled the ladder. And, yes, it certainly was smaller than dishes of yesteryear. It was black and perforated – very Ikea, very eighties. It didn't look at all like the 'squarial', which was just as well, since if it had, it would have been a monument to my consummate failure as a human being. 'Very trendy,' he added as he came down the ladder.

But, no, it wasn't trendy. The day a satellite dish becomes trendy is the day I will clad my house with whatever that horrible stuff is called. Cladding, I believe. Though in a sense, now that I have a satellite dish, I might as well have the full horror make-over. An old mattress for the front garden, a wardrobe consisting entirely of stained singlets and jogging pants.

It got worse when I went inside to watch the stuff. I had paid £199.99 to be upgraded. For a couple of years I had cable TV, but Digital seemed to offer me more. Now I receive nearly 200 channels. My extremely grand package also included six kinds of Discovery Channel (not one exclusively devoted to meerkats but that, surely, is a matter of time), six sports channels, 12 for movies, a dedicated games show channel, five music video channels. True, 44 channels are audio only. To be honest, though, if I ever want to hear a dedicated German music station while I dust the living room, I will seek the kind of interactive psychiatric care that Digital TV providers don't yet offer. What's more, there are about 50 so-called channels which in fact are screenings of pay-per-view movies – the same films broadcast at different times throughout the day. But, still, there is a great deal of choice. I know this because authoritative entertainment paramedics have told me so.

My new Digital handset is big and colourful, but it has so many buttons that I feel sure that it doesn't only activate my digibox. There are charter flights landing at Luton, I fear, which have been diverted from Edinburgh because I've pushed the wrong buttons. The handset makes me nostalgic for my cable TV remote. Oh, how I loved that cable remote! It was like a Lada, but with fewer wheels. It was big, simple and had buttons the size of shot-putters' fingers. My favourite cable remote control button, in a hotly contested contest, was the button called 'Last'. I used it a great deal. If, say, I was watching Villa v Fulham, but lost the will to live halfway through and wanted to watch *Seinfeld* instead, I would push 'Last' and it would take me from Sky Sports 1 to Paramount. Then, when *Seinfeld* went to a commercial break, I would push 'Last' and it would take me back to the football.

No such simple facility exists with the Digital handset. Instead, I have to key in three digits to take me from sport to *Seinfeld*. 127 to take me to Paramount; 401 to take me to the football; 310 to take me to the relevant movie. Three key strokes where once there was one. Or I can go to the on-screen TV guide and make a selection in that laborious way. This makes negotiating the wonderful world of Digital much harder than flipping around cable.

All of this is rather unfortunate, since surely one of the main points of Digital TV is that it should give me what I want as fast as possible, if not faster. 'It's going to completely change the way we watch television,' said the enthusiastic man at SkyDigital. 'The beauty of it is that it is there to give you what you want. You come home and you want to see a film, then you have 12 movie channels to choose from 48-plus screenings of films on the home box-office to choose from. You want to watch sport, then you have six channels to choose from.'

Digital TV will indeed change the way we watch television. Lord Reith once said that good broadcasting gives people what they do not yet know they need. He would have hated Digital television because its founding philosophy is very different from his. Digital television gives people what they want.

Or maybe it isn't as simple as that. Perhaps Digital gives me not what I want but what other people think I want. Or most likely, it serves up specific demographics for advertisers. UK Gold for people who buy reproduction furniture. Bravo for sex toy enthusiasts. Granada Plus for 'Chubby' Brown videos and Saga Holidays. Genre channels that pre-package their entertainment and pre-package their viewers for consumption by demanding advertisers.

I feel I am being set free from the constraints of paternalistic, Reithian television and immediately imprisoned in a scarier world in which I have greater choice, though nothing is worth choosing because so little of what is on offer is tailored for me. I can choose from two business news channels, though one would have been more than enough. I can choose from three 24-hour news networks, though really I was happy with at least two fewer. Digital does not meet my demands. What I want is philosophy on TV, an Iranian film retrospective, a 24-hour *Flowerpot Men* repeats channel, Larry Sanders over breakfast, a repeat of the Aston Villa-Bayern Munich European Cup Final any time soon. This will never happen. But then how could it? I am too eclectic to be satisfied by the limited choices on offer, and so is everybody else.

In the pre-Digital age, we might have watched BBC1 all night but in so doing we would stumble across things we didn't expect. We were exposed to things rather than protected from them. Our demands were not met but created, which was partly what justified and justifies public service broadcasting. How could we have known that we would want to watch David Attenborough whispering in the bushes? Or sheepdogs herding sheep? Or Alan Titchmarsh getting his finger nails dirty?

In the Reithian vision, television was not tailored to your ever-changing moods and instead was imposed on a sometimes exasperated, sometimes enchanted viewing public. The BBC had an Auntie-knows-best philosophy which well fitted the post-war patrician climate. Only on November 2 1982, with the arrival of Channel 4, did the notion of niche programming – serving up specific demographics for advertisers – first become significant in Britain.

Even more importantly, in the pre-Digital era of television, TV was one of the things that structured our lives. We used to worship the sun and its movements structured our lives. Then the liturgy overlaid that structure: it helpfully divided up our lives into times, rituals, even public moods. Television, since the coronation in 1953, has offered us a structure that borrowed from both the sun and the Church: it had its seasons, its reassuring parade of moods and events. TV sport, for instance, had its year – the Boat Race, the Grand National, the English and Scottish cup finals, Wimbledon – events which had a national character since they were broadcast throughout Britain. 3 p.m. on Christmas Day meant the Queen's annual message. We were nationally unified in the second half of this century by means of such television. It gave us a fund of common memories, shared heritage and a vernacular that came out of the cathode ray tube into our living rooms and into our hearts, then out into playgrounds, factories and offices. Nice to see you? To see you nice!

As the Digital vision takes over, we will lose all this. Digital makes television just like shopping: like Iceland or Woolworths, though, it is a crude attempt to meet sophisticated demands and not a very nice place to be.

The Digital vision of television became very clear to me as soon as I started negotiating my way around the on-screen TV guide with my handset. It pre-packaged my choices; it gave me what someone else thought I wanted. I went to a menu in which channels were listed under seven headings – Entertainment, Movies, Sports, News and Documentaries, Children, Music and Specialist, and Other Channels. I scrolled down the menu and chose one of these, then was presented with a list of channels and the times. I scrolled across the screens and found out what was on each channel throughout the day. I pushed another button and it gave me a synopsis of each programme.

'You see this?' asked the man who had screwed a dish to my chimney, brandishing my *Radio Times*. 'You won't need this any more.' Personally, I didn't care for his tone. Nor for what his boots had done to my hall carpet. But he did have a point. The on-screen TV guide was very absorbing; more engaging than watching the programmes themselves. For me, the characteristic experience of watching Digital TV has become one of flipping around the listing screens, unable to decide which of 200 types of unabsorbing cobblers I want to watch. I feel like a jaded roué at a vulgarly appointed brothel. There is lots of choice but nothing that proves sufficiently enticing.

What is most striking about the on-screen listings guide, though, is that the terrestrial channels – BBC1, BBC2, ITV, Channel 4 and Channel 5 – fit into its thematized viewing menus like square pegs in round holes. All five are to be found under the Entertainment heading. But in what sense is the Nine o'Clock News entertainment? Perhaps in the same sense that *Cybill* is a comedy. Isn't *Match of the Day* sport?

What does fit in well with the Digital vision of television, though, are interactive services. They allow me to do my banking and surf the Internet on my TV. I can order goods from Iceland and Woolworths. But, even before Digital TV, I never bought anything from Iceland, and only light bulbs and pick 'n' mix sweets from Woolworths. If interactive services helped me buy clothes from the next Nicole Farhi sale without leaving my sofa, Digital might have improved my life, but not otherwise.

I don't want to be that roué at the threshold: I want to be challenged, to find out new things, perhaps be entertained and in that entertainment build up a bank of common experience and shared memories that link me with other Britons. These are a few of the favourite things that I have wanted and sometimes got from television. Not lots of choice of things that I don't really care about very much.

Instead, the Digital vision stops television being special. The picture quality and sound are better, but that doesn't make it any less dreary. I wander Digital's choices rather as someone might wander the freezer cabinets of Iceland, morosely looking for something reassuring to defrost a cold Wednesday evening. I know that *The Simpsons* will be on Sky 1 at 7 p.m. each weekday; I know that *Seinfeld* is on Paramount at 9.30 p.m.; I know there will be news whenever I want it. Everything is in its proper time slot ready to be activated by me if I can work up the enthusiasm. I know too that if I miss a film on Sky, I will be able to catch up with it later – they're all repeated in a short cycle. Thanks to Digital, television is no longer engaging, no longer an event.

When Sideshow Bob threatened to bomb Springfield, he was exasperated by a city that seemed transfixed, by a community linked by nothing stronger than a box in the living room. But Digital isn't like that: it hardly ever captivates us, still less does it challenge or unite us in the superficial way television used to do. In the Digital age, no one will need to nuke a city to stop people watching TV addictively. By making the television experience much more impoverished because it offers lots and lots of only mildly interesting choices, Digital TV will help us to make our lives richer. We will reduce it to the corner of our lives, rather than let that corner of the living room where the TV sits dominate our lives. When I feel lonely and the house is quiet, I will be less likely to turn on the television thanks to Digital. Despite a lifetime's experience of watching television, I am being cured of my low-level TV addiction. It may cost £30 a month but I think it's worthwhile. I never thought that I would thank Rupert Murdoch for anything.

In the Digital age, we don't need Sideshow Bob to bomb us into turning off our TVs. In the near future, television will end – not with a 10-megaton atomic bang, but with a shrug of the shoulders.

TVography

(Dates are given for the first screenings.)

DREAM ON. Meta-televisual US sitcom. Broadcast on Channel 4, 1991–92.

TELLY ADDICTS. Don't read the next sentence if you're of a nervous disposition. *Telly Addicts* is a quiz show hosted by Noel Edmonds. BBC1, 1985–.

PINKY AND PERKY. Children's entertainment show made by Czech immigrants Jan and Vlasta Dalibor. But that's hardly the whole story. As Neil used to say in *The Young Ones*: 'It's the pigs!' BBC1, 1957–68; ITV, 1968–71.

THE TEST CARD. Shown on BBC from 1967 to 1983 with Carol Hersey, her rag doll and the blackboard.

THE HERBS. Children's series with puppets in an English country garden of Sir Basil and Lady Rosemary. A Caribbean spin-off, Righteous 'Erbs, was never commissioned. BBC1, 1968.

DR WHO. Long-running science fiction series, whose chief villains, the Daleks, could be easily evaded by going upstairs. More importantly, who sells jelly babies loose these days? BBC1, 1963–.

THE WOODENTOPS. Children's series featuring Spotty Dog, 'the biggest spotty dog you ever did see.' BBC1, 1955–58.

CORONATION STREET. Long-running soap opera. Women in hairnets, men who like hotpot – it has something for everybody. ITV, 1960–.

TILL DEATH US DO PART. Sitcom in which an East End bigot is treated with contempt by his liberal daughter, militant son-in-law and dim wife. BBC1, 1965–68; 1972–75.

EASTENDERS. Delightfully depressing London-set soap, though the character-to-consonant ratio has not suited all tastes. BBC1, 1985–.

THE MORECAMBE AND WISE SHOW. Comedy variety show that brought a nation sunshine, for a while. Not now, Arthur. ITV, 1961–68; BBC1, 1968–78; ITV, 1978–83.

CHAPTER 1

BILL AND BEN THE FLOWERPOT MEN. Disturbing psycho-drama. With puppets. BBC1, 1952–54, 1957–58.

ANDY PANDY. As above. BBC1, 1950–1957, 1970.

BAGPUSS. As above. BBC1, 1974.

BLUE PETER. Ah memories! John Noakes hanging upside down from Nelson's Column, Bleep and Booster, the dancing feet of Lesley Judd, Sarah Greene modelling Victorian corsetry. Down Shep, down! BBC1, 1958–.

THE PHIL SILVERS SHOW. In Kansas, as far as any American serviceman could get from real conflict, Sergeant Bilko fought his war. US sitcom, shown on BBC1, 1957–61.

CAMBERWICK GREEN/ TRUMPTON/ CHIGLEY. Puppet dramas or social conditioning? You be the judge. BBC1, 1966/1967/ 1969.

DAD'S ARMY. Critique of the British class system during wartime. Funnier than it sounds. BBC1, 1968–77.

THUNDERBIRDS. Drama in which Gerry and Sylvia Anderson's hi-tech puppet vigilantes safeguarded geopolitical stability. Implausible, but true. ITV, 1965–66.

MONTY PYTHON'S FLYING CIRCUS. Inventive comedy series whose sketches can be quoted verbatim by the kind of people you don't really want within earshot. BBC2, 1969–74.

CAPTAIN PUGWASH. Each week Pugwash wrangled with his inner demons, Cut-throat Jake got his and Tom the Cabin Boy said nothing. BBC1, 1957–66; 1974–5; 1998–.

HERE COME THE DOUBLE DECKERS. Kids have fun on a double-decker London bus. Notable for introducing Brinsley Forde, later lead singer of reggae combo Aswad, as Spring. BBC1, 1971.

SOOTY. He is the hollow bear, he is the stuffed bear. Headpiece filled with straw, alas! And other bits filled with Harry or, latterly, Matthew. BBC1, 1952–68; ITV, 1968–.

THE CLANGERS. Squeaky socks who live under bin lids on the moon. On another planet, other vengeful, angry socks planned a mission to take back those bin lids. For years they lived with only bin bottoms, which was no good at all. BBC1, 1969–74.

MAGPIE. Though mostly a poor kid's *Blue Peter*, Mick Robertson did have a hairdo that prefigured Brian May's which, with hindsight, gives the programme some cultural cachet. ITV, 1968–80.

NOEL'S HOUSE PARTY. The saga of a big rubber doll, a Crinkly Bottom and a man who never changed his beard. BBC1, 1991–.

THE SIMPSONS. A meta-televisual critique of the medium. But funny. US cartoon comedy series. Sky 1, 1990–; BBC1 and 2, 1995–.

TELETUBBIES. As colourful as *The Simpsons*, but with bulkier participants and less readily understandable jokes. BBC1, 1996–.

TOP CAT. A cartoon version of *The Phil Silvers Show*. Broadcast on the BBC as *Boss Cat*, 1962–63.

THE WOMBLES. Bernard Cribbins narrated. Puppets kept Wimbledon Common clean. Mike Batt had chart success, with songs such as 'Remember You're a Womble'. Could any of this really have happened? BBC1, 1973.

CHAPTER 2

THE WORLD AT WAR. Twenty-six-episode series about the Second World War narrated by Laurence Olivier. ITV, 1973–74.

THE LIKELY LADS/ WHATEVER HAPPENED TO THE LIKELY LADS? Two men fail to come to maturity. BBC2, 1964–66; BBC1, 1973–4.

MEN BEHAVING BADLY. Two men fail to come to maturity. ITV, 1991–94; BBC1, 1994–99.

RIPPING YARNS. Michael Palin's series of stories for British boys. Who could forget the heartening story of how stiff-upper-lipped British chaps crossed the Andes by frog? You did? BBC2, 1977–79.

LOVE THY NEIGHBOUR. Race comedy from the team who wrote *Never Mind the Quality, Feel the Width,* about a Jewish jacketmaker and an Irish trousermaker. Laugh? I'd rather deploy a UN peace-keeping force. *Love Thy Neighbour* was every bit as sophisticated. ITV, 1972–76.

THE OPRAH WINFREY SHOW. US talk show. Channel 4, 1986–.

RANDALL AND HOPKIRK (DECEASED). Detective drama in which one of the duo was dead. Rather like Starsky and Hutch, but with less knitwear. ITV, 1969–70.

CHEERS. The place where everybody knows your name but is too drunk to pronounce it. US sitcom. Channel 4, 1982–93.

INDOOR LEAGUE. Pubs and pipes, men in zip-up jumpers. Bar sports, too. ITV, late seventies.

CHAPTER 3

IT'S A KNOCKOUT. Games with foam, water and plimsolls. There was a continental version, too, which single-handedly kept European monetary integration in check for nearly two decades. BBC1, 1966–82; 1999–.

MASTERMIND. Fact quiz for regionalised autodidacts. BBC1, 1972–.

COUNTDOWN. Consonant, please, Carole. And another consonant. Vowel. Vowel. Consonant. Put them together and what does that spell? That's not very nice, Carole, not nice at all. Channel 4, 1982–.

CHAPTER 4

ARE YOU BEING SERVED? Unintentional critique of post-imperialist culture and British sexual repression. BBC1, 1973–85.

FAWLTY TOWERS. As above. BBC2, 1977, 1979.

THE GENERATION GAME. The most popular game show in British TV history, hosted by Bruce Forsyth, Larry Grayson and Jim Davidson. BBC1, 1971–82; 1990.

THE AVENGERS. Science fiction/crime drama. ITV, 1961–9.

PORRIDGE. Sitcom in stir. BBC1, 1974–77.

BIRDS OF A FEATHER. Essex-set sitcom. BBC1, 1989–.

THE DICK EMERY SHOW. 'Hello, Honky Tonk. How are you?' BBC1 1963–79.

MINDER. Comedy drama featuring shifty Arthur Daley, burly Terence, but not 'Er Indoors. ITV, 1979–85; 1988–94.

FRASIER. US sitcom set in Seattle. Responsible for coffee fetishism among Channel 4 viewers. Channel 4, 1994.

THE LIVER BIRDS. Scouse-set sitcom. BBC1, 1969–78.

YOU'VE BEEN FRAMED. Video howlers with links by Jeremy Beadle that can easily be edited out. ITV, 1990–.

ONLY FOOLS AND HORSES. One of the funniest and most popular British sitcoms. The headline 'Peckham wry' was used on articles about John Sullivan's show with annoying regularity. BBC1, 1981–96.

HANCOCK'S HALF HOUR. The existential struggle of a man stuck in west London. BBC1, 1956–61.

STEPTOE AND SON. As above. BBC1, 1964–73.

FATHER TED. The existential struggles of a man stuck in the west of Ireland. Channel 4, 1995–98.

BUTTERFLIES. The existential struggles of a woman stuck in domestic infelicity. BBC2, 1978–82.

THE BENNY HILL SHOW. Racist, sexist bilge. Very popular for a time. ITV, 1969–89.

HARRY HILL. One man, one breast pocket, many pens. Channel 4, 1997–.

VIC REEVES' BIG NIGHT OUT. One man with a stick, two men in suits, but only one man in a white coat. Channel 4, 1990–92.

THE FAST SHOW. Sketch comedy programme starring the comic genius Paul Whitehouse. A little bit dodgy, a little bit tasty, a bit of a geezer. A little bit whoar. A little bit whay. BBC2, 1995–97.

THE SMELL OF REEVES AND MORTIMER. A northern comedy. You could tell it was northern because of this rhyme from one of the songs: 'I love the smell of manure. And I love the smell of the poor.' BBC2, 1993–95.

HARRY ENFIELD AND CHUMS. Sketch show also starring Paul Whitehouse, Kathy Burke and a lovely little chimney sweep. BBC1, 1994–.

SHOOTING STARS. Post-modern critique of the game show with some lemon on drums in a romper suit. BBC2, 1995–.

HAVE I GOT NEWS FOR YOU. Satirical comedy which upset nobody. BBC2, 1990–.

THAT WAS THE WEEK THAT WAS. Satirical comedy which upset the then Home Secretary. BBC, 1962–63.

RORY BREMNER . . . WHO ELSE? Satirical comedy best satirised by Harry Hill: 'Now I wonder what Mr Frank Dobson thinks of that?' Channel 4, 1993–.

MICHAEL MOORE'S TV NATION. Satire on the US and the media. Channel 4, 1995–.

WORLD IN ACTION. Investigative news magazine. So investigative that it didn't fit in the era of news as entertainment. ITV, 1963–98.

THE MARK THOMAS COMEDY PRODUCT. Trotskyist satire. You know, for the cause. Channel 4, 1996–.

SATURDAY NIGHT LIVE. Comedy show hosted by Ben Elton, that served to turn alternative comedy into the establishment. Channel 4, 1986–87.

THE THIN BLUE LINE. A sitcom analysis of the virtues and vices of British policing. BBC1, 1995–96.

THE YOUNG ONES. A faithful depiction of student life. BBC2, 1982–84.

BLACKADDER. British history reduced to absurdity. At last. BBC1, 1983–89.

EVER DECREASING CIRCLES. The sourest of Esmonde and Larbey's suburban sitcoms. BBC1, 1984–89.

CHAPTER 5

BRIDESHEAD REVISITED. Adaptation of Evelyn Waugh's novel. ITV, 1981.

INSPECTOR MORSE. Crime in the most photogenic parts of the Thames Valley. ITV, 1987–93.

PRIDE AND PREJUDICE. Adaptation of Jane Austen's novel by Fay Weldon. BBC1, 1980.

PRIDE AND PREJUDICE. Adaptation of Jane Austen's novel by Andrew Davies. BBC1, 1995.

SONGS OF PRAISE. Once, they set this religious show on ice. But only once. BBC1, 1961–.

MIDDLEMARCH. Adaptation of George Eliot's novel by Andrew Davies. BBC1, 1993.

VANITY FAIR. Adaptation of William Makepeace Thackeray's novel by Andrew Davies. BBC1, 1998.

CHAPTER 6

BROOKSIDE. Liverpool-set soap opera. Channel 4, 1982–.

CROSSROADS. Birmingham-set soap opera. ITV, 1964–88.

VICTORIA WOOD – AS SEEN ON TV. Sketch comedy, marred only by interludes for songs that made Peter Skellern sound cutting-edge. BBC2, 1985–87.

EMMERDALE FARM/EMMERDALE. Yorkshire Dales-set soap opera. ITV, 1972–.

WHACK-O! Sitcom set in a public school. BBC, 1956–60, 1971–72.

GRANGE HILL. Drama set in a comprehensive school. BBC1, 1978–.

GANGSTERS. Crime drama that started each episode with a stand-up comedy routine. But that's not important now. BBC1, 1975–78.

EMPIRE ROAD. Mixed-race soap set in Handsworth. BBC2, 1978–9.

BOYS FROM THE BLACK STUFF. Alan Bleasdale's drama anatomising the impact of unemployment on men in Liverpool. BBC2, 1982.

CRACKER. Jimmy McGovern's drama series about a police psychologist who was nearly as dysfunctional as the psycho-killers he sought to profile. ITV, 1993–97.

CROWN COURT. UK legal drama. ITV, 1972–84.

LA LAW. US legal drama. ITV, 1987–92.

ALL CREATURES GREAT AND SMALL. Nostalgic drama set in the Yorkshire Dales. BBC1, 1987–90.

HEARTBEAT. Nostalgic drama set in the Yorkshire Dales. ITV, 1992–.

LAST OF THE SUMMER WINE. Nostalgic sitcom set in the Yorkshire Dales. BBC1, 1973–the end of time.

THE WHEELTAPPERS AND SHUNTERS' SOCIAL CLUB. Bernard Manning's finest moment. It was that bad. ITV, 1974–76.

THE FAMILY. The mother of all docusoaps. BBC1, 1974.

SYLVANIA WATERS. The bastard offspring of the mother of all docusoaps. BBC1, 1993.

THE HOUSE. Posh docusoap. BBC2, 1996.

ASTRONAUTS. Fly-in-the-cockpit documentary that didn't quite take off. Channel 4, 1996.

THE BILL. Drama series about a London police station. ITV, 1984–.

ANTIQUES ROADSHOW. A programme that knew the value of beauty is not monetary. As if. BBC1, 1979–.

CHAPTER 7

THE GREAT PHILOSOPHERS. Discussion programme about philosophy. BBC2, 1987.

THE LIFE OF BIRDS. Natural history documentary. BBC1, 1998.

LIFE ON EARTH. Natural history documentary. BBC2, 1979.

CIVILISATION. Kenneth Clark's series on the achievements of humanity. BBC2, 1969.

THE ASCENT OF MAN. Jacob Bronowski's series on the achievements of humanity. BBC2, 1973.

CHAPTER 8

THE MARY TYLER MOORE SHOW. US sitcom set in WJM – TV studios, Minneapolis, and starring Mary Tyler Moore as Mary Richards, perhaps the first US TV heroine to be single by choice. Created by James L. Brooks (who also had a hand in *Taxi*, *Cheers* and *The Simpsons*). BBC2, 1971–75.

RHODA. Mary Richards' best friend, the window dresser, Rhoda Morgenstern, spun off into this sitcom. BBC2, 1974–80.

SCOOBY DOO, WHERE ARE YOU? Velma, Daphne, Fred, Shaggy and Scooby tracked down wrongdoers. Darn kids. BBC1, 1970–72.

THE STREETS OF SAN FRANCISCO. Crime drama starring Karl Malden, Michael Douglas, but mostly San Francisco. ITV, 1973–80.

THE WALTONS. Wholesome American family drama. BBC1, 1974–81.

THIRTYSOMETHING. Fashionable drama about voguish neuroses. Channel 4, 1989–92.

ELIZABETH R. Historical drama series about virgin queen, starring Glenda Jackson. BBC2, 1971.

ALLY MCBEAL. Fashionable drama about self-absorbed woman. Channel 4, 1998–.

TWIN PEAKS. Murder mystery set in Washington State. The whodunnit was less interesting than more important matters to do with coffee and cherry pie. BBC2, 1990–91.

ER. Hospital drama devised by novelist Michael Crichton about an emergency room in a Chicago hospital. Channel 4, 1994–.

FRIENDS. Sitcom about six New York twentysomethings. Channel 4, 1995–.

SEINFELD. Sitcom about four New York thirtysomethings. BBC2, 1993–98.

ROSEANNE. Sitcom about a working-class American family. Channel 4, 1989–97.

REN AND STIMPY. US cartoon. BBC2, 1994–.

WACKY RACES. US cartoon. BBC1, 1969–70.

THE FLINTSTONES. US cartoon. ITV, 1961–66.

DALLAS. US soap. BBC1, 1978–91.

BEVERLY HILLS 90210. US soap. ITV, 1991–.

CHAPTER 9

'ALLO 'ALLO. Sitcom set in war-torn France. BBC1, 1982–94.

M*A*S*H*. Sitcom set in war-torn Korea. BBC2, 1973–84.

CULLODEN. Drama-documentary about the last battle fought in Britain. BBC2, 1964.

THE WAR GAME. Drama-documentary about a nuclear strike. BBC2, 1985.

THE DAY TODAY. Comedy critique of TV news. BBC2, 1994.

KNOWING ME, KNOWING YOU WITH ALAN PARTRIDGE. Comedy critique of TV chat shows. BBC2, 1994–95.

THE MRS MERTON SHOW. Comedy critique of TV chat shows. BBC2, 1994–97.

THE LARRY SANDERS SHOW. Comedy critique of TV chat shows. BBC2, 1995–98.

CHAPTER 10

HOLLYOAKS. Teenage soap set in suburban Chester. Channel 4, 1995–.

THE SINGING DETECTIVE. Dennis Potter's semi-autobiographical drama. BBC1, 1986.

NEIGHBOURS. Australian soap opera that was responsible for launching Jason Donovan and Kylie Minogue on an unprepared world. BBC1, 1986–.

THE SAINT. Damsels were in distress, Volvos were groovy and Roger Moore was sexy. Time is pitiless. ITV, 1962–9.

THE SWEENEY. Shat it! Do one! An extended homage to the virtues of the Ford Granada and slip-on shoes. ITV, 1975–78.

JASON KING. Paisley shirts, paisley ties, sideburns that rhymed with the descenders of the eponymous hero's Zapata moustache. It all made sense at the time. ITV, 1971–72.

CHAPTER 11

CHANGING ROOMS. A domestic makeover programme hosted by Carol Smillie. BBC1, 1996–.

GROUND FORCE. A domestic makeover programme hosted by Alan Titchmarsh. BBC1, 1997–.

SIGNS OF THE TIMES. A documentary series about how people have decorated their homes. BBC2, 1992.

THE GOOD LIFE. Esmonde and Larbey's most popular suburban sitcom. BBC1, 1975–78.

KEEPING UP APPEARANCES. Sitcom by Roy Clarke, starring Patricia Routledge as a woman trapped in a floral dress. BBC1, 1990–95.

THE REAL FANNY CRADOCK. Documentary about the life of the Lenin of British TV cuisine. Channel 4, 1998.

CONCLUSION

WHY DON'T YOU JUST TURN OFF YOUR TELEVISION SET AND GO OUT AND DO SOMETHING LESS BORING INSTEAD? Self-defeating, proselytising kids' show. BBC1, late seventies, early eighties.

ASK THE FAMILY. A question now for mother and younger daughter only. If Robert Robinson was so clever, why did he have such a grotesque comb-over? BBC1, 1967–84.

ONE MAN AND HIS DOG. For eighteen years, Phil Drabble wore the Wellingtons. Then he handed them over to Robin Page in 1994. A soothing rural idyll in which men in flat caps whistled their instructions to sheepdogs, and sheep rarely risked spontaneous self-expression. BBC2, 1976–99.

CYBILL. US sitcom, with little com. Channel 4, 1995–98.

BIBLIOGRAPHY

BIBLIOGRAPHY

David Attenborough, *The Life of Birds* (BBC, 1998)

Jane Austen, *Pride and Prejudice* (Penguin, 1996)

Roland Barthes, *Mythologies* (Vintage, 1993)

Roland Barthes, *Image-Music-Text* (Fontana, 1982)

Jean Baudrillard, *The Gulf War Did Not Take Place* (Power Publications, 1995)

Cary Bazalgette and David Buckingham, *In Front of the Children: Screen Entertainment and Young Audiences* (British Film Institute, 1995)

Sue Birtwistle and Susie Conklin, *The Making of Pride and Prejudice* (Penguin/BBC, 1995)

Pierre Bourdieu, *Television* (Pluto, 1997)

David Burke and Jean Lotus, *Get a Life! The Little Red Book of the White Dot Anti-Television Campaign* (Bloomsbury, 1998)

Frances Cairncross, *The Death of Distance: How the Communications Revolution Will Change Our Lives* (Orion Business Publishing, 1997)

Bruce Dessau, *The Funny Side of Billy Connolly* (Orion, 1996)

Billy Connolly's World Tour of Australia (BBC Books, 1996)

Umberto Eco, *Travels in Hyperreality* (Picador, 1986)

Terry Eagleton, *Literary Theory: An Introduction* (Blackwell, 1983)

T. S. Eliot, *Collected Poems* (Faber, 1974)

Jeff Evans, *The Guiness Television Encyclopaedia* (Guinness Publishing, 1995)

Susan Faludi, *Backlash: The Undeclared War Against Women* (Chatto and Windus, 1991)

Sigmund Freud, 'Beyond the Pleasure Principle' (in Volume 11 of the Penguin Freud Library, *On Metapsychology*, 1991)

Paul Gambaccini/Tim Rice/Jonathan Rice/Tony Brown, *The Complete Eurovision Song Contest Companion* (Pavilion, 1998)

Paul Gambaccini and Rod Taylor, *Television's Greatest Hits* (BBC, 1993)

Richard Hoggart, *The Uses of Literacy* (Penguin, 1991)
Graeme Kay, *Life in the Street: Coronation Street Past and Present* (Boxtree, 1991)
Hilary Kingsley and Geoff Tibballs, *Box of Delights: The Golden Years of Television* (Macmillan, 1989)
Jacques Lacan, *Écrits: A Selection* (Tavistock, 1977)
John E. Lewis and Penny Stempel, *Cult TV, The Essential Critical Guide* (Pavilion, 1993)
——, *Cult TV: The Comedies* (Pavilion, 1998)
Marc Lewisohn, *Radio Times Guide to TV Comedy* (BBC, 1998)
Darian Little, *The Coronation Street Story* (Boxtree, 1995)
David Lodge, *Nice Work* (Penguin, 1988)
Alison Lurie, *The War Between the Tates* (Abacus, 1986)
Ian McIntyre, *The Expense of Glory: A Life of John Reith* (HarperCollins, 1993)
Bryan Magee, *The Great Philosophers* (BBC Books, 1987)
——, *Confessions of a Philosopher* (Weidenfeld and Nicolson, 1997)
Ben Pimlott, *The Queen: A Biography of Elizabeth II* (HarperCollins, 1997)
Bill Podmore, *Coronation Street: The Inside Story* (Macdonald, 1990)
John Prebble, *Culloden* (Penguin, 1967)
Marcel Proust, *In Search of Lost Time* (Chatto and Windus, 1992)
Phil Redmond, *Brookside: The Official Companion* (Weidenfeld and Nicolson, 1987)
Edward Said, *Culture and Imperialism* (Chatto and Windus, 1993)
Roger Silverstone, *Television and Everyday Life* (Routledge, 1994)
John Updike, *Memories of the Ford Administration* (Penguin, 1992)
Ivor Yorke, *Television News* (Focal Press, 1997)

ACKNOWLEDGMENTS

I am very grateful to the *Guardian*, where friends and colleagues have allowed and sometimes encouraged me to write about television. Thanks to Laura Cumming, who invited me to write for the *New Statesman* and got me going on this book; to Rosemary Davidson, who encouraged me to write a book about television, if not quite this one; to Mandy Kirkby and Philip Gwyn Jones at Flamingo; to my agent David Miller. Thanks to my partner Kay, without whom nothing.

INDEX